The Economic and Social Growth of Early Greece

The Economic
and Social Growth
of Early Greece
800-500 B.C.

Chester G. Starr

New York

Oxford University Press

1977

Copyright © 1977 by Oxford University Press, Inc.

Library of Congress Cataloging in Publication Data

Starr, Chester G 1914–
  The economic and social growth of early Greece,
800–500 B.C.

  Bibliography: p.
  Includes index.
  1. Greece—Economic conditions.   2. Greece—Social
conditions.   I. Title.
HC37.S7   330.9′38′02   76-57265
ISBN 0-19-502223
ISBN 0-19-502224-6 pbk.

To Willem and Phien den Boer

IN FRIENDSHIP

Preface

In this work more than most others from my pen I am touching on economic and social issues the theoretical aspects of which still excite controversy. My picture may be judged by some to be unconventional or heterodox; let me stress, accordingly, that I am seeking to understand the development of early Greece, not to draw lessons for the modern world or to buttress doctrines which are widely held today.

Throughout, I have sought to keep in view the interwoven complexities presented by three centuries of change, not always illuminated as sharply as we might wish; at times, too, the Greeks who animate these pages are portrayed as inconsistent in attitudes, beliefs, or behavior. That does not make them the less fascinating or diminish the exhilaration which one senses in looking at their manifold achievements.

During the summer of 1975 a number of colleagues in Europe gave me freely of their time and advice on many aspects of my investigations. At various points in the footnotes I have acknowledged specific indebtedness but would here express generally my gratitude for counsel. I am also grateful to the agencies and individuals which provided the photographs for the plates and to the University of Michigan, which granted me sabbatical leave.

Chester G. Starr

Ann Arbor, Michigan
April 1977

Contents

Contents

Plates

(after page 146)

I Early Landed Wealth
A. *Clay granary model* B. *Gold earring*

II Aristocrats and Horses
A. *Chariot scene* B. *Young noble on horseback, "Leagros Kalos"*

III Warriors
A. *Bronze figurine of warrior*
B. *Rival phalanxes with an* aulos *player*

IV Rural Life
A. *Plowing and sowing* B. *Harvesting olives*

V Coinage of Greece
A. *Naxos* *(grape)* B. *Metapontum* *(barley)* C. *Sybaris*
(bull) D. *Himera (cock)* E. *Aegina (turtle)* F. *Zancle (harbor)* G. *Croton* *(tripod)* H. *Derrones* *(helmet)* I. *Terone*
(vase) J. *Zancle (prow)* K. *Thebes (shield)*

VI INDUSTRY
A. *Bronze figurine of smith beating out a helmet* B. *Female
worker in a metal-vase shop* C. *Manufacturing a bronze statue*

VII Commerce
A. *Merchant ship chased by pirate galley*
B. *Weighing and shipping wool before king Arceslas of Cyrene*

VIII *Phrasikleia with elaborate chiton,
crown, necklace, earrings, and bracelet*

The Economic and Social Growth of Early Greece

Chapter I

Preliminary Guidelines

During the three centuries before 500 B.C. the Greek world underwent tremendous economic and social changes. Initially the Greeks lived in rural self-sufficient villages about the shores of the Aegean, in a fractured landscape of stark mountains and small plains; their social distinctions were simple, limited, and rigid. Processes of alteration were barely under way at this point. Three hundred years later Greek life was framed in a complex economic structure embracing much of the Mediterranean and centered in cities which were socially differentiated; on this base rested the great outburst of classical civilization in the next two centuries down to Alexander.

Neither the economic nor the correlated social aspects of this evolution, taken as a whole, have received much attention. This is really odd. Economic historians and theorists are now much interested in the problems of economic growth, and in defining the necessary conditions for economic "take-off" in underdeveloped countries. This interest reflects an effort to understand the Industrial Revolution in western Europe and America, which has been a powerful influence on the world down to our own day; economists also trust that their explorations may enable them to offer useful prescriptions to the developing countries of the other continents. Yet no student of modern economic change seems ever to have cast his view back to the most remarkable example of economic growth and structural alteration in western history—that of Greece between 800 and 500 B.C.—even though it was a land initially lacking in all but the simplest techniques. Greece was also limited in its natural resources; as the Spartan king Demaratus put it, "Greece has always had poverty [*penie*] as her companion." [1]

If a subject is thus neglected despite its importance, there must be obvious reasons. Ancient Greece lies distant in the course of time, beyond the ken of scholars interested in the present and future world. The information on its history, if written, is in a difficult language which not many scholars now read; or if the evidence is archeological, it is presented in a technical fashion, with special terminology, and accompanied by site plans, vase profiles, and other forbidding illustrations.

Classical scholars themselves have given little guidance for students from other fields; only esthetic, intellectual, and religious developments have been extensively studied for early Greece. Valuable surveys have been made of colonization and a few other marks of economic expansion; but the whole range of economic progress has usually received only brief comment and has not been appreciated in its entirety.[2] Those investigations of the interconnected social changes which have been published have all too often been based on modern sociological and anthropological theories and have overemphasized the amount and effects of slavery.

Moreover, scholars of classical bent who have been drawn to consider ancient economic and social history have sometimes painted gloomy pictures of stagnation and oppression which fully warrant the famous description of economics as the "dismal science." In truth, later periods of antiquity were lacking in innovation, but the Greek age of expansion was far different: cities, coinage, workshops, tradelines within and without the Aegean world, and a richly articulated social structure existed in 500, but not in 800. Exploitation of political power was known in early Greece; Hesiod had told the tale of the hawk and the nightingale to illustrate the moral, "He is a fool who tries to withstand the stronger." [3] Yet Hesiod went on to show that abuse of position brought its punishment; history is not a tale solely of continuous crimes against the weak.

The following pages reflect a view that great advances were made by the early Greeks, even though they had normal human failings; and the study is written in the belief that we have sufficient evidence to suggest the character and tempo of changes. Scholars who demand quantifiable data or intimate detail will find much lacking in the story, but it is worth exploration even on a level which must usually, though not always, be somewhat general.

THE LITERARY EVIDENCE

Down to about 500 the Greeks wrote only poetry. The work of many poets survives in fragmentary form, and none of it was directly intended to serve as economic analysis. The greatest literary achievements tower at the beginning of our period, the *Iliad* and the *Odyssey*.

For historical purposes, however, the use of Homer (as we may term the author or authors of the epics) presents very serious problems.[4] Heinrich Schliemann, the excavator of Troy and Mycenae, was fired by a faith that the Trojan war took place and that Homer described it accurately, but not many students now would share that belief. The attack on Troy, granted its existence, occurred about or before 1200, in a very different era of Aegean history called the Mycenaean age. For that period extensive archeological exploration and the decipherment of the Linear B script permit us to see a picture of palace-based economic and social concentrations, which employed writing for bureaucratic purposes; the Homeric epics simply do not reflect that pre-Greek world.[5]

In recent years Homeric scholarship has reached a fairly general agreement that the *Iliad* and the *Odyssey* assumed their present form within the eighth century, and that their author or authors deliberately pulled out of a long developing epic tradition themes, poetic formulas, and even whole passages to create the powerful, absorbing tales of the wrath of Achilles and the adventures of Odysseus. If this consensus be valid, then the real historical question is the utility of the epics for the beginning of the period with which the present work is most concerned. That is to say, can we gain from Homer, a realistic picture of society at the end of the Greek Dark Ages, which extended from the fall of the Mycenaean world late in the second millennium down to about 800?

The Homeric world is a simple one in which the heroes, the Zeus-sprung kings, occupy almost all the stage in their demonstrations of military prowess or ingenuity in mythical travels. The objective of the heroes is *arete,* which at that time meant glory and repute, gained by victory in individual duels, in heaping up booty (both physical objects and female slaves such as Briseis, the bedmate of Achilles), and in peacetime hunting. Exchange takes place by means of mutual gifts. Truly economic interests are virtually, though not quite, lacking; the *Odyssey,* which is generally considered a generation later than the *Iliad,* does suggest a broadening out of Greek geographical awareness and overseas ventures. A very few crafts are mentioned in the epics and related stories, but the dominant form of life is rural.

In many respects the Homeric world does accord with the contemporary archeological evidence, but in others it lamentably does not. A fierce debate, for example, currently rages between scholars who would accept the epic depiction of a gift-society and those who deny its reality.[6] In seeking a solution to our present concern, we must always keep in mind the fact that the epic tradition evolved over centuries. Its formulas and descriptive passages, such as the washing of hands when a hero reaches the end of a trip, became stereotyped; almost one-third of the epics consists of repeated phrases. The epic dialect evolved as an artificial construct which corresponded only in a most general way to the forms of Greek spoken on the coast of Asia Minor.[7]

Homer, moreover, had as his function the glorification of a heroic past. He was not expected to engage in personal comment or to exhibit his own point of view; we know nothing whatever of his exact date and place of origin and can only guess his attitudes. The subject matter of the epic was traditional, and conscious innovation was discouraged by the nature of the poet's audience. All in all, it is historically unsound to call the epics a precise reflection of any one point in early Greek development; nor can one safely conclude that *all* parts of their picture ever existed in real life— the artificial character of epic dialect, just noted, may serve as sufficient warning in that respect. On the other hand, the

Homeric world did exhibit, *modo grosso,* the major enduring characteristics and intellectual attitudes of the early Greeks. A modern student must be cautious in building specific reconstructions on any one Homeric passage, but he may properly feel that the whole spirit of the epics—once allowance is made for their poetic concentration on individual heroes—does provide useful guidance for the conditions at the beginning of our story.

Once one has made his way through the many and hotly debated Homeric controversies the remainder of the available literary evidence can be appraised more succinctly.[8] Later Greeks always coupled Homer and a second poet, Hesiod, because the latter wrote in epic hexameters and in epic style. Hesiod, however, who lived in Boeotia about 700, expressed a personal outlook in his work. Among the many poems assigned to him, not all of which probably were his product, the significant one for our purposes is the *Works and Days.* This poem, a fairly lengthy one, was a reaction to the success of his brother Perses in defrauding Hesiod of his share of their father's farm, but in true Greek fashion it rose from the plane of the specific injustice to the general; Hesiod discusses economic rivalry, gives a picture of rural "works" through the agricultural year, and ends with a running commentary on activities proper for the days of the month. Although Hesiod's purpose was primarily ethical, his poem is rooted in the economic and social patterns of Greek life of his day far more directly than are the Homeric epics.

Hesiod is often called a peasant poet, a description which ill accords with his work, as we shall see later. His poetic successors, however, do certainly and clearly manifest a conscious aristocratic outlook, beginning with Archilochus of the early to mid-seventh century, Alcman thereafter, and Sappho and Alcaeus at the end of the century. Toward the close of the sixth century Theognis exhibited this point of view in a jaundiced, grumbling form at a time when men of ancestral standing had to face the rise of the *kakoi*, the rich but ill-born. The figures just named throw more light on contemporary social conditions than on economic developments; the one poet who does briefly but brightly illustrate the terrific economic tensions which emerged in the expansion of the era is Solon, archon of Athens in 594.

These poets of the seventh and sixth centuries wrote in a great variety of meters and expressed their own feelings in a manner impossible for Homer, though the nature of their audience had a powerful influence on their pens. Homer probably lived before the Greek alphabet was created, a step which seems to have occurred about the middle of the eighth century; only at that point does its presence begin to be evident in the incision or painting of hexameter lines on vases.[9] Yet of all the authors of the era only Hesiod and Theognis survive to the present day intact; and the compendium of short poems passing under the name of Theognis is in reality the work of many conservatives across the late sixth and fifth centuries. For Archilochus, Solon, and others we must depend on the citation of fragments in later literature and commentary, or the survival of papyrus scraps from Hellenistic and Roman Egypt.

Greek prose became a literary vehicle only in the mid-sixth century. The major prose writer for present purposes is Herodotus, the Father of History, who wrote in the later fifth century but preserved oral memories reaching back into the sixth century. Herodotus is so outwardly transparent in his indefatigable curiosity, which led him to set down everything heard or seen, that his critical ability is too often minimized; without Herodotus' guidance even those modern historians who depreciate his worth could scarcely treat the political history of the sixth and fifth centuries.

In the fourth century Plato and more especially Aristotle occasionally looked back to earlier days as they constructed their philosophical analyses of ethical and political problems. Platonic dialogues are so polished and Aristotle's intellect so magnificent that general students of intellectual history too often take them as completely safe guides to Greek views of life. In reality both figures lived in a century of internal and external strife which seriously affected their views of the past; that bias needs to be kept especially in mind when one consults Aristotle's *Politics* and the *Constitution of Athens* which passes under his name. It is, more generally, impossible to avoid extrapolation backward from classic Greece to earlier centuries, but this process needs always to be carefully guarded; Athens, in particular, underwent very extensive changes after 500.[10]

To Aristotle, incidentally, was also ascribed a small work entitled *Economics,* which certainly is not Aristotelian and consists mainly of stratagems to extort money from the citizens of a state. Xenophon had already written early in the fourth century a pamphlet, *Ways and Means,* to suggest plans by which Athens could balance its budget; but neither work shows much evidence of conscious economic analysis.[11] The English word "economics" has a Greek root, but in ancient Greek it meant no more than household (*oikos*) management. Public debate was vigorous in Greece and led to extensive exploration of political theory; the economic system gave less room for conscious contention.[12]

Modern students, nonetheless, sometimes draw too sweeping conclusions from the fact that economics did not become a discipline in its own right either in early Greece or in later ancient centuries. This lack does not in any way mean that Greek authors and politicians were necessarily ignorant of, or disinterested in, economic problems and potentialities—"in spite of what is often said, Greece did produce 'economists.' "[13] It would also be well to recall that economics, under that title, has been a formal discipline for less than a century, and that so-called economic decisions in recent generations have often been reached primarily on political or social grounds.

ARCHEOLOGICAL EVIDENCE

The second main type of evidence for our present line of investigation is the fruit of extended and ever more precise archeological exploration.[14] This evidence must be contemporary if it can be dated and accidental or intentional intrusions are identified and removed from consideration. Yet historical use of the results of archeological activity is very difficult for both formal and conceptual reasons.

Archeological reports are published all over the world in a variety of journals and treatises, written in many languages and not always easy to locate. The reports themselves are normally a mass of specific observations and descriptions couched in terms such as "Red-on-White Ware," which may be almost meaningless to all but fellow experts. Generalizations are rare, though sometimes they are tossed off in a manner neither logically nor historically well founded. Archeological evidence is also always incomplete. The accidents of destruction and the limited degree to which men of the present will devote resources to discovery of the past usually prevent a complete excavation of even one specific site; reports often end with a sentence suggesting that "further study [or excavation] will be necessary to define fully the bearing of these discoveries."

From our point of view it is unfortunate but true that as a rule Greek archeology has been directed toward illumination of cultural achievements; social and economic aspects of the discoveries have often been scanted or even ignored. Athens has received an undue amount of attention, partly because of the feverish expansion and constant rebuilding of the now huge modern city, partly because of its cultural importance.

Parenthetically, this overemphasis on Attica is far too common in studies of Greek history; one must always remember that in antiquity Greece was simply a geographical area, occupied by many independent states which did not develop at the same rate or even necessarily in the same direction. In the present study the decisive area is the Aegean world, as against the Greek colonies, which were in many respects affected by their situation amid native populations; [15] but within Greece proper conscious effort must be made to keep Athens in balance with Corinth, Miletus, Sparta, and other states.

Through archeological work, however, we do now have a far-flung record not only of states in the Aegean homeland but also of the overseas settlements and trading posts. In combination with the literary evidence, and often quite independent of that source, archeological reports provide invaluable clues to many economic and social changes, and assist particularly in defining the tempo of these alterations.

The chronology, indeed, for the earlier part of our period rests primarily on archeological guidance. Herodotus' account occasionally runs back into the mid-sixth century, and Thucydides gives a précis of the Greek colonization of Sicily, which does not in some points fit the ceramic record; but the reconstructions of early Greek history by later ancient chroniclers are often evidently erroneous or ill-based. The first fixed date which most, though not all, modern scholars would accept is the archonship of Solon in 594. Although minor debate still exists over the dating of successive stages of Corinthian and Attic pottery, their general schemes are sufficiently solid to permit reasonably certain chronological assessments wherever a sufficient bulk of these wares appear.[16] Fortunately, absolute precision in dates B.C. is not a vital matter for the present discussion, but fairly clear appreciation of the speed of changes is certainly necessary.

QUANTIFIABLE DATA

Our inability to quantify any major series of data in early Greece stands in the way of applying interesting approaches devised by modern economists and sociologists. If one applies rigorously the dictum that "it is not possible to study economic growth without some sort of quantitative yardstick to indicate the timing, directions and pace of economic change at the national level," then a meaningful study of early Greek development is impossible.[17] There are no price series for archaic and classical Greece; it is difficult to determine the prices at which items could have been exchanged at any one point, or even to think in modern terms of pricing. The gross national product of any Greek state is totally unknown in statistical terms; and in any case the concept of GNP is of little utility in assessing a pre-industrial society where production lies largely outside the scope of markets. Demographically, we cannot establish the population of any one area, let alone Hellas as a whole, nor can we determine in numerical terms percentages of increase or decrease.

These limitations are distressing, and they must be kept in mind whenever one advances general propositions; but they do not constitute a total bar to reflection on early Greek economic and social changes. A classical student may wryly observe, without malice, that when he turns to surveys of early modern periods he often finds their statistical bases very weak. The price and wage series which have been prepared, for example, for England from the Middle Ages to the Industrial Revolution rest on shaky foundations; even for the eighteenth century the study of British economic growth just quoted goes on to observe that "our quantitative conclusions are heavily dependent on our interpretation of qualitative evidence."[18] National income accounts, as another judicious author has noted, begin no earlier than

World War I, and often rest on extrapolation back from post-World War II statistics.[19] Demographic analyses can make use only of occasional quantitative information down to practically the close of the eighteenth century, when England and the United States began formal, regular censuses.[20]

Recent enthusiasm for quantitative methods of historical research is not a passing fancy, one hopes, for it can lead to uniquely illuminating conclusions in many fields. From the Middle Ages onward a variety of harbor, parish, manor, and other records gives a proper base for statistical methods of analysis—but over all the studies of early modern European economic change are largely qualitative, impressionistic, even subjective. Our investigations of early Greece will necessarily be of that type; yet at times there is some evidence, particularly of vases and temples, which can be quantified usefully. For other major issues it will occasionally be possible to establish cross-checks which limit the areas of uncertainty.

MODERN PARALLELS AND THEORIES

Significant methodological aspects of the line of attack employed in following pages deserve to be clearly stated at the outset. I have found useful an exploration of economic and social developments in modern Europe, from the revival of the mid-fifteenth century on to the later decades of the eighteenth century, when the Industrial and French revolutions begin to add complications of too modern a type; [21] even the period of expansion in the high Middle Ages has interesting parallels at some points. This evidence is particularly valuable for our purposes in furnishing a large volume of detailed information by which we can establish parameters of the possible, as in agricultural yields or demographic movements. Modern studies also can raise questions which might not otherwise be immediately suggested by the ancient sources.[22]

In adducing modern parallels there are traps. An evident danger is the likelihood that one may rely on obsolete or inadequate studies. More important is the fact that early modern Europe does not provide exact parallels to ancient Greece: the essentially unified Catholic church, the concept of large national states, the survival of cities at least in Italy across the whole of the Middle Ages, and a host of other differences stand in the way of easy equations. Yet the population of Europe from about A.D. 1450 to about 1800 did exist in a relatively simple social and economic system, resting for the greater part on self-sufficient agriculture. Men lived in close group structures, and their life expectancy did not extend past the 30's. Scholars of the western world in the twentieth century cannot directly appreciate the manifold important consequences of these factors, but if we look from time to time at early modern history we may be able to sense their possible bearing for early Greece.

Early modern factual skeins are one thing; theoretical constructs of the nineteenth and twentieth centuries, quite another. These latter are the fruit of great physical and psychological upheavals in the French and Industrial revolutions, and later of Marx and Freud; however useful they may be as tools of analysis for the modern world, they cannot be applied directly to ancient Greece. That, however, does not mean they have not often been so misused. Much has been published by scholars of Marxist persuasion, and views of this tint have considerable influence even in outwardly non-Marxist approaches.[23] Such work is suggestive inasmuch as it turns developments, as it were, upside down or strips off conventional beliefs. Yet it also is often seriously blinkered, and writers so influenced cannot avoid imposing a straitjacket of modern ideology on available evidence from an era of very different character.

Economic and social analyses of earlier societies which

rest on bourgeois and capitalist beliefs are scarcely less distorted. Again and again in recent literature one will find "trade" for capitalistic reasons advanced as a prime motive force in the eighth, even the tenth and eleventh centuries B.C.—eras in which such a concept could not consciously have been influential.[24] The Greek language did not even have precise words for labor, capital, or entrepreneurs in their modern senses. The forces lying behind these concepts existed but not always in a conscious manner; any discussion which often employs their modern equivalents will introduce unwarranted connotations arising from the work of Adam Smith, David Ricardo, and a host of later economic analysts. I shall not hesitate to use modern terms where they come easily into play, but these pages will not be phrased primarily in terms customary in modern economics and sociology. Several very important institutions or concepts will be given only in transliteration (*polis, chremata,* etc.), and such words as city, peasant, aristocracy, and others on the definition of which no two scholars may entirely agree will be employed as precisely as possible in order to limit the effects of modern thought.

A specific example of the difficulties in this area may be useful. Late in the nineteenth century Karl Bücher, following out suggestions in earlier German economic thought, advanced a scheme of economic stages according to which the ancient world lay on the primitive level of *Hauswirtschaft*.[25] This view angered two great scholars, Eduard Meyer and Julius Beloch, who argued that, on the contrary, antiquity was essentially modern and capitalistic in its economic structure.[26] Further debate continued to the 1930's, when M. I. Rostovtzeff could still assert that at least the Hellenistic economy after Alexander "differed from the modern economy only quantitatively, not qualitatively" in his criticism of the renewed and even intensified assertion of Bücher's views by Johannes Hasebroek.[27]

Since then there has been no significant addition to the debate, and one recent commentator has observed that "the relationship between trade and politics in classical Greece still seems to be treated most of the time as if there were no conceptual problems . . . that means, necessarily, that the concepts and generalizations which are constantly being brought to bear, expressly or tacitly, are modern ones, even when they hide beneath the mask of 'common sense.' " [28]

A PERSONAL POINT OF VIEW

From the point of view which will appear in succeeding chapters this debate is absolutely meaningless, though dangerous. Antiquity, by definition as well as in a chronolog-. ical sense, is not modernity; and abstract schemes of stages do violence to the fundamental qualities of history. Moreover, Bücher and his opponents lay under the spell of the concept of *homo oeconomicus*. The theoretical explorations of the rise of modern capitalism associated with the names of Weber, Sombart, and others are stimulating for the study of early modern Europe, but they cannot help us extensively in searching out the characteristics and motive drives of early Greek economic growth. The deliberate, calculating pursuit of profit, specialization of economic activity in narrow ranges, bookkeeping, and credit will not be found in our period—not at least with the clarity in which they can be assessed in modern economic history. They should not even be expected in so very different a world as that of early Hellas, where economic and social conditions and changes were intimately tied to parallel and interrelated political, religious, and cultural characteristics and alterations. For purposes of clearer understanding we may separate out economic and social threads, but their context exerted a tremendous influence on their structure and the speed of evolution. And that context, though it can only be occasionally briefly sketched in later pages, was not the same as that of Europe in either the fifteenth or the nineteenth century.

To return to an earlier observation, we do have sufficient literary and archeological sources to be able to discern at least the general lines of change in Greece from 800 to 500 B.C. Evidence, after all, is important; it often has a happy faculty for upsetting or verifying theories. No amount of specific data, to be sure, will be sufficient to provide crushing, irrefutable answers to major issues of contention, but every now and then a smaller aspect of these debates can be decisively settled. An excellent example is the effect of the downdating of early Greek coinage, which must totally remove any possibility of explaining the rise of tyrants or the disturbed conditions in the time of Hesiod or Solon in terms of the effects of the introduction of money.

Yet specific information must always be set within a general conceptual framework. As an English novelist has recently put it, "There are certain areas of scholarship, early Greek history is one and Roman law is another, where the scantiness of evidence sets a special challenge to the disciplined mind. It is a game with very few pieces, where the skill of the player lies in complicating the rules. The isolated and uneloquent fact must be exhibited within a tissue of hypothesis subtle enough to make it speak." [29] Whether such a tissue can be provided here for all aspects of our subject is doubtful; but let me suggest some parts of the framework which will be implicit in the specific analyses of subsequent chapters.

Although the focus will be the economic growth of early Greece, we shall have to range further afield into political, religious, and intellectual history at many points in order to understand its background. A thoughtful observer of modern simple societies has recently commented: "Structurally, 'the economy' does not exist. Rather than a distinct and spe-

cialized organization, 'economy' is something that general-
ized social groups and relations, notably kinship groups and
relatives, *do*. Economy is rather a function of the society
than a structure, for the armature of the economic process is
provided by groups classically conceived 'non-economic.' " [30]
Interwoven with economic developments, as this passage suggests, are the social structure and its components; and these
elements will require special discussion at several points,
particularly but not exclusively in Chapters VI and VIII.

We may, thus, seem to have come to those old friends of
modern analysis, social classes, as the operative vehicles for
change. This is indeed essentially the result; how could it be
otherwise in a civilized society? Yet we are not thereby compelled to accept modern theories of *Klassenkampf* or to interpret Greek economic changes solely in class terms. [31] The
expansion of early Greece, insofar as we do define it within a
context of economic and social groups, must be described
with more delicate nuances.

Let me suggest four of these qualifications. First, the concepts of upper classes/aristocracy and lower classes/peasantry
did not in early Greece mean exactly what we might be
inclined at first sight to take as their definitions; somewhat
unconventional interpretations of these terms will be advanced later. Secondly, neither peasants nor aristocrats were
homines oeconomici of modern stamp, and the tendency in
some modern studies to assign to them far-reaching economic motives is totally unwarranted. [32] Other scholars,
however, have created an equally impossible picture of
Greek artists and aristocrats as disinterested in wealth or
economic gain. We shall perhaps not find ruthless capitalistic entrepreneurs endowed with modern economic rationalism, but landholders and others could be ruthless in
seeking their own advantage and so provided a mighty impetus to the forces of expansion which lay in the general
progress of the eastern Mediterranean and of Greece itself.

Thirdly, due appreciation of the influence of this drive must be set within a primarily agricultural context—a requirement which has very generally not been applied by modern students, influenced by the myth of the bourgeoisie.

Finally, sharp class opposition must not be postulated for our period. In the kaleidoscopic confusion of the great age of change, aristocrats, commoners of industrial and commercial character, and slaves were spun apart into far more consciously differentiated elements of the social structure, but the inheritance from the earlier simple world of Dark Age Greece prevented this process from producing total fragmentation. The upper classes, indeed, of early Greece unleashed forces which eventually ran beyond their control. Intellectually and artistically they placed an indelible stamp on Greek culture, but politically and economically they no longer had absolute power by 500.

Chapter II

Motive Forces in
Economic Development

In the fifth century the Greeks could use only their imagination and a few survivals to visualize their early background, but Thucydides' picture is essentially supported by the archeological record:

> The country now called Hellas had no settled population in ancient times; instead there was a series of migrations, as the various tribes, being under the constant pressure of invaders who were stronger than they were, were always prepared to abandon their own territory. There was no commerce, and no safe communication either by land or sea; the use they made of their land was limited to the production of necessities; they had no surplus of wealth, and no regular system of agriculture.[1]

During the age of expansion the volume of industrial output increased tremendously compared with that of the Dark Ages, and was much diversified in types and styles. Through burgeoning commercial activity the Greek world had created a relatively advanced economic system reaching out to trading posts on the civilized shores of the Near East and to a network of Greek colonies on the more backward coasts of the western Mediterranean and Black seas. Luxuries were an important part of seaborne trade, but bulk items— metals, timber, wool, and, by the close of the period, grain—were also significant. Trading and industrial elements emerged as distinct parts of the economic system, and at least some men concentrated on either long-distance or local commerce.

Abroad and at home the advanced centers of economic life became urban communities. After Cyrus the Persian king had conquered Asia Minor he received a warning from the Spartans not to molest the Greeks of the seaboard, and incredulously inquired who these presumptuous people might be. On getting a reply he observed, "I have never yet been afraid of any men, who have a set place in the middle of their city, where they come together to cheat each other and forswear themselves." [2] The tale may well be apocryphal, but it will recur in these pages as a leitmotif, so succinctly does it summarize the vital differences between Greece and the Near East; only Hellas had stationary markets in which enterprising individuals played important economic roles. A modern observer would also stress the fact that the Greek standard for measuring economic values had by Cyrus' day become coined money, even if coins were not always actually used in the exchange of goods and services. Animating this structure was a conscious interest in gain; though or may not describe this vital spirit in terms of modern ent preneurial rationalism, Greek evolution did produce

able to seize opportunities and eager to do so, at times in the sheer delight of gaming.

The various lines of progress can be observed with some clarity, at least in their general dimensions; agricultural changes, though equally important, are not so easily surveyed. In their more detailed aspects they will concern us in later chapters, but first we must isolate the mainsprings or causes, and distinguish attendant circumstances or results from the motive forces themselves.

To illustrate this latter point: trade has often been urged as a primary ingredient by those few students who have turned from modern economic history to consider Greek economic development. Yet trade—or at least interchange of goods—had long existed; and the increase in such interchanges must fundamentally be accounted an outward indication of general economic advance, important though it was in encouraging continuous industrial evolution. Colonization, again, provided important overseas markets and safe harbors for seaborne activity, but it was certainly a visible reflection of the general expansion in the Aegean homeland. Moreover, students of early modern European history agree that the main sources of demand and supply, except for exotic items, must be sought for that period in western Europe itself; and the same was true of the ancient Aegean. The rise of cities, the invention of coinage, and the concentration of political power in the hands of tyrants, all of which have been singled out from time to time as motive forces, are even more clearly consequences, both logically and chronologically, though again each could help fuel the outburst already under way.

More fundamental factors must be sought, and they will largely be found beyond the economic sphere proper. We must look at the general progress of the eastern Mediterranean in the first millennium, at the political and religious changes in the Greek world itself, at possible demographic alterations, and at the dominant social element in the Aegean, which could provide leadership and impetus.

REVIVAL IN THE
EASTERN MEDITERRANEAN

During the second millennium B.C.—the Late Bronze Age—the ancient Near East attained an impressive height, concluding a line of evolution reaching back in some areas two thousand years. Egypt, which long had been civilized, acquired for a brief period hegemony in Palestine and Syria; Mesopotamia saw first the power of Hammurapi, king of Babylon and famous law-giver, and thereafter an abortive expansion of Assyria in its northern reaches. In Asia Minor the Hittite realm held power over central and southern districts and vied with Egypt for the control of Syria. Even in the Aegean the lords of the Mycenean fortress-palaces reached the fringe of civilization by using writing for their palace bureaucracies and by supporting a variety of advanced arts.

Then toward the end of the millennium this advanced world crumbled, partly through internal decay and dissension, partly through interstate rivalries. The coup de grâce was delivered by barbarian invaders by land and sea, Indo-Europeans from the north and Semitic-speaking peoples from the desert. In the Aegean and in Asia Minor civilization was so tender and so recent a plant that it was destroyed; in Egypt, Mesopotamia, and the connecting corridor of Syria and Palestine there was widescale destruction of urban centers, some of which disappeared forever, but the civilized tissues of life were not quite crushed.

The ensuing period from about 1100 to 900 was a dreary one. Kings, warlords, and priests could no longer heap up great buildings and patronize the arts. When the super-structure of life was shaken, peasants and artisans, as well as the upper classes, suffered, and life continued only in tiny, local units.

Eventually, however, the Near East regained its strength and launched out on new ways, born of the past but far different in many respects from the patterns dominant down through the Late Bronze Age. To give a specific but significant example, iron came into common use, as smiths grew acquainted with the complicated techniques of repeated heating, quenching, and hammering which were required to make iron (or steel) tools and weapons.[3] Iron objects, sometimes of meteoric origin, had been known since the fifth millennium, but only after 1000 was iron metallurgy widely understood. Wares manufactured from iron do not appear on a large scale until about 800. Whereas the availability of bronze had been limited by shortages of tin, iron ores existed in many areas and could be utilized for more ordinary purposes, though iron still remained a somewhat valuable metal.

More generally, a revival of economic activity can be detected from 900 onward. Among the leaders were the Arameans of Syria and northern Mesopotamia, who traded by land, using camels rather than donkeys,[4] and the Phoenicians, who lived on the narrow plain between mountains and sea in what is now Lebanon. Here the inhabitants of a number of cities, including Tyre, Sidon, Berytus, Byblos, and Aradus, all of which had ancient roots, launched out on the sea, reaching Cyprus and parts of the western Mediterranean before 800.

Phoenician craftsmen also gained a wide market by developing an amalgam of earlier artistic ideas, especially of Egyptian origin, which they executed in bronze, ivory, wood, textiles (often dyed a Tyrian purple), and other materials. Together with objects of true Egyptian origin, such as faience and glass, and parallel achievements in Syrian and other Near Eastern workshops, these wares, often mass-produced in repetitious patterns, became very popular. In fine, an artistic *koine,* though differentiated in subtle ways, was coming into existence by 800 in the eastern Mediterranean.[5]

The consequence of the commercial and artistic integration of the Near East was a political unification, which was carried out by the warlords of Assyria. During the ninth century the kings of that small principality engaged in great raids, especially westward toward the forests and trade routes of Syria; but after a temporary quiescence early in the next century the powerful leader Tiglath-Pileser III (744–27) gained control of Babylon, where he was crowned king, took Damascus, and led his armies as far west as the Mediterranean. Successors including the usurper Sargon II, Sennacherib, and Esarhaddon extended Assyrian power even into Egypt. Under Ashurbanipal (668-after 633) the Assyrian empire was outwardly at its apogee, the largest state the Near East had yet seen.

The Greeks of the Aegean never knew the Assyrian empire directly, even though some of their kindred who had settled in Cilicia and Cyprus had to give fealty to the Assyrian kings. For Hellenic progress, however, the political stabilization of the Near East was a potent factor. Assyrian warlords exacted tribute and booty, but they also gave security to routes of trade and greatly promoted demand for the civilized arts which embellished their many palaces with furniture, sculpture, and other luxury goods.

To a far less degree, but a significant one, the upper classes of the Aegean world were by the mid-ninth century also showing their first eagerness for those products of Near Eastern workshops; but the extent to which the Greeks could acquire luxuries depended on their ability to proffer raw materials, especially metals, to the expanding and more advanced Near Eastern centers. As exchange developed, it took place mainly by sea routes; the Greek trading post at Al Mina in Syria was established by 800. Skilled techniques once known in the Aegean but long forgotten were likewise revived by drafts on Near Eastern technology, though Greek commercial and industrial activity cannot be taken as a simple imitation of Levantine models. The general subject of the connections between Near Eastern and historic Greek civilizations I have explored at length elsewhere; at this point it will suffice to suggest that the Greeks could not have progressed as swiftly as they did had they not renewed their ties with the Near East, but that the manner in which Hellenic culture developed was to be very different.[6] Above all, internal Aegean progress was requisite for the Greeks to be able to look outward in any direction; though the beginnings of contact can be put back into the ninth century, really influential relations commenced only in the eighth century.

During the earlier centuries, when the Near East was reordering its structure, the Aegean turned into a Greek, homebound lake. That unity had not existed in the Minoan and Mycenaean eras of the second millennium, for in those periods many local, diverse cultures existed on Aegean shores; linguistic survivals also suggest the early presence of a variety of languages. During the Dark Ages all languages but Greek disappeared save in isolated districts such as eastern Crete; coasts and islands alike took on a common Hellenic cultural stamp.

To some degree this unification was the consequence of the upheavals during the invasions which closed the second millennium. Greek tradition preserved legends of frenzied migration across the Aegean to escape the barbarian conquerors of the mainland; and even though, in detail, any of these stories is suspect, still physical evidence supports the picture of settlement on the coasts of Asia Minor in the Dark Ages.[7] Equally important was a process of cultural osmosis in an era when old patterns had been shaken or destroyed. The clearest illustration of this fusion is provided by pottery styles: during the tenth century Attic Protogeometric forms spread widely throughout the Aegean, and in the next century the Geometric style, largely of Attic origin, became dominant in almost all Greek pottery workshops. Yet even the pottery demonstrates another enduring quality of Greek civilization of the highest importance, that is, the strength of local adaptations and variations. Just as the Greek language was spoken everywhere but always in local dialects, so too Geometric pottery was designed in a basically uniform manner which was subtly differentiated; Cycladic, Rhodian, Corinthian, and other individual wares can easily be distinguished at a casual glance.

On the one hand there was a Hellenic unity. The word "panhellene" appears very early, in the poetry of Archilochus; during the Persian invasion the Athenians had occasion to comment on "our common language, the altars and sacrifices of which we all partake, the common character which we bear." [8] But always as counterpoise there was a strong attachment to local communities and to their special, even unique, political, religious, and cultural stamps. In that tension lay one of the major forces promoting progress; experiment in any part of the Greek world could take place independently, but was likely to reverberate with sympathetic echoes in other regions.

Further survey of Greece in the Dark Ages is unnecessary save to point out one other conclusion which inevitably follows from examining its pottery. The era was a simple one which appears almost static if considered at any one time, yet Hellenic pottery styles developed continuously from the beginning of Protogeometric wares, about 1050, onward. The structure of Greek life and thought contained dynamic elements which could be powerful, if unleashed and strengthened. First, however, the damage to society which had been occasioned by the upheavals at the end of the Bronze Age had to be repaired, and that restoration required centuries.

GREEK POLITICAL
AND RELIGIOUS DEVELOPMENTS

By the middle of the eighth century the Greeks were ready to leap forward on many fronts. The hundred years that followed brought the most dramatic alterations in all Greek history. Change was many-sided and intricately interconnected in all fields. Swiftly, with simple but sharp strokes, the Greeks erected a coherent, interwoven system, politically, religiously, and culturally, which endured throughout the rest of their independent life. In field after field we can trace back to the early seventh century or late eighth century, but no further, the developed lineaments of the Hellenic outlook; beyond lie only primitive, almost inchoate foundations.[9]

In the arts, for example, pottery shed its rigid Geometric dress; Protocorinthian and Protoattic potters, and others, created the forms and elaborated the motifs which were to be used by their successors for centuries. The major mould of Greek architectural thought, the stone temple, made its appearance. Sculptors began to work on a large scale in stone and metal; from the first simple modeling of human forms in small figurines they advanced swiftly to such noble types as the female *kore* and the nude male *kouros*. While the epic tradition long continued to affect literary creation, new poetic meters appeared in the seventh century, and the

Greek view of human personality gained new depth in lyric verse.

From the economic point of view the most obviously relevant developments were the political and religious alterations of the Greek world. During the Mycenaean age the inhabitants of the more advanced parts of Greece had been subject, perhaps not always willingly, to the lord of one or another palace-fortress, who held the title of *wanax*. In the simplification of life thereafter the Dark Ages knew only tribally organized peoples; the question often put to a stranger in Homer is, "What is your *demos?*" Although a *demos* or *ethnos* occupied a certain limited part of the Greek landscape, its visible political bonds were tribal unity and obedience to a particular chieftain or *basileus*.[10] The *basileis* did not stand far above their fellow tribesmen in either economic or political power, nor did their way of life and social customs differ radically from those of the upper classes who fought, hunted, or feasted beside them. Royal revenues consisted almost solely of food from their own land and the booty gained in raids on neighboring peoples. Most significant of all, the *basileus* did not absorb all the political powers of the community. In the lawsuit depicted on the Homeric shield of Achilles judgment lay in the hands of village wise men.[11] Priests and seers conveyed the will of the gods, who could speak to any man if they so desired. Assemblies of the folk and of greater men occurred sporadically for political, religious, and other purposes; but these gatherings proceeded on no regular rules and had no specific functions.

By the time of Aristotle and Plato Greek political theory was couched in terms of a far more consciously and firmly organized entity, the *polis*. Aristotle, indeed, went so far in the introduction to his *Politics* as to make the famous assertion, "Man is by nature an animal intended to live in a *polis*." Yet even in his day many Greeks still lived in *ethne;* so far as our scanty evidence goes, the *polis* form of political organization had crystallized rather swiftly in the southeastern parts of the Greek mainland during the eighth century, but after the time of Homer. In the epics the word *polis* means only a central geographical point, often a citadel, not a consciously organized, sovereign state.

The machinery of government in a *polis* was quite limited at the outset. A council which may be said to represent the upper classes had extensive powers. In most Greek states the *basileus* disappeared, and executive power was parceled out among several officials, usually chosen for one year. Whether the nascent *poleis* all had formal assemblies of the citizens is quite doubtful, but eventually such assemblies became customary at Sparta, Athens, and elsewhere.

A fundamental characteristic of the *polis* was the concentration of all major activity at one point within its territorial bounds (the old Homeric *polis,* now usually called *asty*). In the earliest days that center was marked by no more than perhaps a walled hill (the Acropolis at Athens) and an open space or agora for assembly; but as the Greeks began to build temples they normally located the shrine of the patron deity of their state at that site. The focal point was *not* a city—the translation of *polis* as "city-state" introduces serious semantic confusion and will not be used in these pages—and the consolidation of its political machinery was not motivated in any significant degree by economic factors. It should also perhaps be stressed that the *polis* was essentially a native development in the Aegean world, which owed little or nothing to Near Eastern states such as those of Phoenicia.[12]

Throughout all later Greek history the presence or absence of an urban center was incidental; what was vital to a *polis* was a certain attitude of its inhabitants which was embodied in their political and social organization, a union of human beings not on a basis of personal loyalty to a leader but as a firm communal entity. Citizens felt that the state theoretically embodied or safeguarded justice (*dike*), whose sister was *eunomia*—not democracy or social equality, but the maintenance of traditional right. The claims of *eunomia* could be raised equally against *basileis* and tyrants, against aristocratic excesses (as in Solon's elegies), or even later against the pretensions of the lower classes if they sought to overthrow the inherited position of the upper orders. Law restrained individual caprice: "The law-abiding *polis*, though small and set on a lofty rock, outranks senseless Nineveh." [13]

This ideal had not been openly expressed in the Homeric epics, but from Archilochus onward it is palpable in archaic poetry and is well summed up by Aristotle: "A state aims at being, as far as it can be, a society composed of equals and peers." [14] In reality the rural upper classes very often were dominant, and the evolution of the *polis* was intimately connected with the consolidation of the aristocracy—but this latter factor is not the sole explanation of its appearance. The new political form was not designed as a tool for the hands of oppressors; it was rather a reaction of the citizen body as a whole to the breadth of change in the era.[15] Whenever the aristocrats went too far, the *polis* was likely to support a lawgiver or reformer, or even to accept temporarily reversion to one-man rule in the form of a tyrant who checked the abuse of privilege by his fellow aristocrats.

Tighter political unity was a reflection of the quickening of Aegean life and of the need to make innovative decisions. Still, the *polis* proved to be so important a framework for later history, a hothouse for forcing Hellenic culture as it has been happily described, that it must be accounted a prime motive force in Greek expansion.

Changes within the *polis* system were also of importance in the seventh and sixth centuries. We cannot write a connected political history of the Greek world, or of any one state, during this era; but clearly interstate rivalries passed beyond mere frontier raids into formal wars very soon after the *poleis* had appeared on the Greek mainland. The earliest war known from Greek tradition which would fit into this pattern was a conflict between Corinth and Megara in the years around 720; soon thereafter came the protracted Lelantine war in Euboea.[16]

By the early seventh century the relatively loose forms of fighting which dominated Homeric battlefields had given way to a closer structure of infantry organization, the serried phalanx of heavily armored hoplites. Plate III.a shows an individual hoplite striding determinedly forward, with greaves, breastplate, and crested helmet (his shield, which he held by a thong and grasped in his left hand, is missing); the Chigi oenochoe, painted at Corinth soon after 650, is the earliest certain representation of phalanxes, with a musician to pipe the step. Leaders remained important in the new style of combat, but less so than previously; the communal unity of the *polis*—or at least of its landholders who could afford the armor—perhaps displays itself best in this military reform.[17] Very often in recent scholarship the concept of a "hoplite class" has been advanced to explain political and social changes in the seventh century; but, as will be more fully discussed in Chapters VI and VIII, the term "class" is ill-advised, and the purported pressures of this group require close scrutiny.

The rise of tyrants, the expansion of state machinery, and other political phenomena may also be reserved for later pages; at this point we may stress the more general economic effects of the *polis,* which were both favorable and unfavorable. The state gave local security for traders and artisans, and its central focus provided an attractive site, frequented by the citizenry on varied occasions; true cities often eventually developed at these points. Pressures by the state on its citizens were, however, far more limited than in the Persian or Roman empires, and room for any private enterprise which might be undertaken correspondingly the greater. The machinery of the *polis* was rudimentary, usually unpaid; only if a state tried to support a navy was significant financial organization required. Yet for a variety of public purposes coinage finally became desirable in many states, and facilitated the growing flexibility of economic life.

The other side of the picture was less encouraging. While the essential spirit of the *polis* encouraged in many ways the free activity of its citizens, nonetheless it imposed communal solidarity and hemmed the unrestricted play of economic forces. Greek *poleis* emerged in an era when almost all their inhabitants were farmers; political rights were often directly tied to ownership of land, and not infrequently remained so even after non-agricultural economic sectors had developed. As a result the policies of the states were not particularly directed toward promoting trade and industry, though this limitation has been overstressed in modern studies of Greek history. Foreign traders and artisans were to be found in many of the more advanced *poleis,* but they were rarely allowed to gain citizenship. The ideal of the *polis,* as it appears both in fourth-century political theory and at times in practice, was in the end one of *autarkeia* or local self-sufficiency.

The major unfavorable aspect of the *polis* system was very much the same as that which became evident in early modern Europe as the nation states evolved. That is to say, each Greek state was absolutely sovereign and lived uneasily with its neighbors; war was endemic. The fragmentation of Greece was even more extreme than that of modern Europe, for a *polis* generally covered only a very few hundred square miles—Athens, with 1000 square miles, was one of the largest. Some 200-odd *poleis* eventually existed in the Aegean (the island of Ceos, six by ten miles, was divided into four states); reckoning the colonies and other farther settlements, the total reaches some 1500 independent political units.

Modern historians, embued with secular and scientific attitudes at least on the rational plane, must have difficulty in comprehending how vital religious attitudes and institutions were in earlier ages. Greek life, in particular, was largely organized in groups, from the family upwards, and the outward marks of these groups as well as their inner cement consisted of shared religious observances and beliefs. In no realm of activity do the stresses and changes of the Greek world from 800 to 500 manifest themselves in more diverse and important fashion than in religion. Here we can comment briefly only on certain aspects which may be said to relate directly to economic matters, especially the rise of festivals, the building of temples, and the connection of religious attitudes and economic ethnics.

The dichotomy between panhellenism and localism existed in religion as elsewhere. International religious festivals either came into existence after 800 or were much elaborated. On the Cycladic island of Delos, where Apollo was born, the long-robed Ionians met in his honor from early times "with their children and shy wives; mindful, they delight you with boxing and dancing and song," and an observer "would be pleased in heart gazing at the men and well-girded women with their swift ships and great wealth." One of the first harbor works thus far known in Hellas was a mole constructed at Delos by about 600; it is not difficult to postulate that traders as well as the faithful attended these *panegyreis*.[18] The festival at Olympia in the western Peloponnesus was said to have been founded in 776; if so, it remained local until after 700 but then expanded swiftly as the western colonies became strong. Other festivals or "games" appeared later at Delphi and elsewhere; and all served not only religious and athletic objectives, but also as meeting places for aristocrats and undoubtedly for traders.

More important, however, was the development of cults of local heroes, semi-divine human figures of the legendary past, and of the deities of the *polis*. During the eighth century and even earlier the Greeks built very small shrines, usually of mud-brick and wood, to their gods. In the seventh century temples grew in size but were still often of the same materials. Stone was employed in an early stage of the Heraeum at Samos and for some small temples such as that at Dreros, but its use became common only in the sixth century, when temples also normally had colonnades. From the mid-seventh century onward the roofs were covered with tiles, an innovation which had considerable influence on design. Corinth was a leading center in the production of rooftiles; when the temple of Apollo Laphrius at Calydon was re-roofed about 530, the tiles came ready-made from Corinth, each piece numbered for its place.[19]

The provision of earthly homes for the gods required the use of communal manpower, to a greater degree than any other public activity except warfare. Early stone temples were usually built from small blocks, but by the sixth century temples at Acragas in Sicily and elsewhere were constructed of such huge blocks that it has recently been suggested they were maneuvered up earthen ramps, as was done when the Egyptian pyramids were built; on this theory the common use of hoisting devices, which needed less manpower, came only in the last decades of the sixth century.[20] Cash outlays, on the other hand, were obligatory only for foreign sculptors and architects or for alien marbles, timber, and rooftiles. A silver tablet of about 530 from the Artemisium at Ephesus lists receipts in gold and silver derived from gifts, from dues on salt, wood, and goods imported by sea, and "from the city." [21] Later on, temples were erected by means of small contracts under the control of building committees, but the stone itself was provided by the community; we do not know whether formal contractors for the detailed work were needed in earlier centuries. Both the occasion for the erection of a temple and such cash resources as were expended on its completion rested to a considerable degree on victory in war; but the observation that "without wars, few of the temples and other sacred buildings of Greece would have been built" applies more to the great fifth-century temples of Syracuse, Acragas, and Athens than to the religious fervor of earlier generations. [22]

It would be very useful to have an accurate and complete list of all temples erected in the seventh and then in the sixth centuries, for this would provide a truly significant index of the vigor of Greek public life and of its underlying economic strength. Such a list does not appear to exist, but an approximate estimate can be drawn from surviving architectural members or grounds plans. Evidence for some 39 temples constructed before 600 can be adduced if one includes a number of very small shrines. The numbers are so great for the next century that modern architectural handbooks cite only typical examples, but at least 88 are certain; several of the sixth-century temples, at Ephesus, Samos, and Acragas, were among the largest ever built in Greece, and many were elaborately decorated. Accordingly the proportions for resources committed to temple building in the sixth as against the seventh century might best be estimated in the range of 3 : 1. [23]

In celebration of athletic victories, success in war, or personal piety, men (and women too) dedicated bronze tripods, cauldrons, figurines, and after 700 large-sized statues in ever growing abundance at international and local shrines and also at graves. If one counts the male and female statues listed in two recent and thorough publications, very much the same conclusion emerges as for temples.[24] For *korai* 35 are assigned to the seventh century and 144 to the sixth, a ratio of 4 : 1. For *kouroi* 31 are of the late seventh century, 157 of the sixth, a ratio of 5 : 1. In both cases we must reduce the ratios to some extent to compensate for the fact that stone statues were not carved all across the seventh century. Vases and figurines from Greek workshops are so numerous, and often not even published, that one cannot derive from them a statistical check; but the ratios we have derived from temples and statues do not appear unreasonable in these other areas of Greek production. Undoubtedly one must make proper reserves for accidents of preservation; it is also necessary to keep in mind that this quantitative base is both limited and connected to some degree to the sphere of religion. Yet the Greeks were not more religious in the sixth than in the seventh century, and after weighing a variety of other possible qualifications I would judge that a ratio in the range of at least 3 : 1 for the sixth as against the seventh century both suggests the great economic expansion of the age and provides a reasonable order of magnitude for that advance in physical terms.

This activity, true, might have had an unfavorable economic aspect insofar as the precious and base metals available to Greece were thesaurized in temple precincts and treasuries; but gold and silver dedications appear to have been extremely rare until king Gyges of Lydia embellished Delphi and other shrines. Treasurers of Athena existed at Athens at least by the mid-sixth century, but temple treasuries became rich there only in the days of the Athenian empire. Excavations of temple sites have turned up mainly dedications of figurines, both bronze and clay (the latter at times made in workshops near the sanctuary), cauldrons, and in a few cases collections of iron spits, an early form of currency. These dedications had more influence in encouraging industrial activity than in immobilizing its resources.

We have no specific examples of the tapping of temple reserves for secular needs, but Hecataeus at least could be bold enough to suggest conversion of the riches of the temple of Branchidae during the Ionian revolt.[25]

Religious beliefs had visible effects in encouraging the arts and crafts, and also letters, of early Greece. Of equal importance psychologically was the provision of manifold vents and reassurances for the tensions and fears of contemporary life. These stresses will appear more fully in Chapter VIII; but in summation Greek religion fundamentally gave support to human confidence. On this matter one could stray far afield; I trust it will be enough to point out that the Greeks could never have ventured abroad in colonization and overseas trade had they not felt that divine forces favored them.

Keeping in mind the recent economic interpretations of the Protestant Reformation and the Puritan work ethic, one must also note that Greek religious concepts did not distort or seriously affect the economic attitudes of men in the age of expansion. By the close of our period the Greeks had a rich, diversified religious structure; but they remained too earth-centered, too keen of thought, and too materially successful to yield themselves utterly to religious preoccupations. Morality was not totally dissociated from the gods, but in practical aspects was anchored mainly to the institutions of the *polis* and to the aristocratic code of life. Hesiod provides evidence that one neighbor should help another, at least to some degree, and the strong group ties of Greek society encouraged mutual assistance; Solon's friends thus were willing to contribute to his relief when his father ruined the ancestral estate by undue generosity.[26] Greek ethics, however, provided no basic spurs or checks on economic self-assertion, simply the warning "Nothing Too Much."

DEMOGRAPHIC FACTORS

Modern economic historians agree that demographic characteristics of a population and especially any marked shifts are among the most influential forces in its economic progress or decline. From Adam Smith on through Marx to the present day the classic view has been that population alters as a consequence of economic change and tends to press on the limits of available supplies of food; but in recent years powerful arguments have been advanced for the essential independence of demographic factors.[27]

For early Greece the enduring demographic aspects can be established without any doubt. In the first place, almost all the population was and remained rural, committed to traditional agriculture and to raising small animals.[28] Greece is semi-tropical, at least in its lowlands, with a climate in which it is possible to support oneself relatively easily; but its small, scattered plains of red soil do not today and never have produced the surpluses which could be gained in the river valleys of the Near East. If men were to eat, they generally had to raise their own food.

The percentage of any *polis* which could have been non-agricultural, i.e., supported off its agricultural surplus, can only be estimated. Crop yields and other dimensions of the agricultural system will be considered when we investigate the peasantry more closely, but they were not conducive to large surpluses. At Athens in the time of Solon dependent farmers had to yield one-sixth of their crops to their creditors or masters; this figure, which appears as a serious grievance, was probably near the feasible maximum. Indeed, intelligent creditors would probably have sought control only in the better lands of Attica, so that over all the surplus of this very ill-favored area would probably have been much less. Some districts of the Peloponnesus were better watered and more fertile than Attica, but other parts were even more mountainous.[29] As a working hypothesis we may assume that over 80 percent of the population of most Greek states must have been directly connected to agricultural pursuits, and that probably some 90 per cent or more were so involved, as in colonial America. True urban centers with non-agricultural elements could only be very small in size unless seaborne grain were available—and could be paid for.

A second demographic characteristic of early Greece was the control of its population by the factors which have been dominant virtually everywhere in human history down to the eighteenth century in western Europe, and are still visible today in some parts of the globe. Greek women, that is, probably entered into marriage as early as did Roman girls, somewhere after menarche, at about 14 years.[30] Hesiod urges his male auditors to marry not far short of 30 and to select a wife who has "been grown up" for four years; he also advises the husband to have only one son.[31] Such an arrangement would help to prevent the splintering of farms and would also usually mean that the husband had already gained possession of his own father's farm; the connection between holding a rural plot and the political and economic independence of an *oikos* or family was always close in Greek life. So great a disparity in age of males and females at the time of marriage has been more noticeable in early and modern Europe than in other societies and may not have existed very generally in early Greece; the important point, however, is the likelihood that females married very close to the maximum of their fertility.[32]

Gross reproduction rates may thus have been in the order of five to six and one-half children per female, but only a little more than two children of any married couple would have reached adulthood; infant mortality probably ran over 200 per 1000. Classical scholars, working largely from Athenian evidence, have sometimes suggested up to almost two and one-half surviving children, but such a figure in a monogamous society would have produced an increase of one-third in a population group over a century, an impossible result for classic times and unlikely even in our own era.[33] Death rates in adulthood were also higher than in the modern world; for the males, engaged in harsh physical labor, died, worn out, before their time. Life expectancy at birth in consequence must have been in the range of 30 to 35 years; women died somewhat earlier than men as a rule.[34] Yet better nourished and less strained male citizens who reached the age of 30 to 34 could expect another 20 to 25 years of life; the age of military service usually ran to 60, though field duty was uncommon after about 50, and Solon visualized a man's career as stretching even to the age of 70.[35] Over one-third the population of any Greek *polis* would have been under 15; in fourth-century Athens the young men of hoplite census aged 18 or 19 numbered at one point about 500, but men of this class aged 60 were only 103.[36]

The consequences of these factors ran through all Greek life. Group preservation was more important than individual self-assertion—and so the appearance of this phenomenon at any point or in any class is the more worthy of note—but individual families could not count with any certainty on the production of males who would carry on their rites. The interlocking of demographic forces essentially tended to produce an equilibrium; Greek thought never had to produce a Malthus. So too in early modern Europe the population of an area might creep up, little by little, and then all the increase of half a century would be wiped out in a series of poor crop years which happened to coincide with outbreaks of diseases. We do not, incidentally, have any literary references to specific epidemics in archaic Greece, though one tombstone of the sixth century does refer to a plague (*loimos*). At the beginning of the *Iliad* an epidemic strikes the Achaean host, and Hesiod promises plague and famine to states where injustice prevails; incidental passages in Herodotus and Thucydides show that both evils were conscious concepts.[37] Whether the comment that almost every child born in western Europe about A.D. 1300 "faced the probability of extreme hunger at least once or twice during his expected 30 to 35 years of life" would be applicable to any generation of early Greece cannot be ascertained; but most Greeks experienced at least minor pangs each spring, "when things grow but a man cannot eat his fill." [38]

A third demographic factor is almost always asserted with relation to early Greece, viz., that its population expanded markedly in the eighth century. Such an increase is taken to explain many alterations thereafter, including colonization and rural unrest: "pressure of population on the limited food supply [of the Greek world] has been persistent, and at times severe, and emigration has been common at all periods in her history." [39]

Some evidence has been advanced for a major increase in population. Studies of surviving skeletal material suggested a rise in fecundity and decline in infant mortality in this period.[40] More visible testimony is provided by the great growth in numbers of settled sites during the eighth century; the expansion of the number of wells of the Athenian Agora, it has been argued, indicates that population at this point tripled in the century.[41]

These arguments, alas, do not really prove the proposition. Studies by physical anthropologists must rely on very small samples, especially inasmuch as cremation was used in various parts of Greece; we have no significant information whatever on any change in birth rates or the size of completed families. It is, thus, impossible to engage in family reconstitutions of the type developed in recent decades by demographers, and there is much else which cannot be stated certainly. Even the wider presence of occupied sites could at least in part have been a consequence of the settling down of previously nomadic elements.[42]

Above all, the relation between colonization and a surplus population is more asserted than demonstrated. Colonies, it must be remembered, were established over a century and a half and did not initially entail major migration; if there were large numbers of Greeks in western and other districts of the Mediterranean by the fifth century this was the happy product of an expansion of population in favorable circumstances and perhaps even more of absorption of natives.[43]

Colonization, mercenary service, and internal stresses were all interwoven manifestations of the great alterations in the Greek world in the eighth and following centuries, and they were surely "the product of prosperity rather than of poverty" in the broadest sense.[44] Rural change, as will be discussed more fully in Chapter VII, was primarily the consequence of the concentration of agricultural surpluses in the hands of the upper classes and middling farmers. There was no *great* growth in agricultural productivity, though the area under cultivation did apparently expand to a considerable degree. Here and there special pressures might have been produced by the conjunction of upper-class exploitation and unusual local increases in population, which would have encouraged the rise of rural debt and tensions; but for Greece as a whole the common view of enduring surpluses of population can scarcely stand if tested by demographic theory. "Overpopulation is always a relative, not an absolute concept." [45]

Even so, there is no bar to accepting the theory that the expansion of Greece was accompanied by a corresponding enlargement in its population, though the increase will not serve as an all-encompassing explanation of the manifold developments of the era. This rise, moreover, cannot be pictured as a boom when one keeps in mind the limited agricultural possibilities of the Greek landscape; if the population of England doubled between 1066 and 1344, a village of 300 would have grown by only one individual every two years.[46] The cause of such increases cannot be fully ascertained; after all the great demographic surge in modern England and other European countries began before any improvements in water supply, medical attention, or other demonstrable alterations were made. For Greece one might advance a purely subjective hypothesis that when life again became stable after the upheavals of invasion and forced migration its population could, and did, begin to expand.

We cannot quantify meaningfully the population of early Greece at any one point, nor did the ancient states themselves need very precise population figures until much later. An informed guess, now old but still reasonable, suggested some 2.6 million for the mainland and islands in 432/1; if we reduce Beloch's figures for slaves but in counterbalance include the Greek states of Asia Minor, a population of 2 millions for the Aegean world in our period would be possible.[47] Today Athens with its suburbs has attained about the same figure.

Nor can the population of any one area be determined much more precisely. Conventional figures given by later ancient authors are incredible, such as 100,000 or even 300,000 for Sybaris. Equally conventional is the figure of 1000 full citizens for Colophon, Rhegium, Acragas, and other states, though it certainly leads us toward a more reasonable order of magnitude. Hippodamus of Miletus, in defining a ideal state, put its citizen population at a total of 10,000; aerial survey at Metapontum suggests for that state at some point about 1300 plots of 6 hectares each.[48] Herodotus twice states that in 480 the Athenian population numbered about 30,000, i.e., adult males. Numbers of 600 and its multiples are often conventional in Greek and Latin, but this figure accords reasonably well with Herodotus' other remarks about Athenian manpower in the battles of the Persian wars. The total citizen body in that case would have been some 120,000 plus unspecified metics and slaves.[49] Athens was geographically one of the largest states of mainland Greece, along with Sparta; from its own farmlands, even so, our analysis in Chapter VIII will show that it could scarcely have fed even a total of 60,000 to 70,000 persons.

To conclude our discussion of an aspect which certainly was important and for which any statement must be woefully imprecise, it may be noted that, if the population of Greece did rise during the age of expansion, that factor may have been a significant motive force in many ways, but also could have deepened the difficulties of the age. Hesiod writes that "more hands mean more work and more increase," but modern economic studies show that demographic expansion does not always result in a growth in productivity or even a compensating over-all increase in production; poorer land, for instance, may be brought into use, but only at the price of decreased marginal utility.[50] More important is the question as to whether the "quality" of the population altered in its willingness to undertake foreign enterprise, to adopt new industrial techniques, and so on. The course of Greek artistic and economic progress testifies that this type of improvement did occur.

ECONOMIC INTEREST AND
THE LEADING CLASSES

The most important galvanizing factor in Greek economic changes is abundantly clear in the literary evidence, though modern depreciation of elites and theories of entrepreneurship tend to muffle or minimize its power. There was in early Greece a leading class which came to yearn earnestly after wealth so that it might enjoy an increasing range of luxuries and display its participation in the aristocratic way of life. The world then was young and fresh, and men seized pleasures avidly. True, the leading classes were not able to do so completely or permanently, but their attitudes were not necessarily those of later, conservative aristocracies.

This phenomenon is so important a theme in the argument of the present work that it demands a careful statement, first as to its character and the evidence for its existence, and then as a more general consideration. Full definition of the nascent aristocratic pattern of the age must be reserved for Chapter VI, where it will be pointed out that beside the aristocracy proper, small in numbers, a much larger "semi-aristocratic" group also flourished; the two together may henceforth be termed very generally "the leading classes." [51] Men of this level were no different from aristocrats in many eras in their delight in wealth; but for our period the matter does not end once one has noted that interest. Aristocrats often have been content simply to enjoy wealth; the Greeks searched for it with that intensity which they displayed in other aspects of life. This desire demands stress, for many modern studies accept far too easily the Platonic and Aristotelian disdain for "profit" or for the sordid aspects of making money (*chrematistike*).[52] Theoretically, there is no reason why economic energy may not vary from century to century in any society; the realities of the seventh and sixth centuries were most certainly different from the wishes of fourth-century thinkers. The causes of this interest may be called social and political; the effects were distinctly economic in many ways.

During the Dark Ages, when men struggled to survive and to hold together the tissue of society, the idea of economic gain had small scope. Its major manifestation then was a casual, almost involuntary reaction directed outward against neighboring peoples in the form of raids for cattle, women, and other moveables; yet even in the world of the Homeric epics a concept of securing "wealth" was clearly present. Odysseus at one point was taunted as "one, who faring to and fro with his benched ship, is a captain of sailors who are merchantmen, one who is mindful of his freight, and has charge of a home-borne cargo, and the gains of his greed." [53] In one light the tone of this taunt suggests a disdain for single-minded concentration on searching out gain; in another, it shows that the concept did exist.

As the Aegean world grew more active in the eighth century, the effort to secure economic advantage consciously entered Greek life, not only on the level of the upper classes but also, as Hesiod incidentally notes, on the level of potters and other craftsmen, hurrying after wealth.[54] The emergence of this attitude is a truly remarkable change when one reflects how long traditions had had an opportunity to fix themselves. Yet the transition was perhaps easier than was the breaking forth of a capitalistic spirit in early modern Europe. Greek tribal society had been too simple to evolve the fetters of manorial and guild organization; its religious system did not inculcate the other-worldly, moral virtues that later characterized Christianity; and the upper class was only gradually bound by the limitations of a developed aristocratic code.

By the time of Hesiod the *basilesi* of his homeland were evidently eager to wring advantage from their position by means of bribes and the use even of force; the whole thrust of the agricultural part of his *Works and Days* is toward acquiring "a well-filled barn." A century later Solon catalogued the diverse ways of gaining wealth and concluded that those who are richest "have twice the eagerness that others have." [55] To us this observation may be a platitude, but it was not so devoid of significance in early Greek po-

etry; Solon meant exactly what he said. Only later, as in Theognis' remark that "You can never surfeit your heart with
riches," may it have begun to be a conventional view.[56]
Alcaeus, Solon's contemporary, quoted Aristodemos—
a Spartan, no less—as saying that "Wealth makes the man,"
and went on, "No poor man is noble or held in honor." [57]

The upper classes sought *chremata,* literally "useful
things," which are specified as silver and gold, fields of
wheatland, and horses and mules—largely in rural terms.
The Solonian classification of Athenian citizens ranked them
according to their revenues in measures of grain, olive oil,
and wine; early richly appointed graves often contained
models of granaries in clay (see Plate I).[58] A man who had
chremata could consider himself *plousios,* that is, able to live
without physical labor and to afford the luxuries of the day;
the unfortunate man beset by *penia,* on the other hand, had
to work for his living and could have no share in the good
things of life. All across archaic poetry the contrast between
ploutos and *penia* was an active, bitter one.[59]

How, then, did one gain *chremata?* Men of ancestral
wealth, usually descended from the Zeus-sprung kings,
probably could adequately exercise their strengths in landed
position and political power at home. Younger sons, dis-
sidents, exiled murderers, ambitious men of middling status, and perhaps even dependents of the aristocrats were
presumably the elements who made the most active use of
the avenues which opened at home and abroad as the Greek
world expanded; but their search, if more active and riskier,
was of the same order and undertaken for the same reasons
as those which moved their seniors and elders.

Outside their native community men of the leading
classes could raid their neighbors or, later, engage in more
formal wars; at sea they could engage in piracy.[60] In the
seventh and sixth centuries men not content with the humdrum life of home could also serve as mercenaries for tyrants

in other states or for the kingdoms of the East, though the latter sometimes retained soldiers in permanent absence from Greece. Gyges in the seventh century rose to power in Lydia with the aid of mercenaries; one of the earliest surviving Greek inscriptions, carved on the two statues of Ramses II at Abu Simbel (594–89 B.C.), lists Greek mercenaries who came upstream with the pharaoh Psammetichus II.[61] The dialect is Ionic, as are the origins (if given); but the social level of those named is not evident. Still, the brother of Alcaeus fought for Nebuchadrezzar of Babylon, and in later centuries both aristocrats and commoners took the pay of Persian kings or dissident rebels.[62]

The place of interstate war or foreign service deserves emphasis. As Bolkestein observed, the waging of war was "the most extensive [trade] which Greek society ever knew," a prime means "of securing a fortune or simply a livelihood instead or next to the other means of subsistence, consisting of labour." [63] A law ascribed to Solon names booty-sellers; judging from Aristotle's paraphrase this was a compact of soldiers rather than an organization of professional buyers and sellers of booty like the later *laphropolai* of Sparta. War does not in itself increase economic activity (unless one wishes to argue that it encourages more intense production at least of armaments), but it can result in a forced mobilization of the resources of the defeated side.

These gains were dispersed deliberately for personal pleasures and luxuries. An interesting study of men who participated especially in the Thirty Years' War of the seventeenth century after Christ suggests that their wealth was committed to building mansions and to acquiring adornments such as gold necklaces; only partly to deposits in the emerging banks of modern Europe; and rarely to agricultural improvement. Much the same pattern governed the disposal of loot acquired in the early centuries of medieval Europe, though here religious dedications bulked somewhat larger.[64] In early Greece, as has already been noted, temples were to some degree the fruit of victories, and individuals dedicated their tithes in the form of tripods or statues. One surviving example from the Samian Heraeum, a seated statue in marble, is marked as the product of booty (*syle*), provided by its "overseer." [65] But if tithes went to the gods, nine-tenths remained in the hands of successful warriors or mercenaries.

In the earlier part of our period the distinction between overseas pillage and long-distance trade was a delicate one; men took by force where they could, and bartered where they could not. Greek expansion by sea, however, eventually became more law-abiding, and was fostered at least in its initial stages by enterprising leaders from the upper classes. Safe reception abroad rested to a considerable degree on ties of guest-friendship (*xenia*), an upper-class phenomenon. [66] Logically, too, upper-class participation in colonization and trade is evident, for overseas ventures required surplus resources in the form of food, seeds, animals, and metals. [67] In the eighth and seventh centuries what other elements in Greek society could have provided this surplus, or could have dared to risk it abroad?

Our specific evidence on individuals supports the general proposition to a degree unusual for an otherwise rather nameless age. In colonization there is Archilochus, whose father at least was an aristocrat; the Cypselid scions established Corinthian colonies up the Adriatic coast; and much later Miltiades of the noble Athenian Philaid family was active at the Hellespont. As traders, beyond the Odyssean references, we hear of Sappho's brother Charaxus, who traded wine to Egypt and there fell in love with a courtesan, to Sappho's disgust and perhaps to his own financial loss;

Solon, the great reformer of Athens, also engaged in foreign trade in order to recoup his father's prodigality.[68] Colaeus of Samos, blown off his course to Egypt as far as Spanish Tartessus whence he gained so much that he had to replace his stone anchors by silver ingots, and the later Sostratus of Aegina, who dedicated a statue in the Greek shrine at Etruscan Pyrgi, very probably were both men of the leading classes inasmuch as they entered Herodotus' ken.[69]

True, neither in trade and colonization nor in foreign military service were men of the leading classes motivated solely by economic factors. Curiosity about foreign parts, which stimulated later travels of the Father of History, and an urge for adventure had their effects; the essential point nevertheless remains valid, that economic interest *did* have a role and men of the upper classes *were* the leaders in the expansion of Greece outside its Aegean homeland.

Within any one Greek state these leaders also exerted serious pressures on other elements, especially smaller and weaker farmers. To attribute the appearance of the *polis* system of organization solely to aristocratic elements would be to simplify the drive of Greek political life too much and omit its important religious aspects. Yet certainly the aristocrats usually gained control of the machinery of government and justice and, as is the way of the world, wrung every advantage they could from their power. In Hesiod's outburst against the "bribe-swallowing *basileis*" who defrauded him of his share in the paternal inheritance the resulting possibilities of unjust gains are starkly suggested, as also in Solon's assertion that the rich "steal right and left with no respect for possessions sacred or profane." [70]

The great landholders could use their strength to acquire power over the agricultural surpluses of the countryside unofficially and privately as well. The methods by which they did so will concern us more specifically in the last two chapters; but the ensuing tensions, which are best illuminated in Solonian Attica, show clearly that they very often achieved their objectives.

In doing so, to repeat an earlier comment, the leading classes were most directly moved by social and political reasons. Theognis talks much of wealth and poverty, but when one considers carefully his references riches are to be held in order that their owner be respected and have power. A man cannot take his wealth with him at death, but it should be saved so that he always has it in this world. Concentration purely on economic advantage continued to be generally frowned on, as it had been in the passage quoted earlier from the *Odyssey*. Solon, thus, asserted that he would not exchange virtue (*arete*) for wealth; for *chremata* could belong now to one, now to another man. Yet even he, in the famous interview with Croesus, specified as one quality of Tellus' glory the fact that he spent a life "in which our people look upon as comfort"; and Phocylides could prize first a living, thereafter virtue.[71]

The results of the desire of the upper classes for wealth had major economic effects, which we must inspect more generally. In modern analysis the phrase "economic interest" which I have used in the title of this section is woefully imprecise, but a discussion in terms of profit motives would introduce seriously misleading connotations of the deliberate employment of "capital" and of rational calculation. As we have just seen, a member of the upper classes could well seek gain by means which involved no investment in the strict sense.

Chremata, moreover, were tangible, but they were not necessarily capital in the modern definition of productive assets—nor, on the other hand, could one properly conclude that they were never used to produce a gain (as in overseas activities). What we might consider the disposable wealth of the Greek world came to be concentrated to a considerable degree in able and ambitious hands. These holders did not play the role of deliberate entrepreneurs and seek to maximize their gains by conscious promotion of productivity, but *chremata* were in a real sense "things to be spent" on prestige and luxuries. Men of wealth could eventually hoard coinage, once money was struck; but the great Athenian general Cimon of the fifth century was generous in the manner of tribal leaders in modern simple societies, who serve "as a kind of channel through which wealth flowed, concentrating it only to pour it out freely again." [72] Expenditure on personal luxuries, moreover, had major industrial and commercial effects which facilitated the appearance of cities.

In modern societies, to conclude this emphasis on a very potent element in early Greek economic progress, the aristocratic classes are almost universally condemned as economic parasites, and so they may be. In the Greek world from 800 onwards the leading classes need not be praised as self-sacrificing leaders of the community. Their urge for wealth was unscrupulous in its procedures, for aristocratic morality was brutally frank in many aspects and did not bar loot or extortion. The avenues for gaining *chremata,* nonetheless, were not limited solely to transfer of wealth within the Aegean complex; and over all the upper classes of early Greece, in their energy and daring, were an essential motive force in the progress of the age.

Chapter III

The Rise of
Overseas Trade

The variety and volume of Greek wares, both ceramic and metal, found in modern excavations on many shores of the Mediterranean and Black seas are remarkable testimony to the economic expansion of Hellas in the period 800–500 B.C. These objects were necessarily transported by sea; and by the close of our period it is evident that the Aegean homeland was connected with a great net of trading posts, colonies, and friendly native ports in the Mediterranean world. A recent work on early modern Europe describes as a salient characteristic of the centuries from A.D. 1400 to 1600 the creation of an interlocked structure of economic units which were politically independent but tied within a shipping distance of 40 to 60 days—and its author asserts that such a system had never existed previously.[1] This is to overlook one of the most spectacular and significant examples in western history.

The rise of Greek overseas trade is evident in its results and reasonably clear in its consequences for the homeland. The initial purposes of such interchanges, however, are the field of considerable debate; the volume of trade and the manner in which it was conducted also require investigation.

EARLY SEABORNE EXCHANGES

Throughout Europe and Asia physical objects were carried overland by Paleolithic men for considerable distances. Seafaring in the Aegean likewise goes back to a very early period; obsidian from Melos, which can be precisely identified by physical tests, has been found in Mesolithic levels on the mainland at the Franchthi cave as well as on other islands.[2] By the third millennium drawings of ships were being made, and Cycladic objects of the period have been found in the far-off Balearic islands.

During the second millennium the abundance of first Minoan and then Mycenaean luxuries and pottery illustrates widespread interchanges from Syria and Egypt to southern Italy, Sicily, and the Lipari islands—very much the same area as that which later supported the trading posts and colonies of historic Greece.[3] The last flickers of this seaborne activity appear on the east coast of Attica in the eleventh century; thereafter the Greeks remained at home for a considerable period, and seem not to have attracted foreign visitors. In the world of the Homeric epics anything outside the Aegean was a dim area, full of marvels and monsters. Yet at least by the tenth century connections within the Aegean itself were being revived.

The evidence for the initial resumption of seaborne links consists primarily of the spread of the Attic Protogeometric style to many areas of the Aegean. In Crete, which always clung to ancestral ways, the attractive powers of ceramic changes to the north were not seriously felt until the ninth century, but other districts moved more rapidly in taking over the general principles of first the Protogeometric and then in the ninth century the Geometric style.[4]

By that time objects and materials of non-Aegean origin were also appearing again in the Greek world. Ties between the Aegean and the Near East had probably never been completely broken, but the sole items so far discovered which could suggest such a continuity are beads of faience, blue frit, and glass found in two tenth-century tombs at Lefkandi in Euboea.[5] Throughout the Dark Ages variation in grave goods was very limited; extensive imports came only in the ninth and still more the eighth and following centuries. A bronze bowl, now considered Phoenician in origin, turned up in one of the mid-ninth century Kerameikos graves at Athens; not far away a female was buried about the same time in the Agora with a wide range of local, elegant vases, ivory objects, a necklace of glass and faience beads (perhaps Syrian), and gold ornaments including a pair of earrings with pomegranate pendants (Plate I.).[6] These earrings are considered Athenian in manufacture, but the granulation technique employed was almost certainly Eastern in inspiration.

Gold jewelry in the form of rings and pins appears in the graves at Lefkandi across the ninth century, and more especially after its mid-point; eighth-century tombs in various parts of the mainland attest ever growing delight in Eastern luxuries among the upper classes. Seals of ivory, faience,

and other materials, first of Cypriote or Near Eastern manufacture, also began to be used and may be considered tokens
of "personal" possession.[7]

By the eighth century ivory, necessarily a foreign import
in Greece, was being carved at several places, including
Sparta, Perachora near Corinth, and Athens. A stiff maiden
of ivory which was discovered in a Dipylon grave rightly has
pride of place in the National Museum, Athens, as a precur-
sor to the later *korai.* In eighth-century Crete ivory is accompanied by a well-known series of bronze "shields."
These thin circular plates might have been Phoenician imports at the outset and thereafter drew abundantly on Eastern motifs.[8] Evidence for drafts on Eastern artistic designs,
to some extent via textiles, is visible in the rows of deer and
other animals on Athenian pottery and gold work; some of
the famous Dipylon vases show ships and scenes of naval
battle.[9] Greek pottery and its styles made their way in that
century to many parts of the Mediterranean; the foundation
deposit for the shrine of Tanit at Carthage in the last decades before 700 consisted of native Geometric vases.[10]

This ever more abundant testimony to the movement of
physical objects into or out of the Aegean has often been
surveyed in greater detail than is necessary at the present
juncture. The fundamental questions from the economic
point of view are two: can we call this seaborne activity, at
least in its first stages, conscious trade? and was it motivated by a search for gain? In a chronological sense these
issues lie before our period, but they must be dealt with, albeit briefly, in order to set the pattern of behavior in later
exchanges. Thus I have deliberately avoided using the word
"trade" in the title of this section.

Stimulated by Marcel Mauss's famous work *Le Don* and
other anthropological investigations, several recent scholars
are inclined to see in the first signs of renewed physical in-

terchanges illustrations of a gift society, as described in the Homeric epics. These views are a very useful corrective to the importation of modern capitalistic attitudes into early Greece, particularly the assertion that trade must always have been accompanied by a desire for profit.[11] Interchanges with men of foreign shores may have been motivated at times as much by the need for vital raw materials, in even trade, as by a deliberate search for gain; and at least for men of the upper classes an urge for adventure and even curiosity cannot be left out of our equations. "Are you for traffic," the Cretans were asked in the Hymn to Apollo, "or pirates wandering at random, who put their own lives in jeopardy by mischief to foreigners?" [12]

Yet the epics, our only source for early attitudes, do not altogether support an idealized picture of heroes totally innocent of economic motives. Homeric men, thus, were aware of relative valuations. One of the few grimly humorous touches in the *Iliad* describes the exchange of armor by Glaucus and Diomedes as a token of ancestral guest-friendship: "And then from Glaucus did Zeus, son of Cronus, take away his wits, seeing he made exchange of armour with Diomedes, son of Tydeus, giving golden for bronze, the worth of an hundred oxen for the worth of nine." [13] The exchange was made, but a recognition of values is explicit. So too a recent study of economic life in simple societies shows that foreign visitors can make gifts to local chieftains, and eventually receive presents in return; but as Sahlins notes the visitors do weigh the value of the items given in return, though they do not haggle, and if dissatisfied do not come back.[14] We must also distinguish gifts between friends, which then as now remained outside the commercial sphere, and less personal interchanges involved in seaborne contacts, as of the Taphian chieftain who carried iron with the deliberate intention of bartering it for copper.[15] The taunt against Odysseus as a captain seeking gain, cited in the previous chapter, is enough to show that motives of an economic character could influence seafarers.

All in all, it would be unreasonable to assume that most traffickers endured the dangers of the sea without serious economic intent. Overseas exchanges would not otherwise have grown so rapidly, and the evidence of the archaic poets attests that gain was an objective, even if a Greek trader could not calculate his profit from a voyage by modern bookkeeping techniques. In describing ways to avoid poverty and acquire *chremata* Solon lists "one, for to bring home gain [*kerdos*] rangeth the fishy deep a-shipboard, tossed by grievous winds, sparing his life no whit"— a picture essentially echoed by Semonides and, for that matter, suggested a century earlier by Hesiod.[16]

TRADING POSTS AND COLONIES

Once seaborne activity was under way, for economic and other reasons, it served as a mighty engine for further progress. By the seventh and sixth centuries we may certainly speak of Greek overseas commerce resting upon a far-flung network of trading posts, colonies, and friendly native ports in Etruria and elsewhere.

Trading posts were established in the Near East, where the civilized states were far too strong to allow the Greeks to create independent colonies; and these settlements were surely made for commercial purposes. Al Mina, on the Syrian coast, which was excavated before World War II, has a wide range of Greek pottery from about 800 onwards. This ware is generally considered to have been imported or even locally produced for the use of the Greek traders themselves—for Greek pottery did not spread far into the hinterland—and attests especially the presence of men from the

Aegean islands, led by the Euboeans, and later from Ionia, Corinth, and Aegina. The settlement was destroyed early in the sixth century, probably by Nebuchadrezzar, and was essentially replaced by Tell Sukas, another trading post occupied from the late seventh century.[17]

In Egypt Greeks were active as mercenaries and as traders by the early seventh century. Eventually the pharaoh Amasis assigned to them a specific point, Naucratis, which was rather inadequately dug by Petrie early in this century. Herodotus comments briefly on its temples, the Hellenium built by men from nine states of Asia Minor, that of Zeus by Aeginetans, of Hera by Samians, and of Apollo by the Milesians. The first temple to Apollo is commonly set about 570 by architectural historians; the earliest pottery of the site has usually been dated to the last quarter of the seventh century, but is sometimes lowered.[18]

This pattern of Levantine settlement is that which one would expect. Normally in history men from less civilized regions have taken the initiative in acquiring luxuries from the more developed areas, either by trade or by incursions; Minoans and Mycenaeans had thus sought out Syria and Egypt in the second millennium, not the reverse. The growth, indeed, of trading interests in Greece may have been much spurred by frequenting the far more developed harbors of the Levant, both in weight standards and in attitudes and interests.[19]

At this point we must turn aside a moment to dismiss the argument that it was Phoenician traders who primarily paved the way for the resumption of contacts between the Near East and the Aegean.[20] There can be no doubt that Phoenicians were active in Cyprus before 800 and made their way into the western Mediterranean by that time, but extensive Phoenician activity in the west was no earlier than the presence of Greek traders and colonists in Sicily and south Italy.[21] In the renewal of ties between the Aegean proper and the Levant the evidence from Al Mina and other sites accords with historical logic in suggesting that Greeks were the principal element.

During the century and a half after 750 the Greeks poured out in a spate of colonies, each relatively small but in totality a major manifestation of the expansive powers in Aegean society.[22] On the African coast there were Cyrene and other points; in southern Italy, Sicily, and southern France a host of settlements was founded; other colonies dotted the north, west, and south coasts of the Black Sea and also Thrace.

Whether these colonies were established, like the trading posts of the Near East, for commercial reasons has been a long and fiercely debated issue. Early in this century it was often argued that trade preceded colonization and that traders thus opened up the avenues along which colonies were established. Further archeological exploration, especially in Italy and Sicily, then led to a denial of the priority of trade, and both the siting and the establishment of colonies are now generally explained in agricultural terms. Always, however, an undercurrent has suggested that trade and colonization were not totally disconnected; and explanations of the colonization movement purely in terms of overpopulation will not do. Indeed, evidence has accumulated to suggest that at least some settlements were otherwise motivated.[23]

No doubt the founders of colonies usually had a clear eye toward agricultural possibilities; their followers, after all, expected to gain plots of land (*kleroi*) from which they could support themselves. Yet not a few colonies were established first on islands or at good natural ports. The earliest settlement on the Italian coast, on the island of Ischia opposite Naples, can scarcely be explained except as an effort to tap the mineral resources of Etruria. Ironworking already existed on Ischia in the eighth century;[24] the site had so few other advantages that the colonists eventually moved to the Italian mainland.

At various points Greek pottery shows up shortly before colonization began, but in general major evidence for imports comes only after the nuclei had become firmly rooted. Italian archeologists in recent years have skillfully followed the spread of Greek wares to native communities of south Italy and Sicily; on the latter island the process varied greatly, from the apparently amicable relations of the Chalcidian colonies inland toward Morgantina to the more ruthless conquest of the hills behind Syracuse.[25] Greek products could and did make their way without the support of colonies; in Etruria Greek potters set up workshops, and the coastal port of Gravisca had a temple to Hera by the early sixth century.[26] Nonetheless, colonies provided a wide network of relatively sure markets and safe harbors; and doubtless they had an interest in this trade. The mint of Zancle even placed a stylized depiction of its harbor on sixth-century issues (see Plate V.f).

Trade was usually a result, not the cause of colonization, in the broadest sense; but the success of the colonizing movement owed much to the parallel rise of commerce. Greek colonists settled in areas where the climate was very similar to that of their homeland so that agricultural adjustments were not difficult; they were organized into *poleis,* which united their strengths; but they would scarcely have been as successful if the natives had refused to tolerate or encourage their presence, partly for the goods they provided, and if they had not been in continuous contact with their Aegean source.

Unlike early modern colonies, the new *poleis* were generally independent of their parent states except in a few religious duties.[27] Some modern studies have suggested that

Rhegium and Zancle/Messana on the strait between Italy and Sicily controlled trade therein, or that Corinth had special advantages because colonies such as Corcyra, on the route west, were Corinthian in origin; but these theories are born of modern colonial experience with trading monopolies and have no real support in ancient evidence.[28] Nor is there any reliable testimony to early commercial competition between Phoenicians and Greeks, who moved westward at about the same point in the eighth century. Eventually Carthage gained control over most of the Phoencian west, shut the Straits of Gibraltar, and limited foreign access to other parts of its coastal domain; but even then foreign merchants could come to Carthage without impediment. There is, incidentally, no evidence that Greek merchant ships in western waters commonly preyed on each other in disguised piracy; the Greeks who settled on the Lipari islands and engaged in freebooting are marked out as exceptional.[29]

THE MATERIAL CONTENT
OF OVERSEAS TRADE

In turning to the objects which moved in this network I shall not seek to draw up a catalogue. There have been valuable studies of individual items, such as types of pottery or even of specific shapes. We also have a few, though not enough, accounts of the materials found at certain points (Massalia, Rhegium, etc.) and the radiation outward of Greek objects from these centers, though mostly for later centuries.[30] Much, however, remains to be done along these lines.

The major debate revolves not so much over items of trade as over the volume of interchanges and the degree to which overseas activity came to involve—if at all—mass exports and imports.[31] Seaborne trade had certainly been stimulated in its earliest days partly by a desire for the luxuries of Near Eastern workshops, which appealed especially to the incipient aristocracies of the Greek states—not only ivory, glass, and faience, but also perfumes, ointments, and spices (many of which had names of Semitic root), and even the "wine of Byblos" which Hesiod celebrated. A considerable part of modern opinion tends to restrict seaborne trade to this range of luxuries throughout Greek history.

Yet it is also commonly assumed that the Greeks balanced their Eastern bills by providing raw materials or staples such as "foodstuffs, wood, cattle, and minerals." [32] While luxuries of Eastern or Aegean origin were without doubt an important ingredient of maritime commerce at all points in ancient history, a compensating movement of bulk commodities also existed at least from the eighth century. As far as one can see, bulk trade grew markedly thereafter both in volume and in the variety of items, though coinage and other aids to supple economic activity were not yet widely employed, but in each major area of exchange we must distinguish luxuries from more humdrum objects.

A casual examination of the objects of Greek trade would inevitably concentrate on pottery; vases survive either whole in graves or in fragments better than most materials. When one turns to early modern Europe, he will soon discover that a very different item was most often noted in the trade of that period. Every region of western Europe and eventually of the American colonies, both Spanish and English, produced its own textiles; but each area had an insatiable demand for textiles from another district, often but not always of luxury character. In the Middle Ages Englishmen exported wool to the Low Countries and brought back finished products; Spaniards bought French textiles; silks were specially produced at certain centers and widely exported. In the English colonies of North America during the eighteenth century the major import consisted of textiles—Irish, English, and German.[33]

The picture here is clear, thanks to surviving textiles, customs records, and literary references to cloth of Arras, etc. For the ancient world we lack physical survivals, though in Assyrian trade to Cappadocia and in the Roman Empire textiles can be shown to be important by literary evidence.[34] As I suggested in the first chapter, however, an investigation of early modern conditions may help to raise a question of which one might not otherwise think; in this case it seems very probable that textiles and wool (see Plate VII:b) *did* play an important role in Greek commerce. From the female statues and also from vase-paintings we can be sure that aristocratic ladies like Phrasikleia (Plate VIII) were dressed in robes of complicated decoration; Sappho and others also talk of purple-dyed and other elegant attire for both males and females.[35] References to specialized centers of textile manufacture exist: Amorgos was later famous for its manufactures from Egyptian linen; Miletus gave its name to a type of woolen goods which were widely known.[36] Simple folk undoubtedly made their own clothes of goat-skins and homespun wool, though in the classic period at least Megara exported a form of work clothing; [37] upper-class demands very often, we may guess, called for cloth of foreign origin. It is a puzzle, in passing, to explain how the Greek states which traded with the Near East got the silver from Thrace and Macedonia with which they partly covered the cost of their Levantine purchases, for Greek imports into those regions do not appear extensive through the archaic period; but textiles and other perishable items may help to provide an answer to this problem.

Modern students who wish to restrict Greek trade to the area of luxuries may place most or all textiles (though not wool itself) in that realm, but raw materials also moved by water to supply the growing needs of Greek industries, arts, and construction. Most districts had adequate pot clay; so too stone was usually available, though many temples had to be built of local limestone and then stuccoed. Before 500, nonetheless, the Siphnians and the Athenians brought their own marbles to Delphi to construct their treasuries in the precinct of Apollo, and the great temple itself was made of Athenian marble in its Alcmeonid rebuilding. Statues too were frequently carved from imported marble blocks (or roughed out, as in the quarries of Naxos, before transport).

Timber was needed for roofbeams of temples, stairs, and scaffolding, and for doors and windows (which could later be sold separately from a house); ships and plows required special woods for specific purposes, which are itemized by Theophrastus and earlier by Hesiod.[38] Wood also provided the fuel for domestic cooking, for foundries and potteries, and for cremations. Hesiod visualizes his farmer as cutting timber with his own ax, and the devastation of Greek hillsides, which laid their bones bare, in Plato's famous description, may have owed as much to woodcutters and charcoal burners as to sheep and goats;[39] but in classic times Macedonia and other districts provided by sea much of the timber demands of Greece.

Metals were also required, and their provision must have been a potent force in expanding the skills of overseas traders.[40] Greece had some supplies of silver, iron, and copper, but they were not evenly distributed; gold seems to have been found only in Siphnos and Thasos, and tin was lacking. We know very little in reality about the sources of iron, copper and tin; iron was always sufficiently valuable that it could even be dedicated in the form of spits.[41] In modern times copper and tin can stand the cost of land transport for some distance, but this was less true in antiquity. Cyprus presumably provided copper; eastern Asia Minor and Etruria, iron; a famous tin route from Britain by sea through the Tin Islands and overland (mostly by river) through Gaul seems to have developed before the close of our period.[42] Greek mines themselves, at least in Attica and Thrace, were publicly owned, and leased for exploitation; trade in metals was in private hands, which brought in raw materials and exported finished products such as armor, furniture, or tripods.[43]

Both the texture and the volume of Greek trade altered significantly when agricultural products came to be imported and exported. In inland Boeotia Hesiod had already known the wine of Byblos; thereafter the shipment of wine is attested only as Greek exports from Chios, Thasos, and elsewhere. Wine probably remained a luxury item in most areas, but Black Sea colonists had to import all their olive oil. Athens awarded Panathenaic amphoras containing oil from public trees to victors in its games, but these special vases turn up so often in Etruria and elsewhere that one must wonder whether they all actually represented victories.[44] Although quantitative evidence is lacking, wine and oil exports from Greece probably became significant only in the sixth century; certainly grain from overseas, which will be considered in Chapter VII, began to enter some Greek markets at that time.

Distasteful as it may be to modern sensibilities to label slaves as "items of trade," the Greeks had engaged in the transport of slaves since the Dark Ages; the *Odyssey* refers to the acquisition of Sicilian unfortunates. Slaves were to a considerable degree a luxury object in the form of attractive females and serviceable young eunuchs and catamites for the Near Eastern market; the famous example for balancing Levantine exchanges in this respect was Rhodopis who "arrived in Egypt under the conduct of Xantheus the Samian" to ply her trade as courtesan and was bought free by Sappho's brother.[45] Like her successor Archidice she was really part of the Naucratite settlement, who were not permitted to marry Egyptians; but the enthusiasm of later Persian monarchs for concubines trained in Greek skills very probably extended back into earlier centuries. By the sixth century, however, slaves had become a "mass item" in the provision of labor for the industrial workshops of the more advanced Greek centers, as we shall see more fully in the next chapter.

Finally, there is the ubiquitous pottery, which was partly luxury ware but partly utilitarian. Open vases such as dishes and cups were used in the household, symposia, and temple ceremonies; closed vases were often containers for some other items. Ointment and perfumes could be shipped in the small aryballos and alabastron; olive oil and wine, "the two liquids most agreeable to the human body," were carried in amphoras.[46] Simple, undecorated jars were used for the major transport of these items, as is attested by the growing evidence found in underwater explorations of ancient shipwrecks.

Pottery is so omnipresent in archeological reports that its significance is inevitably exaggerated. It does show lines of communication, or at least the ends of those lines; but significant states such as Miletus do not appear in the pottery record.[47] Partial studies have been made of the distribution of the various types of pottery—Corinthian, Laconian, Athenian, East Greek, etc.—but the material is so extensive and continuously increasing that really adequate distribution charts are not available for any type.[48] An impressionistic assessment would support the conclusion that if one can take pottery as a guide Greek seaborne activity took one leap forward in the seventh century and another in the sixth; [49] and inferences can, with caution, be drawn from ceramic evidence about the way in which trade was conducted.

Textiles, timber, metals and metal products, agricultural products, slaves, pottery—these do not form an extensive range; but then Greek industrial life was of a very simple order, which did not need many of the raw and finished products that move in twentieth-century trade. What is important is the expansion of traffic in the items which did have utility in early Greece. This growth is very apparent, and its significance is seriously muffled if one interprets it only as meeting aristocratic demand or seeks to limit exchanges solely to the field of luxuries.

SHIPS AND TRADERS

The vessel most often mentioned by ancient Greek historians is the rowed galley. This might have been used by early adventurers, who had to fight as well as trade; but Greek merchants normally employed sailing ships for most of their seaborne activity (see Plate VII.a).[50] The season for shipping extended only from spring through fall, when the weather was reasonably predictable; traders may often have wintered over in foreign ports.

Sailing vessels usually ran from 70 to 80 tons burden up to a few hundred tons.[51] There is no evidence that they were markedly improved in design or rigging through Greek times, but that does not mean a total absence of improvement in the efficiency of shipping activities; better knowledge of markets, better organization of ports, and other non-material factors can also increase naval productivity.[52] Physical improvements by land had begun before the close of our period. The Corinthians built a causeway (*diolkos*) across the Isthmus of Corinth by the beginning of the sixth century so that vessels could be drawn across and thus avoid the dangers of rounding the Peloponnesus.[53] The mole at Delos was probably constructed for the use of pilgrims, but other harbor works began to appear even though Athens relied on the open roadstead of Phalerum until the time of Themistocles. Artificial harbors (*cothons*) have thus been found in Carthaginian domains, at Motya and Carthage itself, though these may have been built primarily for military purposes.

The manner in which overseas trade operated is an important subject on which comment may have been expected before this point, but the truth is that we know very little about the day-to-day activities of ship captains. Aristocratic writers were not inclined to dwell on those subjects; even in classical Athens commercial problems appear only when there were lawsuits which gave rise to orations of defense and attack. Archeological evidence is more useful on the "what" than on the "why or how."

Most Greek business was, moreover, conducted orally. The alphabet had been developed by at least the mid-eighth century, but not solely for economic purposes; its characteristic of writing vowels—unlike the Phoenician prototype—was perhaps most useful in setting down poetry. For rural mortgages there was, at least later, visible testimony in the *horoi;* leases and receipts by state agencies and temples were at times inscribed on stone; but trade produced little written material until the fourth century. From the Black Sea there is a sixth-century graffito which seems to record an Ionian merchant's activities; recently published is a letter of the second half of the sixth century written on a lead scroll in which the writer complains about not receiving his *phortegesion*. This word, which does not recur in Greek, perhaps meant shipping charges.[54] How disputes between foreigners and natives were settled is far from clear, though *proxenoi* were beginning to appear by the middle of the sixth century as guarantors and protectors, but not as judicial representatives of alien traders.[55]

It is also impossible to make any useful statements about

prices, or indeed how pricing was carried out; the quality of objects for sale by tramp shippers could be determined only by visual inspection.[56] In the Homeric epics men had a clear idea of the relative value of gold and bronze armor; public fines and sacrifices were expressed in terms of animals and agricultural products. Plutarch's statements as to Solonian valuation of these latter items in money must be in error—for Athens began to coin only after Solon's period—but his comment that the valuations were very low in comparison with those current in Plutarch's own day is of interest. Already in the fourth century it could be observed that men of the highest Solonian property class might be poor; prices evidently rose considerably across Greek history, but we cannot establish a price series for any major item.[57]

Scratched on the bases of some Athenian vases are prices in terms of coinage which must strike a modern observer, accustomed to the high prices paid nowadays by museums and collectors, as remarkably low. An amphora, for example, is marked at two obols (but a hydria at 12 obols), a crater at four obols, a *skyphos,* or cup, little more than an obol.[58] Even in the fifth century a workman usually earned only up to two obols for a day's work, yet these vase prices are both so low and so diverse that we cannot establish any norms or define increases or decreases in price; it is also unclear whether they represented what we would call wholesale, retail, or export prices. In a few cases vases are marked "so many for so many obols," and these examples presumably represent batches intended to be sold together. How much more did Etruscan nobles or Scythian princes pay the Greek traders who brought them to distant shores?

The ceramic evidence does give valuable, though limited, testimony on other aspects of overseas trade. Beyond question some objects were by the sixth century being deliberately manufactured for export. A Chiote vase, for example, inscribed with a dedication to Aphrodite *before* it was fired, has been found in the shrine of Aphrodite at Naucratis.[59] The Athenian workshop of Nicosthenes produced during the years 535–485 a particular type of amphora, now called Nicosthenic, and also a *kyathos,* or dipper, with high handles, both of which copied Etruscan originals; all but one of these *kyathoi* were found in Etruria, and the exception, from south Russia, seems to have been "a shipping error." [60] These items must have been commissioned by a shipper familiar with the Etruscan market; as has been observed recently, we might "rethink our ideas on the sophistication of international trade during the sixth century. Certainly it was not a chance or random operation." [61] Occasionally, too, there is some suggestion that particular mythical scenes may have been chosen with a special market in mind.

Otherwise, however, the vases attest the equally important point that special attention was only rarely paid to export demands. In the late sixth and early fifth centuries Attic vase painters often singled out a reigning beauty in a *kalos* inscription ("beautiful is Leagros" as on Plate II.b); and even the *kyathos* type just mentioned turns up on the Acropolis with *kalos* inscriptions.[62] It is difficult to believe that overseas purchasers had any interest in these names, the appeal of which could only have been significant in the Athenian Agora itself.

The most reasonable, if hypothetical, reconstruction of the general course of overseas trade is that artisans in the Greek homeland made objects primarily for local markets, but that these objects were so attractive they could be exported widely—though more toward less civilized shores than toward Near Eastern markets. Shipowners (*naukleroi*) accordingly purchased a stock of textiles, metalware, pottery, oil, wine, and other items they thought they could dispose of most advantageously—or took on board merchants with these items as well—and then sailed to appropriate overseas markets.[63] In general, traders must have exchanged their goods for native raw materials (including slaves) or, in the East, for manufactured items, and judged the value of their wares so as to reward their risks and efforts. Coinage, as noted earlier, was little used until almost 500, and in any case shippers must have sought return cargoes in order to secure gain at both ends of their trips.

Even in classic times shipowners settled on trade in special lines or on travel to specific centers only spasmodically; in the archaic era there must have been even more "tramp" carriers. Greek commercial terminology always remained imprecise, and we cannot be sure that long-distance and local traders were distinct. It is not even certain that shipowner and trader were often separate, i.e., that shippers carried the goods of others, though I see no reason to doubt that this could take place occasionally in archaic times as well as later.[64] Passengers certainly could be transported; the famous example is Arion, who gained so much wealth on a trip to sing his dithyrambs in the western colonies that the crew of the ship bringing him back to Greece threw him overboard. Unfortunately for them, they allowed Arion to sing a final song before committing him to the sea and a grateful dolphin took the singer on his back, transported him to shore, and so allowed Arion to reach Corinth in time to seize the crew on its arrival.[65]

Shipowners were not necessarily connected with the state from which their cargo originated. If Corinthian ware was eventually driven out of western markets by Athenian vases, this does not in any way prove that Athenian shippers took the place of Corinthian traders. On a number of Athenian vases, from different workshops, the letters SO were painted before firing; the initials of another individual, SMI, were incised on about 50 vases, one found on the Acropolis. These persons *might* have been Athenian traders in Athenian wares, yet other incised marks are in Ionic script, as already noted; and Sicilian evidence shows that "Sicilians who dealt in Attic pots put prices and numbers in Sicilian dialect." [66] The rise in Athenian commerce which is evident in the fifth century must not be antedated; the traders who bustled about the Aegean and farther afield in earlier centuries hailed from many seaboard states and sought their advantage where they could.

Among the major centers of overseas commerce were the Ionian states, active alike in Naucratis and the Black Sea as well as the west, the Euboean *poleis,* and Corinth. Perhaps the one state, however, which came closest to being dependent on maritime activity by 500 was Aegina, which lacked even native clay for good pottery. The grain ships which Xerxes saw in the Hellespont in 480 were making their way to Aegina and the Peloponnesus; the coinage of Aegina appears to have been by far the largest of any Greek state in the sixth century. [67] It turns up widely throughout the Aegean as far as Crete and Rhodes (see Plate V), and one can only infer that issuance and dispersal of the "turtles" were closely tied to Aeginetan shipping.

A final aspect, so obvious that its importance may easily be overlooked, is the independent position of men active at sea. Initially overseas traders had often been of upper-class origin, as suggested in the preceding chapter, for only well-to-do elements could have provided the surplus needed for ship, crew, and cargo. By the sixth century probably men of lesser background carried on most Greek commerce, but there is no evidence to suggest they lost their independence. The demands and strengths of the *polis* or even of the Greek religious structure were too weak to turn merchants into dependent agents, as had often been the case in the Near East. In later centuries bottomry loans could be secured at rates up to 33.33 per cent, but we do not know to what extent shippers of our centuries relied on borrowed capital. [68] Only in two respects was their freedom of action clearly limited: traders may have influenced the route taken by a captain; and at times a crew formed a compact with their master to share the gains.[69]

THE SIGNIFICANCE OF OVERSEAS TRADE

The dimensions of overseas trade even by 500 must not be exaggerated. Greece was a simple land; many Greeks had no contact with imported objects; the ideal of the *polis* was autarky. Modern economic theorists are not certain that external trade in itself is a sufficient condition for sustained growth or even a necessary factor; causal forces may be essentially internal.[70] Yet when even a small percentage of an area's output enters international markets the local effects can be very significant,[71] and by 500 the more advanced Greek cities were thus interlocked commercially perhaps more closely than they were to secluded rural villages in the mountains of their own *poleis*.

Beating across the waves and avoiding sudden Mediterranean storms in their small craft for only a few months in the year, the traders during the age of expansion bound together homeland and colonies and provided both basic materials and luxuries. Whereas the interchanges of about 800 had been largely in terms of Eastern luxuries paid for by "staples" or primary products, by 500 Greek commerce especially toward the north and west dealt largely in manufactured and processed items. The shippers who carried these goods were quite evidently motivated to a high degree; because of its importance I must reiterate the inescapable view that trade was profitable, even though traders lacked modern methods of gathering market information and assessing relative advantages. They performed magnificently—the word is strong but no more than valid—in overcoming natural and political obstacles; it would not be too much to claim that Hellas could never have attained a relatively advanced economic structure without its overseas trade. Once these social and economic developments had occurred, the major Greek centers were then dependent on its continuance.[72]

More generally, the expansion of Aegean activity, as far as trade was concerned, was a consequence of its intermediary role between the western Mediterranean and the civilized East, and the effects of this position are worth general speculation. It is not easy to see how Greece balanced its accounts with the Near East by means of slaves, metals, and other raw items. From a modern point of view the continuing export of silver to the East is naturally interpreted as the ultimate mode of settling the debit, but I am not certain either that the Greeks of the sixth century took it primarily as a financial tool or that Easterners, not yet coining, accepted and hoarded silver save as a valuable metal.[73] The desires of Greek upper classes for Near Eastern luxuries spurred trade into less developed parts of the Mediterranean—where Greek manufactured wares could be sold—in order to gain the metals needed by Eastern workshops. The landed cost of Levantine luxuries in Greece may well have been so high, in view of exchange difficulties, that Greek workshops were encouraged to provide local substitutes.

Unfortunately, there is no basis on which we can quantify either fluctuations in imports and exports or the over-all total for any state at any point. The trade of Hellas and of each of its many *poleis* had always to be in balance, even if its leaders did not consciously recognize the need; for international credit and provision of economic assistance did not yet exist.[74] The available evidence suggests that seaborne commerce did expand greatly, and did so essentially continuously. Growing numbers of men must have been engaged in overseas commerce, though better knowledge of routes and markets very probably improved productivity in an economic sense. More certainly there was a corresponding enlargement of Greek industry, including the arts, which could provide desirable objects for export purposes.

Chapter IV

Industries
and Home Markets

To speak of the industrialization of Greece in our period would be to exaggerate immensely. In 500 B.C. almost all Greeks were still farmers; the workshops required little more fixed capital than a small assemblage of tools, a furnace or kiln, and shelter for the workmen and their products. Nonetheless, small groups of artisans did exist in many areas by the close of our period, together with independent local traders; both the variety of crafts and the skills used therein cannot really be compared with the simple world of the earlier ninth century.

These mundane developments, however important, did not attract the attention of ancient sources, which focus on the more glamorous adventures of overseas trade. Yet in early modern Europe the expansion in home markets and production was far more important than was colonial trade, and that was certainly true in ancient Greece as well.[1] After all, the Greeks as a whole have never loved the sea. In the Piraeus today female travelers worriedly cross themselves, and anxious relatives utter encouragement to those boarding ships for the islands; a saying attributed to Pittacus sums up both ancient and modern attitudes, "The land can be trusted, but not the sea."[2] Men probably moved to the nascent cities of early Greece more easily than to overseas colonies, and centers of trade and industry became relatively numerous at least on a primary level. Their abundance can be explained both by the fierce sense of independence in the many *poleis* and also by the serious problems involved in land transport, which severely restricted the local trading area of any one market.[3]

ORIGINS OF THE NEW SECTORS

The origins of Greek trading and industrial elements lie in obscurity. In the ancient Near East artisans and traders had long existed, but normally they had been dependent, to a greater or lesser degree varying with local conditions, on temples and kings. So too in medieval Europe the economic revival after A.D. 1000 was closely connected to religious and secular centers of power and demand.[4] For early Greece, as might be expected, there is also a theory, from Bücher onwards, that production was initially carried on within the noble households (*oikoi*).

Undoubtedly much of the equipment and clothing used by a rural Greek family was always made within the household, whether noble or common, and did not enter into any market system. As far as specialized crafts are concerned, however, there is no clear evidence that the few named by Homer or Hesiod were thus contained within the *oikos* structure. In Homer craftsmen do not seem to make objects for open sale; they work, as Hephaestus did on the shield of Achilles, on specific commission—but not, in this case, within an *oikos*. Hesiod pictures the local blacksmith as an independent artisan; and in discussing the favorable and un-favorable aspects of rivalry he comments that "neighbor vies with his neighbor as he hurries after wealth . . . . potter is angry with potter, and craftsman with craftsman." [5] Recent excavations at Sardis even demonstrate that in this Lydian capital some gold refiners and jewelers worked not in the palace, but near the commercial center. The little that can be said about artisans in the Dark Ages suggests that they occupied an independent niche in the rural economy of the period.[6]

As the upper classes and religious institutions came to demand locally produced luxuries, these were furnished by craftsmen who could not have been contained within any one specific *oikos*. The panoply found in an Argive grave from a little before 700, for example, was skillfully made; the smith represented on Plate VII.a as beating out a helmet was another such craftsman. No noble family could have supported an armorer in full-time activity or would have taken up all the product of a Dipylon potter, who threw his great amphoras and craters almost man-sized. So too, the needs of the religious structure of the early *polis* as well as of international shrines and festivals, and also of the colonies, were relatively impersonal in origin. Stone-cutters, makers of figurines, and other skilled craftsmen became far more specialized than in the Dark Ages and can be said to have been dependent on the upper classes only as a whole, not in a permanent one-to-one relationship; as this world passed into the sixth century potters and other workmen became members of a market structure.

At this point a modern student of economics might well raise the problem of the source of capital for such workshops; but ancient manufacturing methods were extremely simple. Capital requirements were very restricted in a pattern of day-to-day manufacture in small shops, often on materials provided by the purchaser (especially so, probably, in the case of jewelry) or for sale in booths and stalls; and these needs were probably self-financed or acquired by marriage.[7] Loans for productive industrial purposes were almost unknown throughout all Greek history (except, in a sense, as slaves were later set up in business), but in truth any lender would have felt uneasy with only the security of a small workshop and hand tools. The growth of early Greek industry depended far more on technological improvements than on the installation of fixed capital assets.

In this respect, i.e., technological change, the age of expansion was a period of extraordinary progress. It is not too much to say that from somewhat before 800 down to 500 the Greek world acquired the stock of technical skills and methods on which it, and the Romans thereafter, normally relied for the rest of ancient history. This development is often muffled in modern treatments of ancient technology, which tend to emphasize and then to lament the limited improvements of classical and later periods; what happened earlier is quite a different story.[8]

During the height of the Minoan and Mycenaean cultures of the second millennium a variety of skilled workmen had shaped gold, silver, ivory, rock crystal, and other materials into handsome luxuries for the lords of their palaces. When those societies dissolved in the invasions and migrations which closed the millennium the skills disappeared, as did the use of writing; but not all industrial activity ceased. Potters continued to be needed everywhere; so too did workers in wood and leather.[9] Metals also were handled throughout the Dark Ages. At Argos a silver refinery existed before 900; mining at Thorikos in eastern Attica provided silver and lead for local processing; a bronze foundry at Lefkandi made tripods and other objects.[10]

In the ninth and still more in the eighth and seventh centuries came the great technological upsurge in the Aegean world. This was based almost entirely on drafts from Eastern knowledge by Greek craftsmen now spurred by local sustained demand. Goldsmiths reappeared and reacquired such skills as the use of granulation techniques, evident in the Agora earrings of about 850 (Plate I.b). For the working of iron, which became common only after 800, Greek myths of the Telchines and Dactyloi emphasized indebtedness to Phrygia and Crete, undoubtedly as intermediaries to eastern Asia Minor and the Levant; the decoration of huge cauldrons with griffin heads derived from Urartian and other sources.[11] Greek potters borrowed only occasional motifs from the East, but the introduction of moulds for making clay figurines was an Eastern import. Textile designs suggest foreign origins. The degree to which the first sculptors of large Greek statues were indebted to Saite models from Egypt is much debated; but one may at least infer that the very idea of carving almost life-size, like the use of stone in major buildings, owed much to knowledge from the East of what could be done.

Further examples could easily be cited; it is all too simple to ascribe Greek industrial progress entirely to Eastern inspiration and even to Levantine workmen in early Greece.[12] Greek craftsmen *did* go beyond their Near Eastern sources in matters of technique. To give examples only out of stone working, they developed a toothed chisel unknown in the East; and anathyrosis, which appears once at Persian Persepolis, can automatically be assigned to Aegean inspiration.[13] Even in modern technological advance small elaborations and improvements play a very large role in the increase of productivity, perhaps as great in the end as major breakthroughs.[14]

Other aspects of this industrial development demand equal stress. If Greek workers in metal, stone, clay, and probably wool gained mastery abroad and also in home markets, their success was due as well to those characteristics of trade and industry which were not physical or technological. One was the encouragement which Greek artisans received from their society to experiment and to develop continuously their artistic styles: "Whatever the Greeks borrow from the barbarians they improve upon in the end." [15] Another factor was the independent and relatively competitive spirit nurtured in Greek workshops at least from the days of Hesiod, and a third was the rise of fixed local markets which promoted the fluidity of economic life.

The structure, however, of local trade and industry is far from clear in its initial stages. All that we can surely assume is that even before true urban centers had appeared the pattern of life both in the *ethnos* and then in the earliest stages of the *polis* tended to concentrate political, religious, and other activity at a central geographical point within each local area. Here the interchange of goods and agricultural products would also have been centered by means of barter; coinage for market purposes became common only long after the markets themselves had appeared.

Much of this exchange lay outside the profit range, intended only to meet the requirements of producer and consumer on either side; but both for local trade and for overseas demands true market forces had begun to play a role at least by the sixth century. Cyrus was told, it will be recalled, that Greeks "cheat each other" in their marketplaces, and admirably specific testimony to an economic spirit appears in a black-figure vase showing the sale of oil which bears the wish, "Oh father Zeus may I get rich." [16]

In production for overseas sale the manufacturer was probably dependent on a shipper, who at times commissioned a specific type of ware and by buying items in considerable numbers might force a reduction in their price— we assume.[17] It is, however, unlikely that an artisan was enduringly connected to any single overseas merchant for the disposal of all his output. Certain types of vases made by the industrious Nicosthenes were inspired by a trader acquainted with Etruria, but others from his workshop have turned up in Naucratis and south Russia. Potters varied, too, in their abilities or work forces; half the signed Athenian black-figure vases we have are the product of only six workshops.[18]

In local consumption the position of the artisan varied with the type of product. Statues and architectural stonework were commissioned; so too were the great vases set atop Dipylon graves in the eighth century, and probably most gold jewelry. Athenian aristocrats, it has been argued, also ordered special sets of cups and vases for their symposia, but a great deal of pottery, textiles, and other objects of wide use would seem to have been made as stock items, though few artisans could have had space or capital for large stores.[19] More and more, however, neighboring rural areas looked to the cities which supplied their demands as well as providing outlets for their agricultural surpluses; in the eighth century Geometric vases were made at various points in Attica, but by black-figure and red-figure times this dispersal does not appear. By 500 a pattern of production and sale with objectives of gain, fixed at long-established geographical centers, had come into existence in many parts of Greece.[20]

THE SOURCES OF TRADING
AND INDUSTRIAL GROUPS

In classic Athens the booths of the perfumers, fish-sellers, ribbon merchants, and other traders were a backdrop to the comedies, orations, and even philosophical treatises written in the period. All this trade appears to have been small-scale and specialized, though we do not see clearly into the warehouses and granaries of the Piraeus; there is certainly no reason to assume that traders in earlier centuries had been more than day-to-day sellers of the wares they handled.

So too the workshops were small. They were not factories of the types common since the Industrial Revolution—though the scholars who dwell on this difference do so mainly in an effort to depreciate the extent and influence of Greek production. The average industrial establishment in the United States in 1967, after all, had only 63 employees; economies of scale can become insignificant very rapidly if fixed capital is not much needed.[21] Vases show that up to 6 and 12 workmen worked in potteries and foundries (see Plate VII.c); and it is estimated that no more than about 125 to 150 persons were active at any one time in fifth-century potters' shops. Shipbuilding required larger groups, especially if warships were under construction; but temple columns and architraves could be raised, once pulleys were in general use, by small groups.[22] Some specialization existed; Xenophon could later comment:

> In small towns the same workman makes chairs and doors and ploughs and tables, and often this same artisan builds houses, and even so he is thankful if he can only find employment enough to support him. . . . In large cities, on the other hand, one trade alone, and very often even less than a whole trade, is enough to support a man: one man, for instance, makes shoes for men, and another for women; and there are places even where one man earns a living by only stitching shoes, another by cutting them out,

another by sewing the uppers together, while there is another who performs none of these operations but only assembles the parts.

Xenophon is here thinking in terms of the quality of the product, as are most modern commentators; [23] but the shoemaker himself may also have been well aware of increased productivity. Such detailed division of work probably did not exist in the archaic era, but the scenes of potters' workshops show a number of hands at work in separate stages; and potters and painters signed vases independently.

For the composition of these industrial and trading groups we lack the variety of epigraphical evidence available for the Roman Empire; only scattered testimony from vases, dedications (especially on the Athenian Acropolis), and a few literary references give any guidance. As a consequence modern ideologies and points of view have had free range for the creation of rather remarkable pictures.

It is, thus, a common statement that traders and artisans in the Greek cities were usually resident aliens. The problem here is not the widespread presence of such metics—they have been identified in some 80 *poleis*—but the exaggeration of our Athenian evidence to suggest that trade and industry generally were in the hands of foreigners.

At Athens metics were so numerous that they were formally registered, paid a metic tax, and had the obligation of serving in the army within Attica. [24] Metics, however, could not themselves enter Athenian courts and required a spokesman, nor could they own land unless they received the coveted status of *isoteleia*. A recent calculation suggests that at least half the potters and vase painters known at Athens during black-figure and early red-figure production had foreign names, though they all worked firmly within the Athenian artistic tradition. Other Greek potters are known to have resided in far-off Etruria, and moulds for figurines were transported by their owners to other states. [25]

A thin film of professionals bound together the many centers of Greek life both culturally and economically. Arion of Lesbos made a trip with his lyre into western waters and gained "great riches"; [26] the Homeridae of Chios traveled about, reciting the epics; more original poets, such as Stesichorus, Anacreon, and Simonides, moved from one tyrannical or aristocratic milieu to another as opportunity beckoned. On a lower level, Xenophon later described at Athens a troupe of girl entertainers, including a dancing girl who somersaulted among sword-blades, which was managed by a Syracusan impresario; [27] we do not know if such entertainers existed in earlier centuries, but they may well have toured along with oracle-mongers, exhibitors of unusual animals, and others. Sculptors and technical experts moved as commissions were available; the skilled engineer Eupalinus of Megara drove the tunnel for the water supply of Samos, and Theodorus of Samos worked on the Artemisium at Ephesus. Skilled craftsmen were on the one hand always scarce and on the other could not exist from the work available in any one archaic *polis*. [28] To call these varied itinerant figures "entrepreneurs" would be to inject too modern a note, but certainly they lived by their wits and skills.

This mobility was nothing new in Greek life. In the Homeric world bards traveled freely, vagabonds roved, and men of standing who became outlaws at home sought the protection of foreign lords both in the epics and in the world described by Herodotus. Yet in the end the view that artisans and traders in each state were normally metics from other states is illogical and rests on nothing better than an assumption, to which we shall return, that citizens would not engage in such sordid activities. Metics may have been more aggressive and so more noticeable; today expatriate businessmen are often more active than natives, but the latter do exist. In many small Greek states which had scant attractive powers local artisans and traders were very probably much in the majority.[29] At Sparta, parenthetically, the *perioikoi* are almost always assumed to have been the manufacturers of Laconian pottery, widely exported in the heyday of Corinthian vases (see Plate VII.b), and also of the metalwork which continued popular into classic times; the *perioikoi* were citizens, even if they lacked political rights.[30]

Once Greek trade and industry began to expand to meet internal and external demands, these sectors required ever greater numbers of men. Productivity increased as technological knowledge improved, but the lack of non-human power severely limited possibilities in this respect. Shops and stalls could draw discontented or dispossessed elements from the countryside, especially the *thetes;* but agricultural changes did not lead to a large surplus population which could either be forced off the land or would find the city so attractive that it could not be kept on the farms. Day labor did exist in fifth-century Athens, where men gathered each morning at a certain spot for hire much as they do in modern Tehran and other Eastern cities.[31]

In trade and industry there are interesting suggestions that women were drawn into economic activity. One dedication on the Acropolis was set up by a female who identified herself as a washerwoman; a hydria depicts a woman engaged in making metal vases (see Plate VI.b); at least later there is evidence for female traders in the Agora of Athens.[32] In eighteenth-century London marriage has been called "a business partnership" on the trading level, for wives were expected to bring with them capital and also to engage in shopwork. The same was at least in part true in ancient Greek cities, for the wives of traders and artisans could scarcely have been supported solely in household occupations. Sons also often entered their fathers' shops, as in potteries. A Solonian law even required that a father teach his son a trade, but only at Sparta do we know that at least three professions (herald, cook, *aulos*-player) were legally hereditary.[33]

EARLY GREEK SLAVERY

Metics, *thetes,* women, and others, however, could not provide the workshops all the steady and absolutely dependent human power required; the lack was met by the appearance of industrial slavery. Here a dispassionate modern student must despair of holding an even course.[34] Many scholars consider that industrial slavery in Greece is the single most important economic and social change, and should be emphasized from the outset rather than being tucked away incidentally in the midst of a chapter. Thenceforth, in such views, ancient society was damned—though a sober critic may observe that the damnation took a very long time in reaching its fulfillment. Not all who would hold this view are necessarily Marxist, but Marx and Engels have certainly influenced many scholars indirectly as well as directly.

Though I do not adhere to this position, I would stress that my obduracy is not the bitter fruit of hard-hearted capitalist feelings; one must stick to the evidence—and the information in the present case does not concern the horrible spread of slavery in the late Roman Republic or in imperial Roman households but that in early Greece, which was a very different society.

Slavery is always distorting in its social implications, both for slave and for master. To give only one small example, when contracts came to be written in classic times, often a slave did the writing so that in case of contest his evidence could be taken under torture.[35] Still, the degree of those distortions and even the actual quantity of slaves in early Greece are almost always exaggerated. Household slaves, of whom the females also served as concubines, had existed since Homeric times and continued to be employed in aristocratic families. Rhodopis, the famous courtesan, and Aesop the fabulist were thus both slaves in the same Samian *oikos* in the sixth century; just after our period Themistocles employed the guardian of his children, Sicinnus, to mislead king Xerxes at two decisive points in the Persian invasion of 480.[36] In the *Odyssey* Eumaeus appears as a rural slave, who owned his own slaves; but rural slavery did not develop extensively in historic Greece. The dependent farmers known as *penestai* in Thessaly, helots in Sparta, or *mnoitai* and *klarotai* in Crete were tied to their land, and we might cautiously label them "serfs" rather than slaves.

The new departure was the appearance of industrial slavery, which provided the workshops of Greece with the manpower they could not otherwise obtain. Chios is reported as the first state thus to use industrial slaves who were purchased from the "barbarians," and Periander of Corinth was reported to have legislated against slavery.[37] At least later slaves came largely from Thrace and Asia Minor, but Solon's reforms included the ransom of Athenians who had been sold abroad into slavery, presumably in near-by states. Down to 500, however, industrial slavery was of very restricted scope in Greece—no slaves appear in the first evidence from the silver mines at Laurium [38]—and its introduction must be taken as evidence first that the artisans of the more advanced Greek states had a steady enough demand to warrant the purchase of slaves, secondly that the owners had sufficient capital to acquire such forced labor. In these circumstances there is no evidence that slavery depressed the wages of free workers; slaves after all had to be maintained by their owners whether work was available or not. Differentiation of wages between skilled and unskilled labor, incidentally, does not appear to have been significant in ancient Greece.[39]

In the legal position of slaves, finally, there were as many variations as in the classifications of citizens in the manifold *poleis;* manumission was very limited in our period.[40] Evil though slavery could become in the long run, its pall did not, by itself, determine the position of arts and crafts in early Greece.

THE STANDING OF
TRADERS AND ARTISANS

Any assessment of the social and political position of artisans and traders in the age of expansion must begin with the fact that capital and labor, in discrete Ricardian terms, were not then sharply conceptualized. True, lucky men could feel themselves *plousioi,* rich enough that they did not have to work but might enjoy the delight of spending their *chremata,* or alternatively were subject to *penia,* the need to labor to gain a livelihood for their family. The concept of work for pay (*misthos*) had also been known since Poseidon and Apollo built the walls of Troy for king Laomedon (though they wound up unpaid in the end); in one Homeric simile appears a poor spinning woman who earns "a meager wage for her children," and in the rural work of the epic hired labor was common. Lines added to the *Works and Days* include the precept, "Let the wage promised to a friend be fixed." [41] But these references do not attest to any clear definition of capital and labor as ingredients of an economic system.

The subjection of one freeman to another was much disliked; from earlier days the Greeks inherited a feeling that each *oikos* ought to be economically independent—but they also knew that many men, the landless *thetes,* were not in this position even in an agricultural world. Eumaeus might be praised by Odysseus for his skill in tending the fire and waiting on table, for Hermes "lends grace and glory to all men's work"; but the epic author does not forget that Eumaeus was a slave.[42] As aristocratic thought was consolidated, dislike of dependence was extended to condemnation of all participation in trade and industry. Herodotus made it clear that in his day traders and artisans had little repute except in Corinth; the term *agoraios* was used contemptuously in Athenian politics.[43] By the fourth century such views had become fixed. In discussing ideal citizenry Aristotle baldly asserted that "a man who lives the life of a mechanic or labourer cannot pursue the things that belong to excellence" and therefore had no right to be a citizen; and Xenophon emphasized the physical disabilities inherent in the life of the workshops.[44]

This latter point was a valid one. Virtually all labor in ancient Greece was provided by manpower, save for very limited use of animals, or of wind power in shipping; men died not only because of diseases, but also because their bodies became worn out.[45] Anyone who could avoid the burden of physical labor was sensible to do so, but on the other hand most men *did* have to work—and labor in the shops or stalls of a city was of much the physical order as working the fields, except in its confinement. Hostility, moreover, to the activities of local traders is also understandable; even today producers and consumers often suspect middlemen of making parasitic profits and of "cheating each other" in the marketplace.

Still, there is a serious issue to be settled, and its solution cannot rest upon a simple acceptance of the developed aristocratic disdain for the life of traders and artisans. Did men hold as firmly this view in the age of expansion? and, in particular, did the commercial and industrial elements of the nascent cities so consider themselves?

These questions might easily lead to the introduction of the concept of a "bourgeoisie" and therewith of unwarranted social and political assumptions—a process which is rather too common in modern discussions of antiquity. Aristotle observes as a general truth for his period that "craftsmen often become rich men," [46] but insofar as the groups in question gained wealth they sought to act socially like contemporary aristocrats. It is far from clear that a *kalos* inscription to the serene, self-assured young aristocrat on Plate II.b connoted the potter's true familiarity with him on the social plane, though such brief inscriptions do not indeed suggest any air of obsequiousness. [47] Politically, as we shall see more fully in Chapter VIII, it is not possible to detect a powerful new economic element in trade and industry which organized itself and bent state policies to its own profit. The numbers of traders and artisans were in absolute numbers quite small; Athenian potteries, it will be recalled, employed only something over 100 persons at any one point.

In modern discussions Greek craftsmen are portrayed as vying in their artistic skills, and so indeed they did. Artisans exhibited a sense of personal worth in the fact that at least occasionally they signed their vases and statues; the inscription on an Athenian amphora by Euthymides, "As never Euphronius," is an explicit taunt of artistic competitiveness. [48] Yet the motto of the era was "Money makes the man," and the traders and craftsmen of early Greece were no exception. Even if ruthless self-seeking is not attested to and is not very likely, still Hesiod's potters were "hurrying after wealth," and artisans and professionals acquired considerable wealth in their callings.

Mnesiades and Andocides the potters thus felt self-confident enough to erect a bronze statue on the Athenian Acropolis; if this work cost about 500 drachmas and represented a tithe of their estate, then they were worth the very respectable sum of 5000 drachmas, almost a talent. [49] Doctors too could gain great sums; Democedes of Croton was paid from one to two talents a year by Greek states before he made a fortune through the good will of Darius. Architects, however, were essentially "master carpenters," and even in fourth-century records from Epidaurus they received only a limited amount more than other craftsmen (though paid by contract for every day).[50] One can but speculate how Eupalinus perfected the skill and determination to drive his tunnel for the water supply of Samos, and what reward he gained.

The conduct of political life continued to lie in the hands of the upper classes; only Pythagoras, said to have been the son of a gem cutter in his native Samos, might be advanced as an exception after his migration to Croton. Socially and politically the trading, industrial, and professional groups were not independent or powerful; there was, to repeat, no bourgeoisie in ancient Greece. Economically, traders and, still more, the major skilled craftsmen dealt largely with the upper classes and so had to tailor their products to the standards of those groups. Despite this important proviso, which some scholars would probably wish to emphasize, opportunities did exist in trade and industry as overseas and internal demand grew; and there were elements in the Greek world willing and able to seize these chances, thus fueling the continuing growth of workshops and markets. They occupied a very different niche from that of their fellow workers for the Persian monarchs or for that matter in late medieval Europe; as cities and coinage appeared and made economic life more supple, more focused, this independence became the more marked.[51]

By 500 a Greek urban center was a complex of diverse, semi-autonomous groups, and the markets within which these advanced elements operated quickened and influenced the course of life. Already in Pisistratus' day the "city" in Attica had become politically important; in the fifth century it was significant, even crucial.

Chapter V

Cities and Coinage

Two important consequences of the Hellenic outburst were the emergence of cities and the introduction of coinage. Both had appeared before 600 B.C., but they became widespread in the Greek world only during the sixth century. These dates deserve emphasis, for urbanization and coinage have often been assigned to much earlier periods; and once so placed have then been used to explain economic changes of which they were clearly the fruits. Neither, moreover, was the product purely of economic factors, though once in existence they were powerful instruments for focusing the structuring economic alterations. The more rapid progress of the sixth century, as against the seventh, may owe much to their presence.

THE CITIES

The major form of political organization in more advanced areas was in Greek called the *polis*. This was an independent group of people occupying an area with definite borders, but the common translation of *polis* as "city-state" introduces really serious distortions in the understanding of Greek history. Far too often scholars assume that a city-state must have contained—or even have been—a city, and then the way lies open to all manner of misconstructions.

Many Greek *poleis* never had an urban center. If one did develop within the confines of a state, it too might simply be called a *polis* but more precisely was an *asty,* in contrast to a rural village (*kome, chorion*) huddled about a never-failing water supply.

The word "city" is easily used in historical pages, but few historians will agree on a definition for urban centers which will apply whenever and wherever such nuclei appear in human development.[1] To speak only of those in ancient Greece, a city was not necessarily larger than an agricultural village, though it usually became so; the critical difference lay in the far wider variety of functions. Economically, a city is normally considered to be composed of commercial and industrial sectors as well as a continuing agricultural group; socially, its life is far more articulated in a variety of modes; but equally important are its political and religious roles. These last aspects in particular must be kept clearly in mind in looking at ancient Greece.

Physically, a Greek urban center had a concentration of religious precincts, not all of which necessarily were temples; in the mild climate of Greece the devout continued to worship various deities at altars in the open air. The city also had public buildings and areas—eventually these might include a *prytaneion* or other public house for the presiding magistrates (with a sacred hearth); a *bouleuterion* for the council; a theater; a gymnasium; and, above all, an agora or open area for the assembly of the citizens. Our conception of an agora is likely to be influenced by that of Athens, which was a somewhat rectangular area, but in some cities it assumed rather a linear form atop a hill crest.[2] Often the agora was near a major temple not far from the edge of the city; unlike the Roman forum it was interwoven with the pattern of streets as a living heart or focus for urban life.[3] In Athens and many other urban centers streets and lanes twisted in an outwardly random fashion, but more uniform layouts were known before the classic period. Old Smyrna had some regularity, as did some cities founded in the Aegean world in the seventh century; Vroulia on the island of Rhodes had two rows of similar quadrate rooms arranged on the straight lines of two streets.[4] Colonies such as Olbia on the north or Acragas in the west likewise were laid out on rectangular grids.

Old Smyrna had a city wall, or so, at least, it is reported and shown on an often reproduced reconstruction.[5] By the sixth century some of the western colonies were walled. On the Greek mainland we know only of fortified points of refuge, such as the Acropolis at Athens, down past 500 except for recent evidence of a wall around Eretria, where at least its west gate went back to the seventh century.[6] In this matter Athens presents a difficult problem. Both Herodotus and Thucydides state that it was walled before the Persian invasion, and their concurrent testimony is not lightly to be dismissed; yet no certain trace of this pre-Persian wall has ever been found. It is also difficult to visualize the event which would have led the Athenians to undertake the task of encircling their whole city before 480. The conflict here of literary and archeological evidence is one of the most patent in our period, and the problem must lie open in the hope of some happy discovery; but it remains possible that the historians were really referring to the Acropolis fortifications.[7]

The physical aspects of a Greek *asty* which have just been sketched are only its external dress, but they do reflect the sources for its rise. These are not quite what we might expect from a knowledge of more recent cities. A Greek city, thus, was not sundered from its countryside politically and economically as discretely as were medieval towns or modern metropolises; where walls did exist, they were draped around an urban center as a rule, rather than determining its shape.[8] One student has seen in the loose early town patterns of Greece a mark of the free, individual spirits of the citizens; [9] we may take them too as a warning not to visualize the early Hellenic city solely as an agglomeration of traders and artisans, parasitic on backward peasants. The root of the city lay in the consolidation of the *polis,* and as the *polis* gained greater civic unity across the seventh and sixth centuries its physical center sometimes developed the outward marks of urbanization. In the Cleisthenic reorganization of Attica in the late sixth century the city proper received no special structure but remained part and parcel of the division of the state into precincts (demes). In sum, it is perhaps not feasible to speak of Greek cities simply as ceremonial centers, as early Chinese cities have been defined; but political and religious impulses were at least as important as economic demands in promoting the growth of cities. Insofar as Greek cities reflected any planning instincts, the sources for such planning cannot be said to have been economic in origin until the fifth century.[10]

Historians are, indeed, accustomed to stress the existence of specialized economic elements in a city to distinguish it from an essentially agricultural village. When these new sectors burgeoned, their agents needed a secure point for their operations and also a continuing source of demand,

and the cities of Greece provided both. The agora, it must be stressed, was originally a meeting place used for political, religious, and military purposes; but in time either its own space or adjacent areas became an economic market-place as well. At Athens various types of wares eventually had each their own particular section, though industries were not grouped on special streets as they were later in medieval towns.

The rise of cities in Greece seems to owe little or nothing to models available in Phoenicia and other Near Eastern areas, but followed naturally from local developments.[11] Accordingly, the shape and character of Hellenic centers varied as widely as did other aspects of the multifarious Greek *poleis,* and urbanization came at different times to different points, depending in part on their relation to trade routes and the extent of their agricultural resources. If we look only to the outward panoply of temples and public buildings, cities were most uncommon down into the seventh century; if we define a city primarily in terms of resident artisans and merchants, then it might be possible to push some urban origins back into the late eighth century.[12] But on the whole cities became numerous and vibrant only on the turn from the seventh to the sixth century.

The one city about which anything can be said in detail is Athens; but in commenting on its evolution one runs the inevitable risk in Greek history of taking a very untypical state as a paradigm.[13] Down to almost the end of the seventh century Athens consisted of several villages, separated by open spaces in which the dead were buried. One graveyard lay along the road to Eleusis, the area called the Kerameikos by reason of its eventual concentration of potteries. Another cemetery lay on the north slope of the Acropolis, where there were houses, and also in the Agora. We do not know whether at this time there was a temple to Athena or any other deity on the Acropolis; later rearrangements of its crest, especially the Periclean building program, swept away any remains of an early shrine which might have existed. At least in the *Odyssey* the goddess Athena, coming to Athens, "entered the well-built home of Erechtheus," a statement which suggests to some scholars that she did not in the poet's mind have her own home on the Acropolis.[14]

By the time of Solon, archon in 594, the focus of Attic political life was becoming a city; the last private houses in the Agora ceased to exist at that time, and burial had already been discontinued in the area.[15] Only under Pisistratus and his sons (547 on), however, were steps formally taken to regularize and embellish the nascent city. Pisistratus concentrated the cults of Attica in the city as far as possible, or at least built subsidiary shrines for Artemis of Brauron and Demeter of Eleusis in the *asty*. The Acropolis apparently received two major temples; smaller shrines which have yielded sculptural fragments may already have been constructed. The Agora was deliberately marked off by boundary stones, some of which have been found in the American excavations of the past generation; an aqueduct brought water to the fountain of Enneakrounos; and at least a few public buildings were erected, though they were destroyed in the Persian invasions. Outside the city itself a huge temple to Olympian Zeus was begun, though it was not completed for centuries. In Herodotus' account of the rise of Pisistratus, *asty* and *komai* are distinguished, but both "those from the city" and rural elements seem to have supported Pisistratus.[16] Interestingly enough, Pisistratus as tyrant sought to check movement from the countryside to the city by encouraging small farmers with state loans. Other tyrannies such as the Cypselid line at Corinth exhibit the same mixed support of urban centers and distrust of their growing masses.

At the close of the sixth century Athens had become the

home of a considerable variety of crafts and trades, some of which are attested by the Acropolis dedications. Its products were exported all over the Mediterranean as far as Greek trade reached; though its port was still the open roadstead of Phalerum, Themistocles was soon to give its navy and merchant shipping several fortified harbors around the promontory of the Piraeus. As a religious and political focus for all Attica the buildings of the city were beginning to fit its role; in the next century, when Athens became a center for the entire Aegean, those structures were replaced on a far grander scale.

Somewhat the same picture of urbanization can be detected at Corinth, which was "a sprawling community of scattered villages throughout the Geometric and much of the Archaic Periods." [17] As Corinthian potteries, tile manufactures, and metalwork grew, they were scattered among these villages, and it is difficult to speak even of a formal agora down to 500 on the basis of present knowledge. The earliest temple to Apollo was erected in the seventh century; the one still standing in part, about 550. Yet Corinth was a *polis* from the eighth century, first under kings, then aristocrats and tyrants, and finally a conservative oligarchy, which colonized widely abroad and promoted commercial activity by constructing a slipway across the Isthmus of Corinth about 600. The far-flung wall which eventually encompassed the urban center itself was, however, a product of the classic period. Sparta on the other hand always remained, in Thucydides' famous words, "a straggling village like the ancient towns of Hellas." [18]

THE IMPORTANCE OF CITIES

Would one have been able to take an imaginary airplane trip over Greece in 500, he would have seen the urban centers as only minuscule dots in the landscape of mountains and small agricultural plains. Though the cities may have been the hubs of commercial and industrial activity, they also embraced elements which engaged in agriculture, and there is no reason to assume that craftsmen such as potters and smiths ceased to be active in the villages.

The population of the cities can only be guessed, but by piling probability on probability atop a few reasonable figures for Athens we can reach a possible order of magnitude for that center in the sixth century. The potteries scarcely kept busy more than about 150 persons in the fifth century, and in the sixth would have needed fewer hands, not more. This industry was certainly one of the largest; other crafts in metals, stone, wood, leather, and wool, together with such service trades as existed, would scarcely bring the total for adult artisans up to 1000, but to round our figures we may take that as an outside range. Traders in the local market and sailors may, for simplicity, be set at the same number. Some of those 2000 would have been slaves; others, resident aliens who would not always have had families. We might, thus, multiply by three rather than four in order to get a total population, with women and children, of not more than 6000 for the industrial and commercial sectors of sixth-century Athens.

To this must be added the aristocrats living in the city, who by the fourth century numbered no more than 300 (plus families and servants); some other basically rural elements; and a fair number of beggars and other marginal types—later on, the urban officials had a band of public slaves to pick up the bodies of those who died in the streets.[19]

All in all, it would be difficult to put the urban population of Athens as high as 10,000. Miletus, Corinth, and Syracuse might have been larger or as large; but many Hellenic cities were certainly smaller. Old Smyrna had some

400 to 500 houses, and so a population of some 2000, which has been described as largely agricultural.[20] Köln was the biggest city in fifteenth-century Germany, with about 20,000, but before A.D. 1500 90 to 95 percent of the German towns numbered less than 2000 inhabitants.[21]

Another early modern statistic is suggestive: an urban center numbering 3000 required the agricultural surplus of some 8.5 square kilometers—in a less mountainous landscape than that of Greece. Early in the sixth century B.C. dependent farmers in Attica had to yield one-sixth of their crops to their creditors; as noted in Chapter II, this ratio was probably the maximum available from Attic farms and would suggest the percentage of the Athenian population which could have lived without itself farming—provided that the surplus were totally subject to mobilization. This assumption is unrealistic both by reason of the problems in land transport and also because the rural villages had an inherited social and economic structure which would have limited the free disposal of their products. In Chapter VII I shall show that the total population which could have been fed from Attic hectares would scarcely have overpassed 60,000 to 70,000 persons; even an urban population of less than 10,000 would have required seaborne grain for its support. More generally no city of ancient Hellas could rise much past this level without a secure supply of overseas food—for which it could pay—and such sources were only beginning to be tapped by the close of our period.

Size does not fully determine the significance of cities in fostering change within an otherwise static system. In the Dark Ages men lived together, but in villages; the world of artists, poets, and thinkers in 500 was set in an urban framework, and politics took place in the cities. Red-figure Athenian vase painting thus reflects far less of a rural background than did black-figure ware.[22] Unlike medieval and some modern aristocrats, moreover, the leading classes of

Greece preferred to live—or at least to have houses—in the urban centers and concentrated there the expenditure of their rural revenues. In telling the story of Lygdamis' seizure of tyranny on Naxos Aristotle commented that "most of the well-to-do lived in the *asty,* though others were scattered in *komai."* [23] Beside the aristocrats dwelt resident foreigners, artisans, and even slaves, whose free behavior on the streets of Athens the Old Oligarch was to describe with disgust in the next century—all that upsetting mass which Plato wished to ban from his ideal, unchanging community.

To the effects of this concentration of the wealthy and intellectually active elements in the small Greek cities we shall return in the next chapter; the explosive onrush of Greek civilization, in brief, would scarcely be explicable except in such a vigorous environment. "Mind *takes* form," observed Lewis Mumford, "in the city; and in turn, urban forms condition mind. . . . With language itself, it remains man's greatest work of art." [24]

Economically too the influence of the cities radiated out into the surrounding countryside. Urban centers provided a growing range of luxuries and more utilitarian manufactured wares. They also demanded much, in various ways, from the countryside. Shops and stalls needed men and women—though, as noted earlier, tyrants might seek to check the drift of rural manpower, and slaves had to be acquired to provide manpower for the workshops. Cities also required more extensive water supplies than wells and springs could furnish. Fountain houses appear abruptly on vase paintings of the late seventh and earlier sixth centuries; to provide water for these points aqueducts or water courses were built at Megara in the later seventh century and in the sixth at Athens, Corinth, and elsewhere. The famous tunnel of Eupalinus at Samos, driven 3400 feet through a hill, was one of the greatest engineering feats of sixth-century Greece, duly appreciated by Herodotus.[25]

Above all the cities needed food for their non-agricultural elements. The passage of Aristotle just cited goes on to note that people came down from the *asty* of Naxos to a village to buy food, but the local fishermen preferred to give their catch to an estimable, wealthy village resident rather than to sell at a low price; a conflict over a fish led to civil war in which Lygdamis was victor and became tyrant. The contention is in microcosm an illumination of processes widely at work; near-by farmers, fishermen, and other non-urban elements became bound to urban markets and could well feel themselves at times exploited by low prices and other disadvantages.

Modern students often have an ambivalent attitude toward this aspect of cities; Weber and others have stressed particularly their role in antiquity as centers of consumption.[26] In archaic Athens, on the other hand, productive and distributive functions do seem to have been significant. When we come to the agricultural world in a later chapter, moreover, we shall discover that formal legal subjection of farmers occurred only in areas of the Greek homeland which did not develop urban complexes; cities must have served in some measure as safety valves for the pressures of the countryside.

The general effects of the emergence of cities should not be exaggerated. Before urban centers became important focuses for economic activity the Greek world had shown itself quite capable of producing social and economic tensions; cities only added new dimensions to the problems and even helped to reduce their intensity. In early modern times urban demands and economic power altered the character of the encircling rural areas, but only in limited districts. So too in Greece city spoke to city far more than to local rural enclaves. Still, by 500 the intellectual and economic ties of the growing urban centers bound the Greek world together in a manner that would have been inconceivable three centuries earlier.

THE APPEARANCE OF COINAGE

The Near East had long been accustomed to reckon and sometimes to make payments of dues, wages, and interest in measured quantities of a staple object such as barley or metals; the Assyrian king Sennacherib even proclaimed that he had cast half-shekel pieces.[27] These payments, it should be noted, were largely on the level of the temples and kings but could also concern private traders in Phoenicia and elsewhere. In modern simple societies similar forms of "money" appear sporadically, but not universally; early Greece valued objects in terms of oxen, but also used tripods, cauldrons, and iron spits (*obeliskoi*) as measures of value.[28]

According to Herodotus, true coinage, "implying the stamping of such nuggets with recognizable designs, together with a standardization of the weight," was invented by the Lydians.[29] Although it is difficult to draw practical distinctions between Lydian issues and earlier lumps of metal, the statement is true at least in the sense that development of coinage was continuous in the Aegean thereafter. To be sure, when we look at the small bits of electrum found at the Artemisium of Ephesus and elsewhere we find that many of them meet only one of the ingredients of the definition just given. The first issues are clearly set on a weight standard in the proportions of ⅓ (*trite*), ⅙, ¹⁄₁₂ . . . on to ¹⁄₉₆ (of a stater); but they bear no designs. Very soon, however, a great variety of electrum coinage appears in Asia Minor which is marked by reverse punches of "incuse" form and by obverse dies of lions and other animals.[30] The date of the earliest issues, which depends upon the attendant material found at the Artemisium, has been placed from the first decades of the seventh century on into the first years of the sixth; but the last quarter of the seventh century still seems the latest reasonable point.[31]

To distribute the anepigraphic issues among the Greek states of the seaboard is difficult, and suggestions have been made that they were the product of private moneyers; at times it is even assumed that bankers and other financial entrepreneurs already existed in the early sixth century. If such a coin as the one bearing the unknown name "Phanes" was privately struck, the source must rather be found in the circle of great Anatolian aristocrats, predecessors of that Pythius who entertained Xerxes and boasted of holding 2000 talents of silver and almost 4 million darics in gold.[32] More probably, however, the coins are the product of *polis* mints; the electrum issues of Cyzicus, Mitylene, Phocaea, and other states made by the end of the century can be positively identified.

This electrum coinage went on into later times; many Cyzicene staters were struck in a variety of handsome patterns into the fourth century, and they circulated widely.[33] Under king Croesus Lydia itself proceeded to separate the gold and silver in electrum and to issue coinage in both metals; the Persians first continued the Croeseids on a lighter standard and then from about the end of the sixth century struck their own gold darics and silver sigloi. The latter, however, circulated almost exclusively in Asia Minor; insofar as the rest of the Persian empire needed coins, these were of Greek origin until the Phoenician cities began their own issues in the fifth century.

In or near the Greek mainland the earliest silver coinage is generally agreed to be that of Aegina, which poured out simple lumps of silver with a sea-turtle design from well before 550.[34] Corinth began soon thereafter with an image of Pegasus and a *koppa,* the archaic Greek letter with which the word "Corinthians" began; this was one of the first coinages to be precisely identified as to mint. Athens struck with a variety of "heraldic" badges (the *Wappenmünzen* series) and then turned to a pattern which remained essentially standard for centuries—the helmeted head of Athena in profile on the obverse, and her owl with an olive twig and the letters AΘE on the reverse. The innovation of engraving a design on the reverse punch soon became common but not universal.

The dating of these Athenian series is an important matter in its relation to the reforms of Solon, and is still hotly debated. The latter tradition on Solon ascribes to him a form of weight revaluation which might be called inflation, a matter which we shall take up in the last chapter; but the numismatic evidence does not support the view that Athens was striking coinage at the beginning of the sixth century. The *Wappenmünzen* seem rather to come in the period of Pisistratus, and one may hazard an unsupported guess that *if* they are heraldic badges they may be connected with his use of mercenary soldiers. On the famous Athena/owl series we can be even more certain that it was instituted only after Pisistratus' death in 527.[35]

Among the western colonies, Himera and Selinus, the farthest west on the north and south coasts of Sicily, appear to have been the earliest mints; this priority is usually explained by the assumption that they could draw on silver supplies from Spain.[36] The sources, indeed, for the silver used by Greek mints are very uncertain save for the Athenian supply from its own mines at Laurium; much of the Aegean must have used silver from Thrace and Macedonia, but the overstriking of coins from one mint by the workmen in another was fairly common practice.[37]

By 500 a great number of Greek states, both large and small, were issuing their own coinage with a rich variety of types drawn from agricultural and manufactured products as well as heads of divinities (see Plate V). Several south Italian states struck thin plates the reverse of which was marked by the same device as the obverse but in intaglio form; north Aegean communities, still largely tribal, issued huge eight-drachma pieces made from their native silver; and other diversities stud the numismatic record. Some of the most active mints had no particular role in overseas trade; other states which were active on the seas, such as Megara, did not coin at all.

The monetary system of the Greek world was one of anarchy. Each state could enforce the circulation of its own currency in payments into and out of its treasury; but even as far as its commercial markets were concerned there might well be difficulties—we know of at least two decrees in later centuries which required acceptance of the coins of the relevant *polis*. [38] Abroad, currency was taken only on the basis of its weight; and at times dubious issues were cut or punched to prove whether they were good metal or plated; these tests are particularly evident in the silversmiths' hoards of the Near East (see Plate V.i, from Terone).

For the purposes of modern study early Greek coinage is chaotic in another sense. Not all of even the great public collections have been published, let alone the large numbers of specimens held in private hands. The evidence which is available for major mints has as yet only sporadically been assembled and analyzed so that we can make safe use of it. As a result, even the dates of issues before 500 are very uncertain; those which have been given above are for the most part still tentative. Weight standards also are a subject of considerable difficulty. [39] The Ionian electrum coinage was struck on systems ranging from 14.25 grams to 17.2 grams per stater; silver coinage was equally varied. Colonies generally tended to follow the conventions of their homelands, but not always; Syracuse, for instance, coined on the Athenian, not the Corinthian, standard. The natural tendency is to deduce trade links among states using the same weights, but that view rests on fundamental misconceptions of the purpose of coinage and an overemphasis on assumed lines of trade. Finally, the badges and devices used on Greek coinage are conventional designs, the origins of which are sometimes unclear; when the name of a mint is omitted, we cannot always be sure even in the fifth century as to its location.

These and other problems are serious issues for numismatic experts and also for historians seeking to use the evidence of the coinage. Yet coins are contemporary sources, once they can be dated and assigned; moreover, coinage is a source of wider range for the many Greek *poleis* than literary or epigraphic testimony, which is available only for a few states.

PURPOSES AND SIGNIFICANCE OF COINAGE

Once the idea of coinage had been introduced into Hellas, it spread like wildfire—and, let us remember, in a system of very tiny economic and political units, the smallest ever to mint in so many local centers. For this development there must have been compelling reasons, though the causes may not have everywhere been exactly the same. Recent investigations have generally concurred in the judgment that coinage was *not* struck primarily for commercial objectives in local markets until copper coins came to be issued in western mints of the fifth century, and in Greece proper in the hundred years that followed.[40] True, over half the electrum examples found in the Artemisium at Ephesus are so tiny ($^1/_{24}$, $^1/_{48}$, $^9/_{96}$) that they could have been employed for fairly small purchases, and Miletus and other states of Asia Minor issued small pieces of silver in the sixth century;

Herodotus, too, couples the beginning of Lydian coinage with the first appearance of *kapeloi* or local merchants.[41] As a whole, however, Greek states struck mainly drachmas and multiples thereof in the earlier period.

Such issues were primarily occasioned by public needs of the *polis,* which were varied. Distributions of surplus revenues to the citizenry are known.[42] Lydia and other states at times hired mercenaries, who had to be paid, and paid relatively well;[43] in later times coinage often swelled tremendously as military needs dictated. Carthage, for example, did not strike any coins, despite its commercial activities, until forced to do so to pay Sicilian mercenaries; and its issues then were marked in Punic, "for the people of the camp." The building of temples, which, as noted earlier, increased greatly in the sixth century, required mainly labor, but also at least at times required cash outlays. For the Periclean buildings on the Acropolis and the construction of the fourth-century complex of Asclepius at Epidaurus we have extensive records of such expenditures, and cult requirements also were continuing demands.

Revenues came in as well as being paid out. Mints have often been sources of profit, especially for wily, unscrupulous monarchs; and if we can trust a later source Hippias, tyrant of Athens, made money out of calling in and reissuing Athenian coinage.[44] Commerce expanded, and harbor tolls and other charges on the increased trade had to be paid in cash. The earliest epigraphic records of state and religious fines may mention staters, but those references were simply to certain weights; a decree, however, from Eretria of about 525 speaks clearly of *chremata dokima,* and the "constitution of Chios" of about 575–550 also perhaps specifies money fines.[45] Direct taxes on agricultural production were not common and were usually expressed, as in Pisistratid times, in percentage terms; still, they may at least in part have been paid in coinage rather than in produce. Finally, and perhaps not least, the growing unity and self-assertion of the individual *poleis* led them to mark that pride by the issuance of their own coinage, though often only in small quantities and at rare intervals. As Duby remarked of coinage in a very different era, the early Middle Ages, "en premier lieu, elle est affirmation du prestige monarchique . . . par sa munificence, le roi distribue autour de lui des fragments d'or, marqués du signe de la puissance personnelle; ils lui reviennent par la fiscalité." [46]

We cannot determine with any precision whether more coinage was struck in the sixth or the fifth centuries. In the latter period Syracuse, which began to coin only late in the preceding century, and also Athens issued huge volumes of coinage, and mints in Crete and elsewhere first began striking. The silver issues of Asia Minor and other areas declined markedly but probably not enough to counterbalance the increase especially at Athens. On the whole one may feel that not only was there more coinage in the fifth century but also, perhaps more certainly, that its usage became more regular.

In this latter respect an electrum *trite* now in the British Museum arouses speculation. This coin bears an extraordinary number of countermarks; eleven honeycomb the edge of the flan, and five are on the obverse. These are anepigraphic marks (unlike the "bankers' stamps" on fourth-century issues of Cilicia and elsewhere) such as a cross, crescent, and so on. Another *trite* in Paris also has a number of countermarks, as do various other early Ionian issues. [47] The most reasonable explanation for these numerous punches on some coins is that they denote private ownership of the specific piece; the issuing state would not have been likely to mark them as they passed in and out of public funds. Clearly there was a tendency to consider a coin a permanent possession once it had been acquired by a private person; Xenophon later comments regarding silver issues, "When men possess a great deal of it, they bury the part which they do not want." [48] This unproductive preservation of wealth was common enough in his period to receive frequent mention.

Before 500, however, hoards and foundation deposits were not very common, as against much larger numbers thereafter. The totals so far known are 16 from Asia Minor (mostly small, and in electrum to the last quarter of the century), 5 from Greece proper, 2 from Macedon and Thrace, 3 from Italy, 1 from Syria, and 2 from Egypt. [49] The reasons for this scanty evidence can only be surmised; generally a hoard in itself gives little reason for its existence. The constant movement of Greek silver to the Near East will not serve as an explanation, for this serious drain continued in later centuries. [50] Far more likely is the probability that the upper classes came slowly to consider coinage a prime vehicle for their wealth; the *trites* we have been considering may well have passed from one treasure chest to another particularly for the payment of dowries. Even in fourth-century Attica a major cause for the pledge of agricultural land, marked by the *horoi* of the period, was the need to secure the dowry of a daughter in the event that her husband had for any reason to repay it; landholders have always been loath to assign land, as against cash, to daughters. [51]

Evaluations of the effect of the rapid introduction of coinage across the Greek world must, indeed, be conducted with caution. Some studies have ascribed the economic and social difficulties evident in Hesiod's *Works and Days* to the effects of coinage, even though minting did not begin for almost another century. [52] The rise of tyrants in the seventh century, again, has been too often linked with coinage, either as a cause for their appearance or as an innovation which they fostered. Pheidon of Argos, a king who is nonetheless called tyrant in some of our sources, is said to have struck coins, and this purported Pheidonian coinage has been localized in Aegina—but he never ruled that state, and in any event the tie is chronologically impossible.[53] There is no need to cite other examples of this confusion, which in root is more conceptual than chronological.

In the modern world money (and credit) are such evident marks of economic activity and are, at least by the monetarist school of economic theory, given such weight in their own right that it is difficult to turn back to the origins of coinage in the western world and avoid exaggerating its initial effect. One recent scholar has even asserted that money led to the change from a stage of *oikos*-economy to the *polis*-economy, a step he places beside the discovery of fire, domestication of animals, and writing; and grounds for such sweeping views may be found in Marx's *Das Kapital* as well as in capitalistic treatises.[54]

Against such extreme magnifications let us set the dry comment that "the 'rise of a money economy' is one of the residuary hypotheses of economic history: a *deus ex machina* to be called upon when no other explanation is available."[55] In the development of early Greece, as sketched in the present work, the introduction of coinage—like the appearance of cities—is more a consequence of a long, involved chain of expansion than in itself the fundamental cause of tensions: "radix omnium malorum avaritia," but greed does not require coinage to be brought into play.

Yet money in coined form did eventually have far-reaching effects on the economic and social life of Greece. It was struck primarily for purposes of state, and its growing use aided the consolidation and expansion of the machinery of government. When the inhabitants of Attica evacuated their land during the Persian invasion, the council of the Areopagus gave each man not food, but eight drachmas in coined silver. Later in the fifth century came the Athenian empire, which sought to convert the tribute of its subjects from the provision of ships to money payments, minutely recorded on stone; far to the East the staircases of Persepolis portrayed the revenues of the vast Persian empire as a great variety of natural and manufactured items.

Private individuals found currency useful in many ways beyond meeting their financial obligations to the treasuries of the state and its temples. Aristotle summed up exchanges of unlike objects by referring them to money, "the measure of everything," and also saw in money an instrument of justice and a corrective to social disorders. This latter view might not occur to a modern economist, but can be justified.[56] Supple economic activity also had come to require a standard measure and medium of value, though trade itself may often have been conducted by barter; and coinage made it possible to translate even immoveable assets such as land into reckoning assets.

Once again we must observe that not all parts of Greece were drawn into a money economy centered in urban markets, but the willingness—forced or voluntary—of more advanced centers to progress to this stage was of tremendous significance, a qualitative change in life. The acceptance of the idea of coinage was, in truth, not automatic; only an open society, ready to change and to seize on new concepts, could have taken the step with such speed.

Throughout later western history the renewed use of coinage, or changes in its volume and method of employment, have facilitated further alterations in many aspects; but the effects have borne unevenly, and often unjustly, on different classes and on individuals within those classes. Both great landholders and smaller peasants, as well as the industrial and commercial elements in ancient Greece, sometimes benefited from and at other times suffered from the pressures made more evident as coinage became widespread; and, as the last chapter will show, it was not the upper classes who gained in the end.

Chapter VI

Aristocrats and Semi-aristocrats

Interwoven with the expansion of industry and commerce, and with the appearance of cities and coinage, were major social and economic alterations in the agricultural world. Lesser farmers often sank into the position of peasants; the rich and powerful evolved an aristocratic code of life. This latter aspect, which is the more visible of the two, had extensive consequences for all aspects of Greek life.

The heroes whom Homer celebrated were not aristocrats. They were indeed distinguished in birth as Zeus-sprung or the scions of great ancestors; they were frequently given the title of *basileis;* their roles as individual leaders in council and on the battlefield were deliberately emphasized; men and women of this stamp are described as being more delicate and beautiful than the ordinary people. The most evident political bond in the Homeric poems was a personal tie between leader and followers, who usually stand as an anonymous mass; when an upstart such as Thersites, ill-favored in appearance, sought to speak, he was rudely chastised and silenced.[1] Yet the Homeric heroes were not aristocrats in the sense in which the term is used in these pages or as it has been employed in discussions of early modern European society. Both Penelope in the *Odyssey* and Agariste of Sicyon in the early sixth century had eager suitors, who were not dissimilar in their objective; but the disdain of Agariste's father for the drunken dancing of one well-favored youth admirably illustrated the changes in cultural attitudes which had taken place across our period.

Not all students of Greek society would accept this distinction, though some have emphasized its existence. A recent survey of Greek ethics points out that in the Homeric world those who were best were warriors, men of wealth and social position who protected their dependents by their valor in war and peace, and concludes, "This is an aristocratic scale of values." [2] The statements are correct; the inference, however, is premature. For the Homeric world had not yet traveled all the way toward the elaboration of an aristocratic ethos, i.e., an obligatory pattern of life and values *consciously* conceived and shared by a limited group which considered itself "best" and the claims of which were generally accepted, even cherished, by other elements of society.[3]

This distinction is not a matter of hair-splitting. The Homeric world was an artificial, conventionalized construction which lasted over several centuries, and poetic requirements led to an overemphasis on the place of individual warriors whose duels and valorous exploits would command the attention of the auditors. Yet the epic was to some degree connected with the life of the Dark Ages, and we cannot hope to understand how historic Greek society and the *polis* structure survived the terrific tensions of the age of expansion if its social system was sharply divided from the beginning. The Greek world in the dim centuries before 800 did rest on a fundamental unity among its individual peoples, a more potent cement than the Homeric tie of leader and follower; a differentiation socially as well as economically evolved mainly in the centuries which are the primary concern of these pages. In battle the Homeric heroes stood out; but in peacetime Paris tended sheep on Mount Ida and Odysseus plowed the fields of his native Ithaca. The aristocrats of later times deliberately employed their free hours in very different ways.

THE ARISTOCRATS

From the period of Archilochus, in the earlier and mid-parts of the seventh century, the aristocratic ethos which existed in classic times is clearly visible. It does not appear in Hesiod, who perhaps lived in a backwater but also on a different level. When, then, did the distinction of the upper classes begin to take conscious form?

In the graves discussed in Chapter III initial steps toward outward differentiation of the well-to-do can be traced back into the ninth century (see Plate I). The eighth century, however, appears to have been the critical stage in the material evolution of Greek aristocratic ways of life, manifested in provision both of elegant native vases and of foreign luxuries; and by the seventh century tombs of the upper classes at Athens were being embellished with marble steles crowned by sphinxes. One of the earliest testimonies to Greek alphabetic writing is a jug on which is scratched, "He of all dancers who now dances most gracefully, let him accept this," a suggestion of aristocratic competitiveness.[4] If we had other contemporary literary evidence from the advanced Greek centers, we might be able to show that the attitudes evident in archaic poetry were beginning to be expressed in the later eighth century.

It is high time to be more specific about the connotation of the term "aristocracy" in early Greek history, for this subject is usually touched upon only tangentially except in ethical and literary studies. The famous phrase for aristocrats came to be *kaloikagathoi,* as distinguished from the *kakoi* or base; but in the seventh century one cannot be sure that its constituent parts, *kaloi* (beautiful = polished) and *agathoi* (good = preeminent), referred normally to class position rather than to individual merit.[5]

In any event such moral or esthetic standards were a later refinement; more fundamentally an aristocrat was one who was born into an aristocratic family. As Plutarch once commented, "How often in Simonides, Pindar, Alcaeus, Ibycus, and Stesichorus is 'good birth' (*eugeneia*) a matter of praise and honor?" Already in the *Odyssey,* when Menelaus greeted Telemachus and the son of Nestor he observed, "Base churls (*kakoi*) could not beget such sons as you"; one fragment of Archilochus runs, "Enter, because you are well-born [*gennaios*]"; at Athens the aristocratic class was thus called the Eupatrids.[6] After the *basileis* disappeared in most Greek states, there were no hereditary titles, though Sappho could celebrate her friend Andromeda as "the daughter of kings";[7] but in the early generations of the age of expansion the aristocratic families of any Greek *polis* maintained an essentially closed circle and developed a sure sense that their way of life was morally superior.

Landed wealth, however, was a second important requirement, which is reflected in the term *Gamoroi* at Samos and Syracuse. When Simonides was asked who were *eugeneis,* his reply ran, "Those rich from of old," and seventh-century archons at Athens were chosen "on birth and wealth."[8]

How much land did an aristocrat have to have? The simple answer is, enough to maintain his distinct way of life; but at Athens we can perhaps utilize the uppermost level in the Solonian classes, the *pentekosiomedimnoi* (those who had annual revenues of 500 *medimnoi* of grain or its equivalent in wine or oil), as a rough indication. On the basis of possible maximum crop yields at that time, such a landed revenue would imply possession of over 30 hectares of fair farming land. A simple rural family, on the other hand, could make do in most years with some four hectares. The largest estates known in classic Athens actually were in the range of 30 hectares; Greek aristocrats were poverty-stricken by the standards of the great dukes of eighteenth-century England and the magnates of eastern Europe, or for that matter Pythius of Lydia.[9]

Later, when the public liturgies of Athens required the expenditure of cash, it has been estimated that wealth (of any sort) amounting to less than three talents would not attract such responsibilities, but those owning more than four talents were unlikely to escape. Despite the great economic growth of Athens across the fifth century no more than 400 citizens were assigned the burden of maintaining a trireme in the Peloponnesian war; only 300 had such a responsibility in the mid-fourth century. In earlier centuries and in smaller states the numbers of aristocrats must have been even fewer; Polybius preserves the information that no more than 100 "houses" were considered noble in Locri Epizephyri.[10]

THE SEMI-ARISTOCRATS

In any *polis* the aristocrats knew who they were, and who their peers abroad were, though we cannot share their intimate knowledge. So too, they knew that alongside them stood a much larger group, not so well-to-do, probably not so well-born. I have described these men as "semi-aristocrats" in the titles to this chapter and section, but so neutral a term need not be often used; together with men of ancient lineage this level helped to form the upper classes of historic Greece.

Little or nothing can be said about the middling, self-sufficient range of the rural population that lived during the Dark Ages. In archaic literature this secondary level already is suggested in Archilochus' fragment, "Enter, because you are well-born," and certainly it is evident thereafter. Most men of this stamp presumably accepted the political and social preeminence which the aristocrats claimed during the eighth and seventh centuries; yet if aristocrats could seize opportunities in age of rapid change, why could not the more able among those who stood just below? Those who did so earned the pejorative label of *kakoi*. Base-born *kakoi* had appeared in the epics; but the poets of the archaic age, in keeping the old term, invest it with a somber significance. To Solon the *kakoi* are men with some type of power; Phocylides considers them dangerous creditors; Theognis even fears lest they win away his beloved Cyrnus. When Phocylides queries, "Of what advantage is high birth to such as have no grace either in words or in counsel?" we can detect that Zeus-sprung nobles could no longer maintain their exclusiveness if it were deliberately challenged by wealthy upstarts.[11]

Whence came the new type of *kakoi?* The problem deserves careful exploration, for it will clarify the characteristics and drives of the upper classes. Very often the *kakoi* have been identified as the cream of an urban bourgeoisie of commercial and industrial origin; but this solution fits poorly with the landed position of the Greek upper classes.[12] The city folk of early modern Europe gained wealth by divers means, yet the role of this incipient bourgeoisie, properly so called, is often much overemphasized. They secured land at times near the cities, as at Seville, but a study of several English counties suggested that judges and officials, not merchants, were the men who acquired such land as changed hands there.[13]

Within an ancient Greek context derivation of the *kakoi* from urban middle classes is even less satisfactory. If we accept a common view that merchants and artisans were primarily metics, then it is impossible: metics could not own land unless given the status of *isoteleia* (at Athens at least), and could not exercise political functions. As I suggested in Chapter III, however, it is very doubtful that commercial and industrial elements were always or even necessarily usually metic in most states; and potters such as Mnesiades and Andocides had acquired enough wealth to be ranked economically among the semi-aristocrats.[14] In other words, it is possible that some artisans and traders, though fewer in sixth-century Athens than in its great expansion during the classic period, might have aspired to aristocratic levels.

Yet there are still serious bars to any suggestion that they often did so. Acquisition of land by purchase was extremely difficult in the archaic period; some scholars would deny even its possibility. Urban elements, moreover, were far too busy in their occupations to live in aristocratic leisure. In classic Athens we know of very few leaders who came from an industrial or commercial background; in the fourth century Plato could still represent Socrates as asserting that the mass "who support themselves by their labor do not care about politics, owning very little property [i.e., land]." [15]

The assumption that semi-aristocrats as well as aristocrats proper were normally men who held land, especially in the archaic period, is a critical one in the present discussion; but it seems well-based. In an important comment Theognis states that the *kakoi* who much irked him had once worn goatskins, the conventional attire of backwoods farmers.[16]

The men who stood beside the aristocrats in the phalanx of heavily armored hoplites were of rural origin; at Athens Solon distinguished the *hippeis,* with rural revenues of 300 measures, and the *zeugitai,* with 200 measures, about one-third the income of his topmost level.[17] In the early fifth century, to place the role of these groups in perspective, Athens could field a phalanx of 9000 to 10,000; of this total men from the aristocracy itself could not have furnished even one-tenth.

One voice from the age of expansion expresses clearly the attitudes of these middling farmers, but it is one which almost never is recognized as such—that of Hesiod. This Boeotian poet is usually labeled a peasant; and it would be pleasant if he were such, in these days when historical scholarship earnestly seeks to hear the voices of the silent majority of mankind. Yet any thoughtful reading of his *Works and Days* must demonstrate that he is from a different level.[18] In the earlier verses Hesiod does show that he did not belong to the uppermost layer of his society, comprised of the bribe-swallowing *basileis,* and urges them not to exploit unjustly their strength, like the hawk who seizes the nightingale. Thereafter, in describing the course of the agricultural year, Hesiod turns to men of his own standing, who are far from being peasants in the sense of being small farmers dependent on a landlord. Rather he visualizes a well-to-do group capable of finding capital for the purchase of a team of oxen and of female and male slaves and for maritime trips to dispose of surpluses; for himself, Hesiod seeks in the heat of summer "a shady rock and wine of Biblis"— imported from Phoenicia at a time when foreign items of any sort were rare and expensive! [19] Farming in Hesiod's view may not be successful, but "it is idleness which is a disgrace." On the whole earnest toil and dedication will bring their rewards, a well-filled barn and rural security. Even the suggestion that in summer his auditors might take to the sea and sell their surplus is cast in an independent tone, and shows that they themselves controlled the disposal of that surplus. These are men who are not aristocrats but are of some standing.

In later archaic poetry those who are "in the middle" are much praised if they are not too ambitious. "Midmost in a *polis* would I be," asserted Phocylides; Aristotle later argued that "a competence is enough to enable a man to behave in a virtuous manner." [20] Men of this stamp avoided to some extent the "pitiless criticism" of their fellow citizens and probably escaped the dangers of exile or death in civil war; by the late sixth century standing "in the middle" had become a political term for supporting the unity of the community.[21]

The level we have been exploring, below the aristocracy in wealth and birth but beside it in the phalanx, has been much emphasized in recent studies as a "hoplite class," and to it is often ascribed a separate conscious position in the political developments of the age of expansion. To this interpretation I shall return in Chapter VIII; the more able and aggressive men of non-aristocratic backgrounds did seek to have some political voice, but the hoplite warriors were by no means a unified pressure group. After all the aristocrats also served in the phalanx,[22] and the middling farmers were perhaps more divided than united economically.

Rivalry and individual exploitation of opportunities is quite evident in other eras and places where the market has become a major economic factor; yeomen farmers, kulaks, zamindars (in Moghul India), and other middling farmers have shown no hesitation in trampling down both their inferiors and their less successful peers. In early Greece the situation was no different. Hesiod urged his auditors to gain wealth (*ploutos*) "by work with work upon work" and encouraged rivalry as long as it did not use unjust means. Ambitious men, however, were not so limited by scruple, and a hundred years later, in Solonian Attica, small farmers and *thetes* were being sold abroad and other farmers reduced to the level of debt-slaves on their own lands. The *kakoi* preyed on anyone less fortunate—"be not the debtor of a *kakos,* or he will annoy you by asking to be paid before his time." [23]

Even so, the *kakoi* who gained wealth and standing sought to imitate the aristocrats socially,[24] and this social assertiveness was probably their most irritating characteristic in noble eyes, even if it was a compliment. Semi-aristocrats, that is, shared the cultural patterns of men of ancient blood and wealth rather than upholding a distinct social code. This way of life I shall call simply "aristocratic," though the upper classes who adhered to it were not all on the same social and political level.

THE GREEK ELITE

Dispassionate treatment of the Greek upper classes is not easy. They were, to be blunt, an elite, and elites have been much criticized in recent years as a social element in conflict with the basic values of modern communities, especially the urge toward egalitarianism. Modern European aristocracies, in particular, have commonly been damned as packs of luxurious wastrels.

Whatever may be the truth in those charges, the attitude which lies behind them should not be inserted—though it often has been—into a reasoned evaluation of early Greek social and economic progress. This development would not have occurred as it did had there been no upper classes; indeed one may go further and suggest that the leading elements of the *poleis* were vital forces in the great social, economic, and intellectual progress of the era, which we shall examine in part in later sections.

If an aristocratic pattern is to be vigorous, it must be

transmitted firmly from generation to generation. Undoubtedly the major mode was life from childhood within the family and its surrounding groups, but as time progressed formal schools were established.[25] In an aristocratic context the most famous school is that conducted by Sappho for maidens from many parts of Asia Minor, but other instructors taught music and similar skills on a level above that of primary education.

Nobles, consciously guided into the proper paths in childhood, as adults were subject to constant scrutiny by their peers, at times in communal meals, and also by their inferiors in the agora; an aristocrat must exemplify the virtues of his class. Glory and repute were derived from the judgment of one's fellowmen, which was expressed in such adjectives as *agathos* or such nouns as *time* and *kleos*. The poets of the archaic period, the statues in the shrines, and a variety of other sources celebrated and helped to spread aristocratic standards; at the great international festivals and athletic contests, which expanded in keeping with aristocratic development, the upper classes of any one *polis* might measure themselves against those from another state and also engage in more friendly interchanges.

Greek upper classes, indeed, were as interwoven on an international plane as were those of early modern Europe. The marriages of tyrants and their children to foreign wives are particularly mentioned in our sources; but at Athens especially we have evidence for family links to many parts of Greece—foreign marriage, though, could always leave the descendants open to the charge of being "of bad parentage." [26] Guest-friendships continued to be as important as they had been in the Homeric poems; aristocrats never knew when they might be forced into exile or otherwise need friends in other states. A fragment from Solon describes a happy man as one who has "dear children, whole-hooved steeds, hunting hounds, and a friend in foreign parts." [27]

The aristocratic patterns which were thus consolidated on local levels and reenforced by foreign ties led eventually to the fourth-century concept of *paideia*. It is, however, dangerous to read back too much from the pages of Isocrates, Plato, and Aristotle to earlier centuries, though the ethical treatises of Aristotle in particular are useful checkpoints. Also troublesome is the tendency to take *paideia* as a purely aristocratic outlook. Fundamentally, the Greek upper classes shared the values and ethical standards of Hellenic civilization as a whole, though they voiced and exemplified those views in a more conscious manner. So too it has been observed for the Russian gentry of the nineteenth century that "their faith, their tastes, their essential fears and hopes were the same (although they little suspected it) as those of the common people whose ignorance they sneered at." [28] Those historians who explore the lower classes and begin with the premise that their culture is essentially different from that of the elite do not stand in full accord with anthropological studies of peasantries.

For our period, thus, Aristotle's *Nicomachean Ethics* is an excellent expression of aristocratic contempt for "the utter vulgarity of the herd of men," who live the lives of cows, as against gentlemen who seek virtue. Yet Aristotle takes *communis opinio* seriously and even proclaims that, "What all men believe to be so, I say is so; the man who destroys this foundation for our belief is not likely to say anything more convincing." [29]

THE CULT OF MASCULINITY

In taking up the aristocratic code we must pull out one thread after another, though they are all tightly interwoven. Very obvious, at the outset, is the stress on masculine dominance. Valiant efforts have been made in recent generations to discover a matriarchal structure in the earliest days of Aegean history, partly because Marxist thought has taken up the theories of Bachofen to reenforce its idyllic picture of primeval lack of class or sex exploitation.[30] These attempts have never been firmly backed by evidence, and certainly in the age of expansion male domination was a marked characteristic in the consolidation of Greek aristocracy. The ultimate test of membership in this class was derivation from a "well-born" family, and in ancient physiological thought the seed of the father was the only root of the offspring.

In the Homeric epics Agamemnon blasts the entire race of women (especially Clytemnestra), but also in the *Odyssey* there is frequent praise of women, as of Arete, wife of Alcinous, who is honored by her husband and by citizens "who look upon her as upon a goddess." Hesiod was not a man to draw such pictures; his heart was ruled by a cold masculine head—"Do not let a flaunting woman coax and cozen and deceive you: she is after your barn. The man who trusts womankind trusts deceivers." Later, to be sure, he gives sage advice about marrying a maiden much younger than the husband, "for a man wins nothing better than a good wife" and nothing worse than a bad one, "who roasts her man without fire." In subsequent poets of the archaic age womankind is both necessary to man and a curse; the most vitriolic attack is that by Semonides of Amorgos, who likens females to sows, vixen, bitches, and others, and only in one type, that of the bee, can he find anything good to say.[31]

This parade of masculinity was the fruit in large part of an increased social unity within the *polis*. Leaders met often in the agora or in the council chambers, and served side by side in the infantry phalanx; when gymnasia came into existence in the sixth century, men vied with each other in athletic activities, and did so nude.[32] Men of leisure also passed social hours in male symposia, and were at least to some degree organized in such groups as the *hetairia* and phratry. Both of these are present in Homer, and the phratry is commonly considered as a warrior brotherhood.[33] At Sparta and in Crete it may have been the root of the well-known military groupings of historic times, but even at Athens citizenship depended upon presentation of a son to the father's phratry and his acceptance by the "brothers."

The world of bronze figurines of the eighth down through the sixth century, at Athens, Dodona, Olympia, and elsewhere is one populated almost exclusively, as far as human beings are concerned, by warriors and horsemen (see Plate III). Male figures also are far more dominant on vases down to 500 than thereafter, and the physical attributes of male sexuality were portrayed by the arts—on coins, on vases, in wayside pillars of Hermes—without the scruples which have marked most centuries of modern western civilization. Homosexuality does not openly appear in the epics, but at least by the sixth century it was accepted on aristocratic levels. Young aristocrats are hailed as *kalos* on Athenian vases (Plate II.b); to be young and handsome and have friends was the acme of masculine desire—and the counterpart, old age, was the worst of ills.[34] By that time, too, professional prostitution was clearly in existence in major centers, quite apart from its religious presence at the temple of Aphrodite at Corinth and elsewhere; *chremata* built up over a long period, sighs Archilochus, go into the stomach of a courtesan.[35]

Always, to be sure, the words of masculine writers must be taken with some reserve in any appraisal of the relations of the sexes. The rich graves of the ninth and eighth centuries which were noted above were almost entirely of females; perhaps the husband wished to make display of his wealth, but real grief and devotion may also have led to the abundant provision of grave goods. Politically and legally women were dependent and had no part in many aspects of

social intercourse; but they did not live in a harem atmo-
sphere, and their beauty, no less than that of men, was appreciated.[36] Still, the female part of the Greek population
suffered the tensions of the great changes in the age of expansion as much or more than did the men, and women had
fewer vents for their frustrations and uncertainties. If we
had adequate evidence, we might find here a source of enduring family difficulties; yet it is interesting that in the
major female voice of the period, that of Sappho, there is
not one surviving word of bitterness on the relation of the
sexes.

USES OF LEISURE

The doggerel taunt of the late medieval English rebel John
Ball,

> Whanne Adam dalfe and Eve span
> Who was thanne a gentilman?

could have been applied to the peacetime life of the Homeric heroes. Odysseus plowed; Penelope wove. Later Pe-
nelopes continued to spin and to weave, though not through
economic necessity; but the descendants of Odysseus no
longer worked on the land. "Leisure," Aristotle pronounced, "is a necessity, both for growth in goodness and
for the pursuit of political activities." [37]

An aristocrat could live without working, but he was not
thereby physically idle. The duties of the *polis,* as Aristotle
suggests, might take a great deal of a man's time, talking in
the agora with his fellows about civic matters (and gossip-
ing, too), attending assemblies or councils, serving from
time to time as an unpaid magistrate of the state. *Arete* also
involved doing one's duty courageously in battle. Male warriors, as just noted, were a frequent theme of figurines and

vases from the eighth century onward, and war became an endemic, unavoidable part of interstate contentions, though it was usually settled by one encounter of rival phalanxes on open ground. One mark of the happiest man Solon had ever known, Tellus of Athens, was his glorious death in a battle between Athenians and Megarians where he secured the victory: "The Athenians gave him a public funeral on the spot where he fell, and paid him the highest honors." [38]

Yet most of an aristocrat's life was passed in peacetime, and *arete* could be displayed here too in physical activities. Aristocrats hunted, on foot, with their lean hounds, though the prey was no longer the wild boar of Meleager's hunt. If lions had ever existed in Greece, they had retreated to the fastnesses of Macedonia. One Cretan plaque depicts two huntsmen, one with a wild goat on his shoulders; an Athenian cup shows perhaps a more normal trophy, a brace of rabbits with hunter and hound. [39]

Athletics became an ever more regular part of upper-class life, a position it has held to the present day. In the local gymnasia aristocrats vied in running and other individual competition—team sports were virtually unknown—and those who had special abilities could enter the great international contests. [40] In a lengthy fragment the philosopher Xenophanes, who always thought otherwise from the bulk of his contemporaries, assailed the public recognition of victorious athletes, as if in sooth they benefited a state more than did men of wise counsel; but his attack only demonstrates how great was the *arete* which successful athletes could gain. One victor from Sybaris in the mid-sixth century erected a small shrine to Athena with only a tithe of the rewards which he had received for his Olympic victory. [41]

Physically able non-aristocrats might also win athletic prominence, but they could not hope to engage in one very significant range of upper-class physical activity. Raising horses "is the task of the most well-to-do," [42] for only they could afford to own horses and chariots, a prime example of what Thorstein Veblen labeled "conspicuous consumption," inasmuch as horses were difficult to maintain in the meadowless Greek landscape, and were of no economic utility. But horses and chariots appear abundantly from eighth-century figurines and vases (especially at Argos) onwards (see Plate II). A perhaps legendary law of Cyme gave political rights to those who raised horses, and the leading class at Chalcis was called the *Hippobotai*. [43] Names compounded with Hippo- were common on the upper-class level; the young wastrel Pheidippides (also a horse-name) in Aristophanes' *Clouds*, who bade fair to bankrupt his father with stable fees, chariots, and dreams of victory in the races, was the product of centuries of horse-loving aristocrats.

INDIVIDUALISM AND GROUPS

The two preceding aspects of the aristocratic way of life, masculinity and physical activity, are quite visible in our sources; in both is suggested the presence of individual pride and power, that "unsought self-possession, which is a sure sign of good breeding," which stamps the young horseman on Plate II.b and the statue of Phrasikleia on Plate VIII. [44] The leading elements exhibited a strongly competitive or agonistic spirit in their athletic rivalries; in politics the efforts especially of the aristocrats proper to gain prominence and to hold state offices led to bitter factionalism which rent asunder many *poleis*.

Already in Archilochus we can hear an individual human being, living from day to day, returning hate for hate and love for love. The conscious awareness of human freedom and of man's liberation from the more superficial bonds of convention are evident in his work; later poets simply made more apparent and extended more widely the line of thought visible in his savage iambics.

Yet Archilochus himself may warn us against overstressing individual self-seeking on the upper-class level and against accepting a common view that group life had been all-powerful in early Greece but lost its sway in the lyric age.[45] The individualism which Archilochus expressed had its roots in the magnificent heroes of the *Iliad* and the *Odyssey,* but the sense of social unity which lies below the Homeric surface pervades the surviving fragments of Archilochus as well. His verse was meant to communicate the poet's reflections to others and to instruct; he was bound more tightly to the fabric of society than a modern individualist could endure.

The first great voice of archaic aristocracy is illuminating in another important aspect. The upper classes of the archaic age had great confidence in their achievements and abilities; at times a heaven-storming audacity, a sense of unfettered experiments, and an almost anarchic outlook are visible, as in the more extreme forms of Protoattic pottery.[46] In their pride men might sometimes dare to forget the gods and to feel that their future lay in their own hands, whether they ventured afar on the stormy waters of the Mediterranean or exercised tyranny in a Greek state. But fear is never far from pride, and as men grew bolder and richer they also became more consciously analytical.

Fundamentally Archilochus was confident, as Hesiod had been earlier; but he felt no less than did Hesiod and the epic poets that man was a frail creature in an unpredictable world where the gods ruled all. "Such," he advised Glaucus, "becomes the mind of mortal man as Zeus may bring him for the day"; so, he deduced, let us take each day as it may come. If ill befell, Archilochus exhorted his heart, which was confronted by pains without remedies, to bear up and resist its enemies; "Conqueror, do not overexult; vanquished, do not groan prostrate in your house. Savour your successes, mourn your reverses, but not too much. Learn the rhythm which governs the life of men." In sum, when human consciousness grew more acute, human helplessness (*amechania*) was more keenly felt. Various heroes, said Alcman in the next generation, had been conquered by Fate (Aisa); and he drew the moral, "Mortal man may not go soaring to the heavens," but must live day by day.[47] Aristocratic individualism, in truth, rested on very feeble grounds, both religiously and socially. The tissue which bound together the Greeks in the age of expansion was one in which the group was far more important than a single mortal human being.

The *oikos* or family included the physical possessions necessary for its survival and was always the fundamental entity; a colony, for example, may properly be described as "an organic group of *oikoi*." [48] Above or around the *oikos* were territorial units ranging from village to *ethnos* or later the *polis,* religious groupings about local shrines, phratries, ties between aristocrats and followers, and many others. A Greek of any class, male or female, adult or child, was thus linked to his fellow by many ties of different sorts, which he usually accepted both in their limitations and in their support of his existence. We lack reliable ancient evidence to explore in depth these social patterns, important though they were. It is equally impossible to discuss alterations unless we import modern theory from the fields of anthropology, sociology, or psychology; and the results, while superficially tempting as explanations of the obscure, accord poorly with the manifold diversity of the centuries we are discussing.[49]

One form of social grouping, for instance, has been given far too much emphasis as a vehicle for aristocratic political activity. The *genos* or clan, resting on belief in a common ancestry, had undoubted significance in republican Rome or in early modern Scotland, yet in Greek life its presence is far less evident than is usually asserted. The *genos* simply does not appear in Homer; and even at Athens had no place in law.[50] Kinship may have been a potent force in many aspects of early Greek life, but aristocratic ties at least were of a more personal type.

The point stated at the beginning of this chapter, that aristocratic patterns of life only became consciously consolidated after the Dark Ages were waning, needs renewed emphasis. Aristocracies and the *polis* were contemporary in their appearance, and in the new form of political organization all citizens had rights as well as duties. When men of the upper classes engaged in too obvious extortion or threw their states into internal chaos, the concept of the social unity of the *demos* as a whole always revived, as we shall see more fully in a discussion of lawgivers and tyrants in the last chapter.

The question of upper-class loyalty to the *polis* is a delicate one in which theory and practice did not always concur. At no point in Greek history did all citizens support their state, any more than they do in the modern world; aristocrats in particular were jealous of their repute, and if affronted or excluded from power could, like Alcaeus, take foreign gold or go into exile, there to plot their return in traitorous manner. Yet examples of such disaffected behavior do not prove that the aristocracy as a whole lacked a communal spirit. Even in Homer the Trojan hero Hector felt his duty to his "fatherland," though the term, if more precisely defined, is one's father, wife, and children, and one's own estates.[51] As the *polis* developed, its demands on the lives and property of its citizens were strengthened both in theory and in practice; Sophocles' portrayal of the anguished Antigone, torn between religious and political duty, is famous.

The sense of social obligation among the Greek aristocracies was, however, not of a high order—aristocratic fathers, in advising their sons, have usually emphasized outward behavior more than inner elevation. In contemporary Persia young nobles were taught to shoot the bow, to ride, and to tell the truth; but Cyrus did not need to be thinking of merchant morality when he reproved the cheating in Greek agoras. Neither the gods of Hellas nor its nobles ever cultivated truthfulness as a primary virtue. Since Greek ethics always remained connected to religious as much as to political thought, it may be noted that while Hesiod urged that Zeus required just behavior Xenophanes came closer to the mark in his blast against Homer and Hesiod (of the *Theogony*) as attributing "to the gods everything that is a shame and reproach among men, stealing and committing adultery and deceiving each other." [52]

Charity, brotherly love, and other Christian virtues also played no part; Greek views were far franker, as in Theognis' advice, "Speak your enemy fair, but when you have him in your power be avenged without pretext." [53] Vicious verbal attacks on the ancestry or personal life of opponents were customary from Archilochus and Alcaeus on to the orations of fourth-century Athenian politicians. Aristocrats did have a moral code, which was in most ways eventually described in Aristotle's ethical treatises; but as suggested in the earlier discussion in Chapter II, the aristocratic principle of life might be summed up as "Nothing Too Much."

A MODICUM OF LUXURY

In daily life the upper classes were probably distinguishable by their behavior toward each other and toward their inferiors, and very possibly also by their mode of speech. Equally evident were physical marks of luxury. *Habrosyne,* or luxury, is a leitmotif of the poetry of the seventh and sixth centuries; *tryphe* (daintiness) is a contemptuous word that was used later for the most part. The concept, to be sure, is always a relative matter; an Assyrian monarch would have scorned a Greek house as a hovel, and one may doubt that Greek painted pottery would have developed as far as it did if its purchasers had been able to afford to load their shelves with gold and silver vessels. Still, the upper classes of Greece seized all available opportunities for a more elegant life.

Modern hostility toward elites swiftly rises into view at this point in the common assertion that aristocrats seek to spend money, not to improve the economic machinery of their world in an entrepreneurial fashion. So too early modern aristocracies were reproved as being engaged in "the unjust, unhealthy, brilliant and anti-economic utilisation of any surplus produced in a given society." [54] Only one noted scholar, to my knowledge, finds merit in this luxurious expenditure. Writing about early modern English aristocrats, G. M. Trevelyan raises the question as to how else the English nobles could have expended their money in a period when banks, stocks, bonds, and general loans were unknown and land was not easily bought—but then Trevelyan is nowadays generally dismissed as an elitist.[55]

If a phenomenon recurs frequently in different historical societies, then there must be significant reasons for its presence; and an understanding of those reasons will be more useful than the common, scarcely justified expression of indignation or reproof. Braudel, just quoted, also observes that luxury "scarcely changes at all" as a concept accepted both by privileged and unprivileged classes: "Luxury does not only represent rarity and vanity, but also social success, fascination, the dream that one day becomes reality for the poor, and in so doing immediately loses its old glamour." [56] As he goes on to point out, both Mauss and Sombart emphasized the role of luxury in promoting demands in early modern Europe; and the same is as true of the period which we are considering as it has been in those modern societies where the chieftain, as noted at the close of Chapter II, "acts as a tribal banker," collecting the surplus and then pouring it out again. To ascribe all the economic progress of the age of expansion to this one cause is, as I have sought to show repeatedly, too simplistic a view, but the urge of Greek aristocrats for a great variety of luxuries cannot be overlooked as a stimulus both to their own search for wealth and to their patronage of arts and crafts.

In the *Odyssey* Alcinous boasts that "feasting, stringed instruments and dancing, changes of clothing, warm baths, and the pleasures of love are ever dear to us." By the sixth century the picture has become more precise in Xenophanes' condemnation of the Colophonians, who "learnt useless luxuries of the Lydians while they were free of hateful despotism, and went into the marketplace clad in all-purple robes, went not less than a thousand in all, proudly rejoicing in gold-adorned hair and bedewing their odor with studied anointings." Much the same portrait is drawn by the poet Asius of the Samians, "swathed in beautiful vestments, with snowy tunics that swept the floor of wide earth; and golden head-pieces surmounted them, like cicadas; their tresses waved in the breeze and their golden bands and bracelets wrought with carving circled their arms." [57] Sappho talks much of precious textiles, but so do other poets. The statue of Phrasikleia (see Plate VIII) illustrates the outward luxury of elegantly woven robes, jewelry, and elaborate hairdressing; men, it should be noted, patronized perfumers as much as did their wives. [58]

Even in food there was distinction. Alcman boasted that he ate "not what is nicely prepared but demands common things like the rabble"; the Sybarites, who became a symbol of luxury, were said to have given patents to cooks who devised new dishes; by the sixth century Hipponax could label barley as "fodder for slaves." [59] Very probably better and more secure diets permitted the upper classes to live longer than did the rest of the populace, though the results of overindulgence in symposia may have to some degree countered this favorable factor.

For other outward aspects of life we have less secure testimony. The aristocratic dead, as noted earlier, were buried more magnificently than others. Though house patterns are almost unknown, interesting recent evidence has begun to reveal that in classic times the well-to-do of Athens may have lived in large mansions; vase paintings and other evidence attest the presence of well-turned furniture and tableware. [60]

Wealth was used—and had to be used—for external display, including the dedication of tripods, cauldrons, and statues at shrines, and also the ownership of horses and chariots. Aristocrats of all ages, as I have said earlier, do not directly enter into capitalistic, entrepreneurial activities for their own sake, though they are not averse to gain; too many social, political, and religious elements exist in their lives to prevent such narrow concentration. At least in later centuries men of the upper classes had to borrow to keep up their horses (as in the case of Strepsiades of the *Clouds*) or to secure dowries in cash for their daughters, but they neither borrowed nor lent for purely economic objectives; even the continuing search for power over the land, to which we shall return in the next chapter, had aims which were only in part economic.

In this respect a side glance should be given to the Spartans, who are often contrasted to Athenians and others as noble or at least self-sacrificing servants of a rigid political and social system designed to maintain their mastery over the helots. If one looks at the actual testimony of the archaic age itself, this contrast did not exist. When Alcaeus quoted the proverb "Wealth makes the man," he ascribed it to the

Spartan Aristodemos; when Cyrus inquired about the nature of the Greeks, he specifically wished to know about the Spartan way of life, and his distaste for the cheating participants in markets was voiced as a result. True, the Spartans were considered to be just in the sixth century, and a Milesian accordingly entrusted half his wealth, in silver, to the Spartan Glaucus—who sought to convert it to his own possession.[61] The Spartan "Equals" were such only in a political sense, and differed widely in wealth. In the age of expansion they were as interested in the fruits of luxury as other aristocracies until the so-called Lycurgan system began to be tightened.

ARISTOCRATIC ENCOURAGEMENT OF CULTURE

As the *polis* became a unified political and religious structure, the activities of the upper classes tended more to take place on a public stage than within the Homeric households; and as true urban centers developed, the aristocrats commonly lived there—or at least had townhouses as well as rural abodes.[62] Aristotle's evidence on Naxos was cited in the previous chapter; at Athens too the Eupatrids were "those dwelling in the city." [63] Aristocratic ways came to be urban ways. Sappho thus contemptuously dismissed some poor wench as a "farm girl in farm-girl finery . . . even ignorant of the way to lift her gown over her ankles." [64]

Architecturally the towns of Hellas were primitive. Socially they were simple, and the men who inhabited them could step quickly into the world of fields and pastures, of wild animals and the elemental forces of nature which lay all about. The intellectual stimulus, however, of the towns was not thereby limited. While the highly sociable character of the Greeks was a vital factor throughout their history, this trait never played a greater role than in the early seventh century. The close personal association of the upper classes at this time was a tremendous force in promoting the lightning swiftness of contemporary change; in intellectual outlook the upper classes seem scarcely to have boggled at any novelty. With remarkable openness of mind and lack of prejudice they supported the cultural expansion which underlay classical achievements and much of later western civilization.[65] Great masses of superstitition and magic trailed down into historic times from the primitive Dark Ages; it is always amazing to discover anew how limited were the trammels which this inherited past laid on the intellectual and artistic outburst of the seventh and sixth centuries. That past, as exemplified for instance in the epics, was not dismissed in its most fundamental aspects, but writers, artists, and thinkers felt free to explore and to enlarge their horizons. The proximate cause, without doubt, was the aristocratic domination of life.

The upper classes themselves entered freely into this bustle and fervor in various fields. Thales, the first philosopher, came from a noble family and he gave political counsel to the Ionian Greeks when they faced the Lydian threat. His successors down at least to Heraclitus of Ephesus in the mid-fifth century were, with Pythagoras perhaps as an exception, exclusively aristocrats. In another field of learning Hecataeus wrote geographical and semihistorical treatises in the later sixth century and likewise provided wise advice to the rebels against Persian mastery; he counted his ancestors back sixteen generations, to a god.[66] Apart from the slave Aesop, all authors throughout the archaic age of whom we have evidence came from an upper-class background and normally expressed its values in their work. Thinkers, after all, could not expect outside support in an era without foundations or universities, though poets could gain the patronage of tyrants such as Pisistratus and Polycrates.

The origins of artists are as a rule far less clear, and that fact may in itself indicate non-aristocratic birth. The potters of Athens who bore the foreign names of Amasis, Lydos, Skythes, and so on may be accounted either slave or metic in background; [67] aristocrats were not likely to subject themselves to the physical labor of sculpture, pottery, and metal-working. But men of wealth directly commissioned much of the artistic production of archaic Greece, and there is no reason to assume that they lacked interest in the artistic evolution which moved inexorably from primitive beginnings toward the classic synthesis.

In the end, economic and social developments were too much for the old families, though they did not yield all their power. Usually they were forced to unite with men of new rural or urban wealth to form oligarchies, as at Corinth, but at Athens they accepted, albeit not always wholeheartedly, the general participation of the *demos* in the determination of state policy. Even in that model of democracy, however, the leaders of the people commonly remained of upper-class origin across the fifth and even the fourth centuries; and the culture of classic centuries preserved its inherited aristocratic dress.

Modern attitudes toward elites being what they are, some students might desire to emphasize this class character of Greek civilization. It did exist, without doubt; but two qualifications need always to be kept in mind. First, archaic Greece allowed room for many divergences in attitudes; Xenophanes, who assailed aristocratic delight in athletics and scored the dedication of Colophonians to luxury, may serve as sufficient example. Secondly, the basic attitudes expressed in Greek arts and letters were a common quality of all Hellenic thought, latent in part in the Dark Ages but made more conscious and refined across the archaic period.

The human-centered, physically active, essentially rational outlook of the Greek world we may call an aristocratic pattern; for we know that this spirit has been an important force in subsequent noble ways of life. Originally, though, it was a creation of archaic society as a whole, given only its surface dress by aristocratic interests. In their deepest beliefs, small farmers, the upper classes, and city dwellers formed a community both politically and intellectually.

Plate I   Early Landed Wealth

(a) Clay granary model
(*Hesperia,* XXXVII [1968], pp. 94–97)

(b) Gold earring
(ibid. pp. 111–14—both photographs courtesy Eugene Vanderpool, Jr.)

Plate II   Aristocrats and Horses

(a) Chariot scene
(Athenian cup; Tarquinia, Museo nazionale RC 4194)

(b) Young noble on horseback, "Leagros kalos"
(Athenian cup; Antikensammlungen 2620, Munich—
both photographs courtesy Hirmer, Munich)

Plate III   Warriors

(a) Bronze figurine of warrior
(Staatliche Museen 10560, Berlin—
photograph courtesy museum)

(b) Rival phalanxes with an *aulos* player
(Corinthian œnochœ; Museo nazionale della Villa Giulia, Rome—
photograph courtesy Hirmer)

Plate IV   Rural Life

(a) Plowing and sowing
(Athenian cup; British Museum)

(b) Harvesting olives
(Athenian amphora; British Museum B 226—
both photographs courtesy museum)

Plate V Coinage of Greece

(a) Naxos (grape)

(b) Metapontum (barley)

(c) Sybaris (bull)

(d) Himera (cock)

(e) Aegina (turtle)

(f) Zancle (harbor)

(g) Croton (tripod)

(h) Derrones (helmet)

(i) Terone (vase)

(j) Zancle (prow)

(k) Thebes (shield)

(photographs courtesy Mrs. Silvia Hurter, Bank Leu, Zürich)

Plate VI   Industry

(a) Bronze figurine of smith beating out a helmet
(Metropolitan Museum 42.11.42, New York—
photograph courtesy museum)
(b) Female worker in a metal-vase shop
(Athenian hydria; Torno Collection, Milan—
photograph from *Journal of Hellenic Studies,*
LXXXI [1961], pl. VII)

(c) Manufacturing a bronze statue
(Athenian cup; Staatliche Museen 2294, Berlin—
photograph courtesy museum)

Plate VII   Commerce

(a) Merchant ship chased by pirate galley
(Athenian cup; British Museum B 436—photograph courtesy museum)

(b) Weighing and shipping wool before king Arcesilas of Cyrene
(Laconian cup; Bibliothèque Nationale 4899, 2707, Paris—
photograph courtesy Hirmer)

Plate VIII

Phrasikleia with elaborate chiton, crown, necklace, earrings, and bracelet (marble statue not earlier than 590 B.C., carved by the Parian sculptor Aristion—photograph from *Athens Annals of Archaeology,* V [1972], pl. XIII, courtesy E. Mastrokostas)

Chapter VII

The Agricultural World

Nearly all Greeks in all eras spent their lives wresting crops from the soil and tending sheep, goats, and pigs. Agriculture absorbed almost all the available energy input and probably gave the smallest rate of return—but the Greeks did eat. Rural alterations occurred with glacial slowness and were relatively minuscule. Yet the agricultural world was so major a part of the economic structure that even small developments bulked large in their total effect.

Changes did take place. If certain elements in the population, including the upper classes and the commercial and industrial groups, were to live without producing their own crops, then that food had somehow to be provided either by the farmlands of Greece or by imports. Logically we may infer that there was a reorganization of land rights, an extension of agricultural acres, or an increase in productivity—or a combination thereof. The last possibility, a sharp rise in productivity, has been a major factor in the growth of the western world only since about the beginning of the Industrial Revolution; in earlier European history changes in the other two areas were the most rewarding, as they were in ancient Greece.

Eventually rural evolution turned many Greek small farmers into peasants, but before we approach that major step we should establish the enduring characteristics and limitations of Greek agriculture. In fair warning to the reader, I should tell him that we must pick our way across several misty, thorn-encumbered fields ere we reach a clear hilltop from which the Greek landscape as a whole will be visible.

VILLAGE AND LAND

Almost all the population lived in villages from the Dark Ages onward. During the Greek summer ever-flowing water sources are limited; needs of protection as well as the desire for community life further encouraged village settlement in ancient times. In Asia Minor and even in mainland Greece there is some evidence that rural *pyrgoi* or towers were scattered across the countryside; but individual farmsteads began to be more noticeable only in the fifth and fourth centuries as agriculture became commercially oriented or subject to greater landholders.[1] Yet Greek farmers, unlike Near Eastern villagers, cultivated individual plots; in the Near East irrigation and drainage required the cooperation of great masses of rural laborers who worked under a common direction.

The villages and countryside had rural shrines, but usually of such simple character (at times, piles of stones dedicated to Hermes) that they do not often attract the attention of archeologists.[2] Villages themselves have not often been explored; houses might be of stone or of mud-brick with reed roofs, and the dead were not well endowed with grave goods or external embellishments. It is difficult for a modern observer to credit how limited the equipment of a farmer was before the Industrial Revolution gave birth to the vast amount of machinery employed on modern western farms. Where the few have much, the many must have little, or so runs the zero-sum interpretation of much modern class study; but in fact the rural world had little until almost yesterday.

Even in the mid-nineteenth century "the furniture of the peasant of 1850 was hardly any different from what it had been in the eighteenth century," and this in turn was scarcely more than the limited quantities recorded in medieval texts of heriots and church fines on the dead.[3] The tools of the French peasant of 1850 were almost entirely wooden, as they had been on Carolingian manors and in ancient Greece. Achilles did offer as one prize in the funeral games of Patroclus a lump of iron sufficient for the needs of the victor's shepherd or plows for five years, both a suggestion that iron was employed for the share-beams of plows and also an indication that the metal's agricultural utility was very restricted.

For the rest the Greek farmer had a supply of pots, which he would have had charmed by the village magician, the basic necessities of clothes made at home, and the bench, three-legged table, and simple bed which Ovid assigned to his rural Philemon and Baucis.[4] Power might be provided by donkeys or draft oxen, but probably only for the fairly well-to-do farmers, who were classified by Solon as *zeugitai,* perhaps because they had a team (*zeugos*). Hesiod advises the purchase of female and male slaves to help in the house and in farmwork and makes other reference to slaves; but, as we shall see later, rural slavery was not extensive.

The farmer also had access to land for cultivation and for supporting his animals. Hillsides, mountains, and other fringe areas were often held in common and apparently were open to all citizens of a *polis;* [5] the control of farmland proper, on the other hand, presents thorny problems. To this point I have not used the word "ownership" and shall not often do so henceforth, inasmuch as it implies personal power over land and free alienability; the Greeks did not have a specific term for "real property," land being so special and significant in their lives. [6] We do not even know how an adult son became an independent farmer in a world where new land could not easily be gained. The brief life, and the hard work required of the farmer, must often have opened the way, as well as the relatively advanced age at which the father would have married.

The legal character of the family plot (*kleros*) has been the subject of a continuing debate. In the past generation it has become almost an article of faith that until the fifth century a *kleros* could not be alienated outside the family; and even in recent years this belief is still widespread, especially for Solonian Attica but more generally in the prevailing concepts of the *genos.* [7]

The view, however, accords poorly with a variety of evidence. From the establishment of Scheria in the *Odyssey* onward, the leaders of colonies assigned plots to the settlers both with some eye to equality and also to maintenance of the *oikoi* or families over the generations; yet a tale of the colonization of Syracuse, apparently reported as early as Archilochus, indicates that one colonist bargained away his allotment in exchange for a honey-cake. Hesiod's father migrated from Asia Minor to Boeotia and acquired a farm, all of which Perses filched from Hesiod; and the poet himself advises his auditors to honor the gods "so you may buy another's holding (*kleros*) and not another yours." The Agora at Athens was occupied by private houses to about the end of the seventh century, but then became an open, public square delimited by fixed markers. Dissident Samians bought of the Hermionians the island of Hydrea; the citizens of Apollonia recompensed a man they had blinded by buying him two farms (*kleroi*) and a townhouse which belonged to other citizens.[8]

Inalienability of *kleroi* did exist, at least later, at Sparta, Locris, and some colonies; but the assertion, drawn from Aristotle, that "to part with family estate was one of the things that were 'not done,' " does not prove the inference that it *could* not be done.[9] In any event, as we shall see below, men of strength desired primarily to enlarge their control over the small farmers as well as their crops—land without labor was of minor value.

Normally, to be sure, formal sale or transfer of land rights was uncommon in so rurally based a world; political rights and economic security rested on an independent connection to land. The early legislator Pheidon of Corinth sought to keep the number of family plots equal to the number of citizens, "even if the citizens had all started originally with plots of unequal size." [10] This possession was not marked by title deeds and other modern devices but rested on ancestral prescription and community knowledge; the care taken to see that *epikleroi* or heiresses, who probably were not uncommon in that era of high mortality, married relatives suggests that land was considered in some ways the property of a social unit rather than of an individual owner.[11] Indeed, archeological evidence from southern Italy shows that there the community as a whole provided silos and other "installations of a collective nature designed for preserving or exploiting the products of the territorium." [12]

From the land, by agriculture, herding, and hunting, the

farmers of Greece secured the food necessary for their survival and the perpetuation of their families. There is no need here to describe the agricultural year, on which Hesiod throws considerable light (see Plate IV for typical events in rural life). Half the land was left fallow each year, but one may presume the skills of the farmers, if partly traditional, were as advanced as those practiced in classic Greece.[13] Greek agriculture was well fitted to the Mediterranean climate and to the physical characteristics of the Greek soil, which was often red and productive even if in small pockets. The Greek farmer could feel relatively secure in the application of ancestral techniques to his tasks, though at times the rains might fail or other natural disasters and diseases hit his crops. Attica, in particular, had only half the rainfall of the west coast of Greece and lay on the margin of cereal cultivation.

PARAMETERS OF THE POSSIBLE

It is difficult to establish firmly the minimum food supply required by a Greek farming family and the amount of land which would normally be needed to guarantee that supply. Early modern European conditions can provide guidelines for calculations which must necessarily be somewhat hypothetical; still, they do set the range within which we must think.

A resident of the United States today consumes about 2700 calories per day; ancient Greeks, who were usually of Mediterranean body type and younger on the average, probably needed no more than 2000 calories.[14] These would have been gained largely from cereals, primarily barley and only secondarily wheat (see Plate V.b). The former grew better in the Greek climate and in later centuries cost about half as much as wheat. It was used mainly in broth (*maza*);

in the time of Solon wheaten bread was provided at the Prytaneion only on feast days.[15] Grain requirements for an average ancient Greek have been calculated at 6 *medimnoi* (3 hectoliters) of wheat per year. Even today a Greek peasant can say, "Bread is our only food. It is our milk, cheese, butter, honey, sugar, all in one. What the grass is to the animal, bread is to us. Otherwise we live on air and water." [16]

Actually, however, the ancient Greek diet included fruits such as figs and grapes, wine, olive oil, and some vegetables, especially legumes, which provided protein (also available in cheese) and fixed nitrogen in the soil. Fish was not as common an item as often stated; we do not know precisely when the trade in dried fish from the Black Sea became significant. Meat was consumed mainly at the barbecues held during public sacrifices. One must not forget, also, that all early societies gathered and ate a great variety of plants which grew naturally and were not raised as crops.[17]

Ancient agricultural yields can only be suggested in a general range. In modern times the average for Greece has been about 13 hectoliters of wheat per hectare and 20 to 24 for barley. An estimate based partly on an inscription giving the Eleusinian first fruits in 329/8 would put ancient Attic yields at an average for both grains of about seven hectoliters per hectare, which is perhaps a minimum base line. For ancient Greece as a whole Jardé made a careful guess that yields could be set about 8 to 12 hectoliters per hectare of wheat, 16 to 20 for barley. His estimate is somewhat generous, for early modern information from England presents a range of 11.43 to 16.71 hectoliters for barley; in any calculation one should certainly not go over 16 hectoliters per hectare for barley.[18] Ancient wine production has been estimated at 1140 liters or more per hectare, and olive oil at 114. In view of the yearly consumption for an average Greek given above, a cultivated hectare would provide grain for perhaps less than three persons, allowing for seed reserves, wastage, and animal feed.[19]

If we arbitrarily set an average family size at four and assume that half the cropland remained fallow each year, then a farmer with two hectares could scarcely have supported his family.[20] At the other extreme he could not have farmed more than four unless he drew in outside labor at critical points in the agricultural cycle. That is, we must keep in mind the requirements of man-days of labor, which Columella later itemized as between 9.5 and 10.5 man-days per Roman *iugerum* (about 40 as a minimum for a hectare); activities such as harvesting (6 days per hectare) had to take place at a very specific time and could not be delayed.[21]

Small pieces of information for Attica can be assembled to suggest very interesting conclusions, both about the holding of land and about the population which could be fed from its farms. In the Solonian class system, there were *pentekosiomedimnoi* (500-measure men), *hippeis* with at least 300 measures, and *zeugitai* with 200.[22] These measures could be either dry (cereal) or liquid (olive oil and wine); the latter would require far less acreage, and modern students commonly argue that the leading Athenian farmers had gone some distance toward specializing in olive trees and vines.

If a member of the *zeugite* class had only cereal land, then he would have needed a minimum of 12 hectares (6 in cultivation each year at a maximum of 32 *medimnoi* to the hectare), allowing nothing for seed or animal requirements.[23] For purposes of simplicity, since we do not have any basis for guessing the relative amounts devoted to specialized crops, let us assume the average holding of land which could be farmed, for all men, of whatever rank, above the lowest class of *thetes* was 12 hectares. These were the men who served in the infantry phalanx; by the time of the Persian wars the Athenians could field a phalanx of 9000 to 10,000 hoplites. Some of these would have been pairs of father and adult son; if we reduce the figure somewhat to allow for this fact and also for the possibility that the Solonian population of Attica was significantly less, we could perhaps reckon that there were as few as 4000 hoplite farmholders in 600.[24] The arable area of Attica was about 69,000 hectares; [25] the hoplite part of its population would hold 4000 × 12, or 48,000 hectares at a minimum. The conclusion seems inescapable that a very considerable part of the Athenian populace either had no land or else their plots were too small for a secure livelihood, and so they provided a large reservoir of labor for the seasonal demands of their richer neighbors. In the *Odyssey,* Achilles can think of no lower position on earth than service as a day laborer for a farmer who himself does not have a *kleros.*[26] To avoid the splitting of already small estates, brothers, at least in classic Athens, sometimes kept their farms in common.[27]

A theoretical maximum for the cereal production of Attica can also be calculated, departing from the estimate of 69,000 hectares as its cultivable area. If we make the following assumptions: (a) that half of this was given over to grain production each year, in the proportions for wheat and barley given in the inscription of Eleusinian first fruits; (b) that yields were 8 hectoliters of wheat and 16 of barley per hectare; (c) that half of these yields went to seed and animal requirements and wastage; (d) that the population ate 3 hectoliters of wheat or 3½ of barley per person per year, then the total population which could have been fed by Attic cereals would have been in the range of 75,000.[28] The actual figures for the crops of 329/8 were 39,000 *medimnoi* of wheat and 363,000 *medimnoi* of barley.[29] Whether these returns made allowance for seed and other diversions is not stated, and we do not know if this was a poor year; but the totals would scarcely have fed 60,000. The importance of these conclusions has already been drawn in Chapter V: in view of the very limited surplus beyond a farmer's needs, the fields of Attica could not have fed an urban center of even 10,000; once Athens rose toward that figure, it would have been necessary to import seaborne grain.

CHANGES IN THE FARMLANDS

The primary requirement laid upon this agricultural system was that it support the rural population from generation to generation. In the age of expansion, however, new demands were made of it. The upper classes desired luxuries; whether they were of Near Eastern origin or locally made, they had to be paid for—either in food consumed by native commercial and industrial groups or by transfer of olive oil, wine, and other agricultural products to the Levant. Pressures on the rural population were thus already mounting before cities emerged, but the development of urban centers also provided markets for the surrounding farms. In sum, agricultural surpluses had to be wrested from the countryside for non-agricultural elements.

In western Europe, from the appearance of medieval cities onward, similar demands produced marked structural alterations in the rural world; or in some cases it might be more proper to say that agricultural alterations paved the way for urban progress.[30] If we look at the ancient Greek countryside, we can see without difficulty that there was only limited advance in productivity itself, in the extent of farmlands, and in the available manpower. The really dynamic development therefore must have taken place in other sectors, but before turning to these areas we may take up the three factors just named in order to enlarge our view of early Greek agriculture.

Increases in productivity could result from various changes, but a modern economic historian will think primarily of increased use of machinery, improved stock and seed, and new types of crops. These developments, together with inputs of capital, have been significant since the eighteenth century after Christ, but they were not of consequence in our period. The only addition to the Greek landscape was the chicken, imported from the Near East.[31] Olive trees may have become more abundant, as a very valuable supplement to the Greek diet; but adequate evidence for this suggestion, which has often been made for Attica, has not yet been advanced.[32] If such specialization did occur, it argues for a marked increase in agricultural sophistication, as well as a certainty that grain could be otherwise acquired. Extensive experimentation and progress in the raising of grain cannot be demonstrated for any period of Greek history; irrigation or terracing of fields may have been undertaken at some places, but was not of major utility.[33] Harking back to the earlier discussion of the motive forces in early Greek history, we can repeat that no sudden outburst in productivity took place to support a *rapid* expansion in population.

The technical stagnation of agriculture has been the object of scarcely veiled reproof in some modern studies; it has been suggested that the legal restriction of ownership of land to citizens prevented metics from directing toward agriculture "that very substantial proportion of the money available for investment which was in the hands of noncitizens," and thus increasing capital inputs.[34] Whether the assertion itself is true can be debated; but one must doubt that capital expenditure in cereal production at least, given the conditions of the Greek climate and agricultural knowledge, would have brought major returns. The smaller farmers dared not gamble with their essential livelihood so long as they knew that the ways of their fathers had been essentially successful, but throughout history, aristocratic elements have seen little reason to disturb the technical side of a system which is often sanctified by tradition and even by religious beliefs.

This conservatism is at least in part also the result of a real limitation, as just suggested, for opportunities in rural investment, rather than a lack of capital in itself. Ancient farmers could not calculate efficiently returns from rural investments, but they could sense the possibilities of gain or lack thereof.[35] In the disturbed conditions of Attica during and after the Peloponnesian war at least one family bought up uncultivated farms, improved them, and sold them at a profit.[36] Even in our own period Polycrates imported Milesian sheep and other animals to improve the quality of Samian stock; but on the whole it is unlikely that aristocrats often committed capital to the land except in fostering olive groves and vineyards. For the most part they relied on squeezing their agricultural dependents for a greater share of the crop.

If increase in productivity occurred, then it is more likely to have been a result of greater efficiency in the input of labor. To go back far in human organization, men could cover their vital needs in simple societies by only a few hours a day of hunting, fishing, or farming; but wherever chieftains or landlords arose they compelled their subjects to work much harder, either directly or on political and religious grounds.[37] Positive evidence for any change in rural work habits in early Greece is lacking except insofar as the tone of Hesiod's *Works and Days* attests that farmers who did not wish to enlarge their *chremata* did not labor to his satisfaction. It is quite possible that any alterations in this respect had already occurred long before—Odysseus' accumulated food supplies fed the suitors of Penelope magnificently and interminably—but an increase in productivity, as a consequence of longer work-hours, might well have accompanied a more intensive desire to coax the largest possible results out of inherited techniques.[38]

In early modern Europe the key to agricultural change was "found eventually in the breaking down of old tenures so that peasants could be subjected to economic pressures, or alternatively forced out in favour of market-oriented farmers." [39] The latter, which resulted in the enlargement of farm size, took place to some degree in early Greece to judge from the effort by Pheidon of Corinth to limit its spread; but it certainly was not a major factor in improving productivity. Where better methods have been taken up in other agricultural societies, the size of farms often has shrunk; and recent studies tend to demonstrate that small farms can be more productive per hectare than larger ones.[40] For ancient Greece manpower, moreover, was the chief source of agricultural energy. Any expansion, then, of the size of farms would basically have required a correlated increase in the employment of farm labor (though some unfortunate Athenians in Solon's time were sufficiently unneeded that they could be sold off the land); the major change would have been the conversion of independent farmers into day laborers.

Thus, improvements in rural productivity are not to be totally discounted even if technological change or increased capital input was a minor cause for advances. Far more important in increasing at least the total production of food in any state was an extension of the area under cultivation. Across the age of expansion wild animals were driven back into the hills, and the plains became the orderly landscape known in classic times. In Attica there is evidence that districts called *eschatia* had been turned into farmlands; the story of the farmer who cultivated "rocks" in the days of Pisistratus was famous.[41] Hesiod's father also may have acquired a previously uncultivated plot at Ascra, "bad in winter, sultry in summer, and good at no time." [42] The enlargement of cropland may have involved marginal areas, but this was not necessarily always the case. During the Dark Ages Greek life had often been nomadic; but in the historic centuries of Hellas men came more and more to live by eating grain rather than meat. To some extent the increase in settled life merely meant a transfer of energies, but it may also have permitted an over-all increase, if a slow one, in the population. Here, to be sure, we cannot find a source for a rise in productivity; but a growth in the number of *kleroi* under cultivation would presumably have also enlarged the quantity of small agricultural surpluses available in any area.

After changes in productivity and enlargement of areas of cultivation we may place possible increases in rural manpower. Scenes of agricultural activity almost always show more than one man at work, as on Plate IV; the busy times of the rural calendar forced a farmer to draw on outside labor. Rural tenancy itself is not very evident in our sources, though at least at Athens terms exist which suggest that sharecropping did take place there.[43] More often, however, the larger landowners drew from a pool of landless *thetes* for occasional or seasonal labor. In the fourth century even wives of urban citizens went out to work on the land in harvest time,[44] and the *thetes* at this time numbered over half the population. By that point, however, the city of Athens had grown considerably, and the proportion of *thetes* in early Greece must have been much less, though still quite considerable. One would like to know far more about that class: to what extent did it provide colonists? or move to the nascent cities? Or was it even allowed by social convention to enter urban life? At various times in more modern history changes in agriculture, such as a shift to raising sheep, have thrown masses of vagabonds and ne'er-do-wells onto the roads and into the cities.[45] In ancient Greece, however, methods of farming did not change enough to expel great numbers of men; as I suggested earlier, the owners of industrial establishments found it necessary to buy slaves to provide their manpower.

Rural slavery is as debated a topic as urban slavery. Hesiod urged his auditors to acquire both female and male slaves almost as a matter of course, and some modern scholars find here a source of rural manpower. Yet there is remarkably little evidence after Hesiod for rural slaves and no testimony whatever to a major increase thereof; the slaves of Hellas appear mainly in households and workshops. Aristotle observed that "the poor man, not having slaves, is compelled to use his wife and children," and the holder of only four hectares could scarcely have had either the capital to buy a slave or the surplus food to feed him.[46] The principal source of rural manpower remained the landless *thetes,* who were hired intermittently. Once one removes the unfounded hypothesis of a great growth in population, there is little reason to assume that this group increased markedly in numbers, though minor growth is quite likely.

THE APPEARANCE OF PEASANTS

If really sweeping changes cannot be discovered in productivity, productive areas, and rural manpower, then we must look elsewhere for dynamic alterations in the Greek agricultural system. These occurred primarily in the direction and motivation of the rural economy and produced a peasantry, the small surpluses of which could thus be more easily mobilized for non-agricultural uses. To a large degree the peasants must have been the descendants of earlier self-sufficient small farmers, but unfortunate middling farmers might well have fallen into this condition.

For the farmers of simple societies agriculture "is a livelihood and a way of life, not a business for profit." [47] These farmers may be and probably are connected to an outside world, but they live on a plane of independent self-reliance, controlling their means of production. In anthropological analyses, on the other side, peasants are rural producers who are dependent on a secondary group which uses the surplus for itself and other non-farming groups.[48] At times these analyses postulate the existence of cities, a requirement which would ill match the Greek experience down toward 600; but Wolf at least suggests that it is the state "which marks the threshold of transition between food cultivators in general and peasants. Thus, it is only when a cultivator is integrated into a society with a state—that is, when the cultivator becomes subject to the demands and sanctions of power-holders outside his rural stratum—that we can appropriately speak of peasantry." [49] Where cities do exist, they are always dependent on their surrounding peasantry, a fact which Lydian kings made use of when they tried to subject the states of Ionia.[50]

The *polis* with its tighter form of government emerged, it will be remembered, only in the later eighth century. Already in Hesiod's Boeotia unscrupulous leaders were making use of the machinery of justice to gain unjust powers, though Hesiod's home does not yet appear to have been a true *polis*. In remote mountainous districts shepherds and farmers may always have maintained an economic independence, but along the coasts and around the nascent cities the rural population was vulnerable. In brief, it became tied to markets and subject to external pressures from the upper classes so that we may term it a peasantry in an economic sense—culturally there must be reservations, which will be expressed later.

The result, and the tensions produced, can be seen to some extent, though we cannot quantify how much rural surplus *could* have been taken and how much actually did get into the hands of non-producers. The processes by which these elements were able to extort or acquire more peacefully rural surpluses are murky. To some degree the agricultural produce of any one area may have been siphoned off by the requirements of its *polis;* but major secular buildings and public expenditures, as noted in Chapter II, were of very limited order, and direct land taxes were so uncommon that they do not even need to be taken into account in calculating rural revenues and yields. Rather more expense was occasioned by the building of temples and the maintenance of their cults—especially the sacrifices—though there too demands on the community, at least in building, were mainly in terms of labor, which farmers could provide in the slack seasons of the agricultural year.[51] As urban markets developed, they drew in agricultural commodities in exchange for manufactured items. But in the earliest part of the age of expansion, down into the seventh century or even later, the main vehicle for draining the countryside of its surpluses consisted of demands of the upper classes, operating either through control of the system of justice and administration or in more private manner. Hesiod illuminates the early stages of their drive in his bitter epithet, "bribe-swallowing *basileis,*" and Solon shows an advanced stage of the results a century later.

In several areas the upper classes were able to push the smaller farmers down into such dependence that they became what one may loosely call serfs or, in an ancient term, men "between free and slave," that is, farmers tied to their land and owing regular dues to their lords. Well-known examples of this process are the *penestai* of Thessaly, the helots of Sparta, and the *mnoitai* and *klarotai* of Crete.[52] Thessaly and Crete may perhaps be explained as fringe areas of the historical Greek world, where nobles were unchecked by other forces; in Sparta internal problems forced the aristocrats to elevate the middling farmer citizens to a technical plane of "Equals" and, in counterbalance, to subject both native and Messenian small farmers as helots.

Elsewhere the upper classes moved in a less regular fashion, and we probably should not think solely in terms of aristocratic pressures, even though these leaders had the major role in political life down to the sixth century. If some farmers fell into dependent status, others of the type addressed by Hesiod seized opportunities to expand their hold upon near-by rural revenues. In many historical eras the "nouveaux riches" have been even more grasping and ruthless than aristocrats proper.[53] The process or avenue which was used in Attica is said to have been debt; Phocylides also connected the *kakoi* with loans. How debt could have been so mighty an engine we will reserve for the next chapter, and at this point simply accept its existence.

Farmers also lost their independence but, be it noted, did not become helots when they were "entrapped" in the market structure of the Greek urban centers, which operated most directly on the rural areas about the cities. Merchants and other city dwellers in recent centuries have often sought to buy near-by land, "not so much investing their money in land as buying up the perquisites of a social class" but also turning its uses to urban needs and increasing thus its productivity.[54] In view of the difficulties in transferring land in early Greece one may doubt that this process took place to a major degree at that time, though evidence of specialization in the raising of flowers and vegetables to be sold in the cities can be found in the fourth century and those that followed.[55]

It does not appear probable that foreign grain had any serious impact on agricultural production or on prices down to the close of our period, though the people of some cities were beginning to eat imported food by that time. In the Persian invasion of 480 Xerxes saw grain ships, bound for

Aegina and the Peloponnesus, coming from the Black Sea, and Gelon of Syracuse offered to provide grain "for the whole Greek army so long as the war shall last." [56] Egyptian grain was also imported by the fifth century, but no evidence whatever exists to show that the Greek settlement at Naucratis in the late seventh century was motivated by a need for the agricultural products of the Nile. [57]

Gelon evidently had means of controlling Syracusan exports, but the grain trade as a whole was in private hands. Curses publicly pronounced thrice each year at Teos about 470 were leveled against anyone who prevented the import of grain or re-exported it by sea or by land. [58] Assumptions that this trade ran far back into earlier centuries are too easily made, and Athens and other importing cities were exceptions in Greece. In the early modern Mediteranean world scarcely 1 per cent of the total grain consumption was provided by sea in the sixteenth century, and large-scale systems for its transport and distribution did not appear until the eighteenth century; England fed itself from its own acres almost to the time of the Napoleonic wars. [59]

A recent study of archeological discoveries inland in south Russia suggests little evidence of a Greek presence until virtually the fifth century B.C., and argues that colonization on the seacoast was more to secure land than to provide entrepôts for the grain trade. [60] While this argument rests too much on pottery finds, there is no reason to believe that the Greeks even of the cities were fed by any other than native resources until some point in the sixth century—by which time their workshops were producing the wares which could be used to pay for imported grain.

The changes in the agricultural world, in sum, were locally produced, and their dimensions must not be exaggerated.

The principal forces were not so much enlarged productivity via technological change or expansion in croplands as in an increase in economic interest and motivation, a subjective factor not easily quantified.

In some areas the upper classes drove the small farmers into formal legal subjection; elsewhere their pressures, just and unjust, weighed heavily on weaker neighbors who were both tempted and subjugated by market forces. In mountainous villages farmers remained self-sufficient; in the vicinity of urban centers they became, in the economic sense, peasants. The agricultural system of Greece could not begin to provide the masses of grain available to the masters of the Mesopotamian and Egyptian river valleys, though in recent years the gross product in cash terms per cultivated hectare in Greece has been two-thirds that of an Egyptian hectare.[61] Still, the farming surplus of Greece, once mobilized via the peasant route, proved adequate to fuel a continuing expansion of non-agricultural elements until urban masses became large enough to require foreign grain also.

The rural patterns of Greece, however, did not change so much as to eliminate the need for a large rural labor force, not did they lead to the creation of large estates of the Roman *latifundia* type resting on slave labor. The battle cry "redistribution of land and abolition of debts" recurs often in later Greek history, but to evaluate it properly one must remember that the largest farm known in Attica ran only 30 hectares. In the seventh century the upper classes seem to have been steadily increasing their power over the countryside, but by the sixth their drive slackened. The reasons for that decline will concern us in the next chapter; in any case, by 500 the solid backbone of the citizenry of most Greek *poleis* consisted of small and medium farmers who cultivated their *kleroi* in ancestral fashion, but were intimately connected to the urban centers, where they existed, and to the religious and political machinery of the state.

These farmers may thus be called peasants in an economic sense. Socially they admitted themselves inferior to the aristocratic class, and politically too they usually deferred to their betters, though assemblies at least at Athens could be unpredictable. One final point, however, cannot be emphasized too strongly: culturally the modern connotations of the word "peasants" are seriously misleading when applied to the chorus of the Acharnians in Aristophanes or to any other Greek rural elements. Those Greeks who visited the Persian empire or the Nile valley met abjectly ignorant, downtrodden masses very different from the small farmers they knew at home, who were citizens in the *polis*.

Chapter VIII

Economic and
Social Tensions

Thus far we have examined the social and economic growth of early Greece analytically. First I suggested the motive forces at work; then discussed the rise of trade and industry, the subsequent appearance of cities and coinage, the crystallization of an aristocratic way of life, and changes in the agricultural world. Now it is time to put all these factors and institutions together, as it were in a Greek cauldron with griffin heads, and stir them about with iron spits to illustrate their interactions and conflicts.

A formal economic and social history of Greece from 800 to 500 B.C. would be both an improper and an impossible undertaking.[1] Political, religious, and intellectual advances were equally as important or even more vital in the stirring up of this bubbling world, and in any case quantitative series for prices or demographic shifts cannot be reconstructed. The states of Greece, moreover, did not all follow exactly the same path, nor did they move at an even speed. Still, men must make their living; and changes in the ways in which they do so, and in the social relationships connected thereto, are important elements in the historical chain.

The poets of the archaic age commented on contemporary altercations primarily on the social level, but we can detect at least three areas in which economic contentions were, or could be, important: the relations of the new industrial and commercial classes to the policies and institutions of the *polis;* the effort of the *kakoi* to gain a voice in government; and the difficulties of the smaller farmers in an age of great change. After considering these problems we must endeavor to ferret out the reasons for their resolution without revolution. By the beginning of the classic era the Greek world had generally returned to a state of balance, though on a much more complex level than in 800.

GENERAL STRESSES

Nowadays historians often seek to apply the lessons of social psychology and kindred fields to past eras, and to locate the roots of conflict in such fundamental human relationships as those of parents and children or between the sexes. These efforts are frequently illuminating, but the method cannot be seriously applied to the very limited evidence from early Greece.[2]

Nonetheless men and women who lived then did suffer fears and uncertainties. The poets celebrated with naïve enthusiasm their individual feelings; but they also had a sense of helplessness before the chaotic, unpredictable turns of fortune. The polar opposites, *hybris* and *sophrosyne,* emerged in this era even though they were most deeply explored later in Attic tragedy. More generally it has been observed that the Greeks moved from the shame-culture of the Homeric epics, where social reproof derived from the opinions of one's peers, to a guilt-culture in which the gods punished misdeeds, though both could co-exist in fifth-century Athens.

The most intriguing evidence of human fears is that furnished by the monsters and wild beasts who appear so swiftly and so abundantly in the arts of the late eighth and seventh century. The untamed powers of savage nature, though not conceived sharply in anthropomorphic guise, were a fundamental constituent of Greek religious beliefs. They outlasted the great gods and passed on into modern rural folklore; at the other boundary of Greek civilization their origins must go far back into primitive days. What is significant is that men of the years around 700 felt so pressing a need to represent this demonic quality of their world. Since the human form seemed ill-fitting, artists turned to the rich treasure of wild beasts and imaginary figures of the Near East, took what they needed, and remolded the borrowings with a native esthetic sensitivity. The griffins, sphinxes, and sirens do not illustrate myths: that is, they do not have true histories, nor do they do anything; they simply are, and by their presence manifest a sense of unfettered powers encompassing mankind.

A companion concern over death appears in the plenitude of fierce beasts which paralleled the monsters. On vases lions pounce upon unsuspecting, grazing cattle or turn their snarling heads out at the spectator in grim rows; one brutal composition shows two lions devouring a man.[3] Throughout Greek art, from the middle of the eighth century down well into the seventh century, death intruded frequently, and men responded to the ultimate proof of their weakness not with dignified resignation but with fierce, macabre horror. In the fifteenth and sixteenth centuries after Christ a similar mood recurred, and that too was a period in which magic and religious intensity hovered in men's minds alongside daring advance.

One figure illustrates magnificently many of these themes; the cycle of myths revolving about the deeds of Heracles is the greatest of the period, celebrated in art and literature alike. Heracles is a mortal man, a human being who strides forth to vanquish a series of monsters and wild beasts; he is also a creature of passion and violence. Yet he meets a frightful end by donning the poisoned shirt of Deianira, a tale of a piece with the fearful imagination of the early seventh century, even though he is then translated to Olympus and there "lives among the undying gods, untroubled and unaging all his days." [4]

We may seem to have strayed far from the prosaic area of economic and social life, but nowhere better than in the field of religious sensitivities can one see into the minds of the men who lived and died in the age of expansion. Religious developments, too, suggest another very important conclusion. By the late seventh and sixth centuries, the Greek world had achieved a variety of modes by which to release or appease its fundamental uncertainties and had established a new religious and psychological base for an active existence. Fear had been exorcised, not canonized in patterns of grim myth, restrictive taboos, and rigid social structure. By 500 the Athenians were also celebrating, beside Heracles, the civilized Theseus, who warded off external dangers and "united all the inhabitants of Attica in the present *polis*." [5]

NEW ECONOMIC GROUPS
AND THE *POLIS*

When a modern historian turns to the difficulties attending the economic growth of early Greece, the effects of the nascent commercial and industrial elements on the policies and organization of the state will come first to his mind. We are conditioned, rightly or wrongly, to interpret foreign policies and especially imperialism as a search for raw materials or trading advantages, and we often find the bases of internal political conflict in rival capitalistic factions. In early Greece, too, there must have been a close connection between economic and social life and political structures; as soon as a society permits real change, decisions between contending elements will be expressed on the political level.[6]

Hesiod's outburst against the "bribe-swallowing *basileis*" shows such an interplay, but in the agricultural sector. Here we have no problem, for it is generally agreed that rural developments and political alterations directly affected each other—though the manner of the linkage may be debated. Historians normally deny that there was interaction between the new trading and industrial elements and the policies of the Greek states, however; the accepted judgment is that the demands of these groups had no significant influence on the internal and external activities of the *polis*.[7] The citizen assemblies, aristocratic councils, and magistracies were firmly based on ownership of land; an enduring, fundamental characteristic of the *polis* was its urge to *autarkeia* or local self-sufficiency.

The scholar who upheld this point of view most rigidly was Johannes Hasebroek. In two powerful discussions he reduced, indeed, almost eliminated, the place of trade in Greek economic life; those traders and artisans who did exist, he and others have argued, were commonly resident aliens who had no voice in political discussions. Hasebroek also polemicized successfully against efforts to interpret the structure of Greek economic life as being in any way modern in character. Ancient Greece did not have conscious capitalists; its colonies were not founded primarily to support overseas empires; the assertion, for example, that "trade leagues" of Greek states existed by the time of the Lelantine war, late in the eighth century, is a purely modern concept.[8] A kindred view that tyrants arose through the support of commercial and industrial elements is also antiquated, as we shall see later.

It is not my intention to disagree with this point of view in its broad outlines; obviously we cannot carry back into Greek economic life the role of the bourgeoisie and of capitalism in modern Europe. Yet minor qualification does seem necessary when the followers of Hasebroek blandly eliminate all ties between the *polis* and the new forms of economic activity.[9]

The public sector, in modern terms, made very limited demands on production. Transfer payments did exist in the form of the public meals provided in the Prytaneion at Athens and elsewhere, and in state gifts to victorious athletes; but they were far less extensive than in later classical Athens. Direct control of industry and commerce by the state was also minimal; "administered trade" outside a market system was important in the Near East, but not in Greece.[10] Greek traders and industrialists were confined far more by social custom and intellectual attitudes than by governmental regulation. And yet people had an interest in and paid attention to trade and industry within a *polis;* "all cities welcome as friends those who import things," commented the later Xenophon.[11]

This welcome was in part for fiscal reasons. States assessed a great variety of tolls and fees, including charges for using public weights and measures and for entrance to markets;

these indirect taxes, together with rents of public lands, were vital to state budgets.[12] Landowners in ancient Greece could resist taxation to such a degree that only under tyrannies do we hear of direct levies on production.[13] "Foreign trade, by contrast, is almost always monetized; it is carried on by a class which, though often individually wealthy, is not commonly as influential politically as the landowners . . . and it is physically channeled through a relatively small number of localities, making it relatively easy to mulct." Greek trade provided a great part of the actual cash which flowed into public treasuries; Chios refused to allow refugee Phocaeans to buy the Oenussae islands lest they create an *emporion* there.[14]

Exploitation obviously existed, but it was not the sole relation between the state and trade and industry. In return, the *poleis* provided justice and protection for the commercial and industrial elements which settled in their cities; Solon, Polycrates, and other leaders favored the immigration of artisans, and urban idleness was sometimes officially discouraged.[15] By the sixth century tyrants and other leaders were devoting extensive expenditures to the water supplies of the cities. Provision of food was in private hands, and state interest did not extend as far as it did in the fourth century at Athens; but it was not totally lacking. Solon forbade export of all crops but olive oil, and Teos was probably not the only *polis* to direct its magistrates' attention to the export and import of grain.[16] The regularization of agoras was largely for public and civic purposes, but it helped make a more orderly arrangement of neighboring market stalls and shops. The first harbor works were under way by the close of our period, and already by 600 Corinth had constructed its causeway over the Isthmus of Corinth.

Coinage was not issued primarily for commercial purposes, but it is unreasonable to deny that states had any concept of its economic utility. The enlargement of the machinery of the *polis* and its increasing demands on the loyalty of its members were closely linked both to agricultural evolution and to the rise of industrial and commercial sectors; the latter, after all, provided the cash and also populated the growing urban centers.

At times we can also see some influence of these elements on foreign policy and activities. The Corinthians, Aeginetans, and others sought to reduce piracy. Commercial ties of real importance between distant states are suggested by the almost exaggerated reaction of the Milesians to the fall of Sybaris.[17] The clearest example, however, is that of the Athenians, who made continuing efforts to secure strongholds in the Hellespontine area, through which came the trade of the Black Sea. Sigeum, at the Aegean end, had fallen under Athenian domination in the time of Alcaeus, after long warfare with Mitylene had been ended by an arbitration by Periander of Corinth;[18] Pisistratus regained it after an unexplained lapse of control, and he installed Hegesistratus, his bastard son, as tyrant. The opposite shore of the Chersonesus was ruled throughout the later part of the sixth century by the Athenian noble Miltiades and his descendants;[19] as told by Herodotus, the story of Miltiades suggests hostility to Pisistratus, but modern scholarship generally infers Pisistratid support. The key to this persistent interest must have lain in Athens' desire to hold strong points on an artery of growing commercial importance to her. As noted in the preceding chapter, the Athenians and others were importing grain from south Russia before the end of the sixth century to feed their growing urban centers; to argue only from the Pisistratid activity one might infer that the need for foreign wheat went back toward the middle of the century.[20]

We cannot, however, construct a picture of contending trade interests which expressed themselves in international animosities. Overseas commerce itself was too limited; the treasuries of the *poleis* could not support standing armies (apart from the bodyguards of tyrants) or maintain navies until the time of Polycrates and later. Down to the Persian wars, moreover, the Greek states suffered little external pressure; even within the Hellenic international system they only rubbed continuously against each other at a few sore points.[21] While we may think that economic rivalries must have entered into the wars of Athens and Aegina or of Athens and Megara, they are not directly attested; and in the case of Megara the possession of the island of Salamis appears in our sources as the gravamen of dispute.

The new economic elements, to sum up, are not to be ignored, and by 500 the influence of the cities was radiating into the countryside as markets and money became more accepted parts of economic life. Yet one cannot find here the engine for political alterations; if we ask the poets of the age, we shall hear them speak mainly about a struggle between aristocrats and *kakoi,* and secondarily of the difficulties in which the small farmer-citizens found themselves placed as a consequence of the ruthless activities of rural creditors.

ARISTOCRATS, *KAKOI,*
AND TYRANTS

As Schumpeter once observed, "Secular improvement that is taken for granted and coupled with individual insecurity that is acutely resented is of course the best recipe for breeding social unrest." [22] That remark admirably fits the age we are considering; the period from 800 to 500 was an era of advance, not of decline. Yet it is not easy to expand an inherited, long-established social and economic framework.

The aristocracy was best placed to profit from the springing of old confines; as the *polis* came into existence, the nobles acquired great political powers. But vicious competition for positions of honor and profit inevitably emerged to divide the upper classes into hostile factions. At Athens, the state we know most about, leaders of its several districts even had private armies and formed shifting blocs across the seventh and sixth centuries until Pisistratus and his sons managed to subdue their power and to elevate the unity of the *polis* over all local centers. Similar rivalries and civil strife studded the history of other states—Lesbos in the days of Alcaeus and Sappho, Sparta in the days before the Second Messenian War, and elsewhere. Even when open warfare did not result, the aristocrats vied in their display of pomp and found themselves forced to gain wealth by any feasible method.

While the aristocrats quarreled among themselves; they could not forget that they did not stand alone. Beside them in the phalanx and not far below them in civil life were masses of middling farmers, some of whom were prosperous and some of whom were facing serious difficulties; to a limited degree men of no ancestry also could acquire a certain position through luck and skill in foreign trade, mercenary employment, or industry and trade at home. The non-aristocrats who could afford the armor needed to man the infantry phalanxes of the seventh and succeeding centuries are often labeled the "hoplite class" in modern studies, and placed in opposition to the aristocracies proper, particularly with respect to the appearance of Greek tyrants.

The Greeks gave us the word "tyrant" (though they may have borrowed it from Lydia); in archaic Greece a tyrant was an individual who seized power and held it by force, not necessarily a wicked ruler. Tyrants did not emerge until the seventh century, but they then flourished in several of the more advanced states of Greece and the colonies; the most famous and longest-enduring was the Cypselid line of Corinth.[23] In the mid-sixth century Athens had its tyranny under Pisistratus and his sons, the best-known example in archaic history but not typical in all respects.

This political phenomenon, appearing as it did in the more advanced *poleis* as a rule, must have been a manifestation of deep-rooted conflicts which could not be settled within the inherited political framework. The difficulty arises in deciding exactly what those problems were. A famous English treatment of the 1920's ascribed the appearance of tyrants to the distortions caused by the use of money and the effort of commercial and industrial classes to break the power of the aristocracies.[24] That view still finds expression from time to time, but since the work of Hasebroek the interpretation is obsolete; chronological evidence alone proves that coinage cannot be connected to tyranny.

A more recent explanation points out that tyrants followed very soon after Greek warfare shifted to the hoplite phalanx; Aristotle comments on the enlargement of constitutions once the hoplites had become important.[25] Thus "a sort of middle class, including the more substantial of the small farmers," claimed a voice in public affairs and supported tyrants, if necessary, to that end.

This interpretation has considerable merit in connecting the rise of tyrants with rural alterations, but one might well be cautious about the concealed tendency to introduce *Klassenkampf* into early Greece. Earlier I suggested that those who "stood in the middle" did not form a conscious, unified class in economic terms—by what means could they have established such solidarity in a Greek *polis?*—and in social terms anyone who could afford to do so aped the way of life enjoyed by men of inherited wealth and position. Politically, as well, the term *demos* in archaic literature usually meant the whole citizen body, though by the time of Solon one occasionally finds it employed to denote a faction or the poorer part of the population.[26]

Aggressive, successful men who found it hard to participate in the closed political circles of early Greece may well have sought to break down this exclusiveness for their own benefit; but there is very little evidence that we should connect their efforts with tyranny. As far as we know, no man of such a background became a tyrant in any Greek state, and it is doubtful if tyrants felt they were leading the *kakoi* in storming the seats of power. Wherever tyrants appeared in the seventh and sixth centuries they gained their position because of patriotic discontent over defeat in war, personal ambition coupled with the ability to secure a band of mercenary followers, or division in a *polis* resulting from rampant aristocratic factionalism and oppression.[27] Economic difficulties never entered the picture in any conscious way, though they may have been hidden in that oppression.

Tyrants did limit the power and ostentation of their fellow aristocrats and thereby helped to spring the bonds of social structure; [28] at times they also aided urban classes and the middling farmers of the countryside. Thereby they *may* have facilitated the entry of new men into public positions, though the archon list of Pisistratid Athens, as far as it is preserved, contains mostly nobles from old families.[29] The role of a tyrant was in general more that of catalyst than of independent agency; his own personal objectives were to keep the power he had seized and to acquire the means for his own profit and public ostentation, though these aims did in turn help to increase the machinery and finances of the states.[30]

At Sparta the Second Messenian War forced the aristocrats to amalgamate, at least superficially, with the hoplite elements. Elsewhere unification took place more slowly and perhaps even incompletely. To some extent the interruption of tyrannies broke old ways and aided this process, but equally influential were the slow, continuing pressure of military necessity and the claims of wealth, which could not well be denied in view of the aristocratic emphasis on *chre-*

mata. By 500 even conservative states were often governed by oligarchies, and money counted for more than birth did—though ancestry was never insignificant. Democracy could appear only where commercial and industrial elements did have some strength, but it did not always do so even there.

PROBLEMS OF THE SMALL FARMERS: SOLON

A second source of strife also emerged from those changes in the landscape which affected the landless *thetes,* the holders of small plots, and also less successful middling farmers.[31] We can presume that some men sought new opportunities in joining colonial expeditions, in serving as mercenaries, or in moving to the urban centers; but many remained on the land and fell into debt, or even into slavery. At Miletus there was rural unrest over two generations—at one point the rebellious peasants seized the children of the rich and flung them on the threshing floors, where they were trampled by oxen. An obscure group called Cheiromacha was involved in the struggle against the faction termed Ploutis, but the idea that the former were urban artisans seems unlikely. In the end the Parians, acting as arbitrators, settled the government of Miletus into the hands of those who farmed their land well, i.e., oligarchic elements who were not necessarily of the aristocratic class.[32] Outbreaks of civil strife are also known to have taken place at Samos, Syracuse, and other states, but as a rule the evidence is too limited to distinguish purely aristocratic in-fighting from uprisings by the oppressed elements of the countryside.

The one struggle about which much can be said is the one occurring at Athens in the time of Solon; indeed, it has been the subject of a number of full-length investigations. Wherever we have Solon's own poetry we can speak with some confidence, but outside this specific evidence ancient and modern hypotheses abound.

Even the immediate reasons for Solon's choice as archon and reconciler in 594 are not as clear as scholars often put them. Aristotle and other ancient sources lead us to consider the election as a consequence of serious conflict between peasant debtors and their creditors, an explanation which fits the fourth and later centuries very well but may not be entirely consonant with earlier times. The aristocrat Cylon had tried to seize power at Athens before Solon's period, and after the Solonian reforms contentions among the upper class continued to tear asunder the fabric of the Athenian state until Pisistratus managed finally to twist his way through the factional rivalry to lasting mastery. In Solon's own verse there is adequate testimony that " a city is destroyed of great men," and in a long fragment he grieves over the unrighteous minds of the leaders of the *demos* who produce civil strife.[33] Aristocratic divisiveness, that is, may have had considerable weight in leading the more sober members of the Athenian community to feel reform was necessary.

Whatever judgment one gives, it is true that Solon visualized his problems as embracing a wide range. He emphasizes the extortion and the luxurious life of the leaders, and the consequence of sale into foreign lands of the poor; and in describing his reforms puts first his liberation of the land, "dark Earth," from its marks of indebtedness (*horoi*) and the ransoming of those sold abroad.

If the Earth is dark, so too are the causes of its encumberment, and we must detour briefly to consider the changes in the control of the Athenian countryside and the effects of rural debt.[34] It is today almost an article of faith, that in the seventh century land in Attica could not be formally alienated, and yet we know that rights to the fruits of the

land were being transferred somehow.[35] Various propositions have been advanced, all of which are highly theoretical; it would be better to cut the Gordian knot by admitt-
ing that rural acres *could* change hands and that control over
the labor which produced the crops could be concentrated
for the profit of avaricious masters.

In Attica the process of subjecting the weaker rural elements was clearly involved with debts, even though Solon
does not directly refer to debt as does Aristotle. The class of
hektemoroi bound to turn over one-sixth of their produce to
creditors was large; according to Aristotle loans at this time
were secured by the person of the debtor.[36] Scholars who
feel that land was inalienable in Solon's day argue that this
pledge was the only way by which a creditor could acquire
power over a defaulting debtor's land; but such a line of attack must cope with Solon's own statement that the land itself was enslaved until he destroyed its *horoi,* as well as the
fact that some Athenians apparently could be separated from
the land and sold into slavery.[37]

As long as coinage was assigned to the seventh century, it
was not too difficult to explain the growth of rural debt; but
once this factor is eliminated the manner in which loans became so mighty a machine is mysterious.[38] The vagaries of
agricultural disaster can strike one plot and not another, but
in a simple world one usually can compensate by temporarily turning to a luckier neighbor. Hesiod says, in the *Works
and Days,* that a good farmer will "not look wistfully to
others, but another shall be in need of your help" in the
gray spring when crops are maturing but cannot yet be
eaten; or again he urges, "Take fair measure from your
neighbour and pay him back fairly with the same measure,
or better, if you can; so that if you are in need afterwards,
you may find him sure." [39]

Larger and more permanent debts usually follow entrance
into a market system, where rewards and losses are outside

the farmer's control; and it is possible that Attica was already shifting toward producing marketable olive oil and wine.[40] One scholar has postulated that a drastic decline in oil prices brought the debt problem to a head—an example of the theoretical reconstructions based on modern economic principles which afflict early Greek economic history.[41] Alternatively, one might argue that an increase in population had forced men into marginal holdings or had splintered plots among too many sons; but this line of thought, though equally reasonable, has no direct support in ancient evidence save for the fact that some surplus manpower was enslaved and sold abroad.

Generally rural debt is contracted for consumption purposes, only spasmodically is it used for productive ends; and when debt does begin to appear in a rural landscape it tends to mount inexorably through the processes of interest and fluctuation in crop yields. All that one can be certain of is that lenders in seventh-century Attica were no longer of the Hesiodic type. To judge from Solon's tone they were ruthless in seeking profit from their loans; we do not know whether in poor crop years they were even more usurious, but later ancient landowners were quite capable of being merciless at such times.[42]

Solon's reforms were very broad in scope, encompassing the problems of indebted farmers and contentions among the aristocrats alike. He abolished rural debts as of that time and banned future debts secured by the person of the borrower. We can probably trust the report that he sought to direct rural activity into the lucrative field of olive-raising;[43] but the prohibition of agricultural exports except for olive oil may also have been designed to keep native grain at home to feed the people of Athens.

For the first time in Greek history a call for "redivision of the land" welled up in Solon's time; but he refused to yield to the demand. In various fragments of his poetry he rejects the idea of economic equality and asserts that the gods give each man his due share in life.[44] Solon was far from opposed to the gaining of wealth, though he placed firm limits on its unjust acquisition, and he appears to have favored the growth of urban elements by encouraging the settlement of metics and by ordaining that every son must be taught his craft by a father.[45]

To check the aristocrats Solon reorganized the political structure of Athens by grouping citizens on the basis of their wealth, in terms of agricultural produce; but the calculations from the evidence given in the preceding chapter suggest that even after his reforms the poor still had "no share in anything." [46] Still, the lowest class of *thetes* could thenceforth exercise a voice through participation in the assembly; there and in the law courts the right of investigating a magistrate's actions gave even the commoners a tool of potential significance. More directly, Solon restricted the display of luxury especially in funerals.[47]

A wide variety of other Solonian laws is reported by Aristotle, Plutarch, and other later sources; but the principles of historical criticism must lead one to be cautious in accepting anything not attested directly by the fragments of Solon's own poetry, even though efforts have recently been made to show that the text of his laws survived intact into the fourth century and later.[48] More dangerous is the frequent interpretation of Solon as a far-seeing economic wizard.

For example, Aristotle and Plutarch report a Solonian reform of weights, measures, and coinage which is obscurely put but apparently was interpreted by Androtion in the fourth century as a lightening of those standards to aid debtors.[49] That Solon could have intended such a result is doubtful; the reform itself demands a skeptical approach. Pheidon, the somewhat earlier tyrant-king of Argos, is said to have regularized weights, measures, and coinage; but we now are certain that Pheidon did not coin, either at Aegina or elsewhere. His activity in regard to weights, moreover, is reported only from Ephorus onward; Herodotus mentions solely Pheidonian measures, presumably of liquid and dry agricultural produce.[50] Whether Athens was coining in the time of Solon has been and still is hotly debated, but the most reasonable view is that its mint began to operate only toward the middle of the sixth century and so had no connection with Solon's reforms. The heated arguments over the exact meaning of the texts describing his reforms of weights and measures show modern ingenuity but carry little conviction; in my own judgment Solon engaged simply in a systematization of those measures of wine and grain which were the basis of his political classification of citizens. Measures, after all, are more important than weights in an essentially agricultural world.[51]

In conclusion, it is dangerous to go far beyond anything reported in Solon's own poetry in reconstructing his reforms; even so, he stands forth as a patriotic, dispassionate, and wise reformer of many aspects of Athenian social and economic life. More, indeed, was needed at Athens and it was provided by the tyranny of the Pisistratids. The founder of that brief dynasty supported troubled farmers by extending state loans—perhaps a necessary step once Solon banned loans secured by the person—as well as burdening the rural population with a direct 10 per cent tax on production; down through the fifth century Athens remained a land primarily of small and middling farmers.[52] Also important for the future tranquillity of the Athenian state was his emphasis on civic patriotism, enhanced by his religious, political, and architectural activity, which cut into the strength of aristocratic contentions. He regularized the Agora and gave Athens its first aqueduct; and though the coinage of the period was intended for public purposes, a large supply of Attic "owls" was also used abroad, presumably often for commercial purposes, from Italy and Sicily on the west to the neighborhood of Persepolis on the east. Before 500, as a result of the subsequent reforms of Cleisthenes, Athens had achieved a reasonably stable pattern of political organization. It reflected a social and economic structure which was essentially balanced among small farmers, middling farmers, aristocrats, and urban elements.

CONCLUSION

Periodization is a necessary evil in history. We cannot organize our accounts unless we place them within a framework of chronological divisions; but once a period has thus been set in historical literature it can seriously distort our vision. We then tend to suppress or minimize deviant patterns, and our accounts will make one specific line or evolution appear inevitable and proper. Yet the era from 800 to 500 does exhibit a comprehensible direction of flow along an essentially continuous course, even though inherited constraints or stresses either checked progress at times or brought sudden leaps.

The Greek world was already beginning to move, though almost imperceptibly, by 800. Protogeometric and Geometric pottery styles spread across the Aegean, largely but not solely from Athens, and invigorated local adaptations of a common artistic pattern. The reviving strengths of Near Eastern civilization were slowly becoming known and admired; to the east the Greek trading post of Al Mina was already in existence by 800, and the graves of Lefkandi and Athens show import of foreign objects, materials, and techniques.

In the eighth century movement quickened along the thin lines already established, but ancestral structures remained strong. The epic tradition, elaborated across many earlier generations, reached its final pinnacle in the *Iliad* and the *Odyssey;* Athenian potters created the largest and most magnificent vases made in the Geometric style. The population of Greece may well have grown, though not with that tremendous onrush which the western world has experienced since the Industrial Revolution; for various reasons there were enough discontented or adventurous Greeks to begin western and northern colonization. Native industries expanded; metal workers, to give one example, turned out cauldrons and tripods, small figurines, and armor showing fairly complicated and skillful technique. The more advanced areas of Greece accepted the political system of the *polis,* and graves suggest that the leading members of those states were becoming distinct from the commoners. The upper classes were also laying hands on the surplus of society. To some extent they employed this surplus on colonization, trade, and public works; the degree to which they actually depressed the living level of the poor, as against gaining control of *increased* production, cannot be established.

One must always keep in mind that the Aegean world held a favorable position as a mediator between the civilized East and the backward northern and western shores of the Mediterranean and Black seas. The expansion of Greece was a function of the general progress of the Mediterranean, but, as Alcaeus commented in another connection, there were in Greece "men able to use their opportunity" who did much to enlarge the range of Aegean activity and to focus it more sharply.[53]

At times these leaders were aristocrats who had the resources and daring to lead colonies or to engage in overseas trade and mercenary service; they also were spurred by a growing desire for the luxuries of the Near Eastern and home workshops. Other men, however, could take advantage of the dissolution of old ways as new opportunities opened up—they were the middling range of farmers, artisans, and traders by sea and at home. All sought to improve their standing, though they operated within an inherited or borrowed framework of technology and were constrained by social limitations.

Only in the seventh century, however, when literary works add a new dimension to our knowledge, can we see that the glacial ice of the past was breaking more rapidly in many aspects of Greek life. As I have said earlier one token of a veritable upheaval is the expression of fears and tensions in religion and in the monsters of art and myth. Politically the *polis* sometimes fell into the hands of tyrants; elsewhere lawgivers and reformers acted more constitutionally. Trade abroad expanded greatly; at home sculptors began to carve or cast essentially life-sized statues, and the gods of Greece received more noble homes in stone temples.

By the sixth century the pace had quickened so much that true urban centers appeared and coinage was struck ever more widely. I have sought to differentiate the chronological stages of Greek evolution, as far as they can be seen; it is particularly important for an understanding of the forces at work not to antedate these two phenomena, which were more important for the classic era than for the age of expansion itself.

Likewise I have endeavored to give quantitative parameters wherever possible. If an aristocrat in Solonian Attica held only some 30 hectares and the city itself numbered scarcely 10,000 inhabitants in the sixth century—however shaky the methods by which one reaches these conclusions, the general figures must be in the right range—then our view of the scale on which Greek progress took place must be markedly reduced. A thoughtful description of Athens in the fourth century would apply as well to the sixth: it was "a society in which, except for a small group of relatively very rich men at the top, and a larger group of casual labourers at the bottom, wealth was evenly distributed, and the graduation from the affluent to the needy very gentle." [54]

The halcyon period of aristocratic domination had been the unsettled seventh century, when the aristocrats consolidated their way of life and planted their stamp on Greek civilization for all time. In the sixth, however, the upper classes tended to lose part of their political and economic preeminence. There was no French or Russian revolution to sweep them completely away, nor was there a technological and financial base for an Industrial Revolution to elevate a self-sufficient middle class; yet aristocratic control weakened in most of the more advanced Greek states.

Why this should have happened must be the subject of speculation, but the cause, I would suggest once more, is not to be sought primarily in economic shifts such as the rise of commerce and industry. The aristocrats were not very aristocratic if one compares them to Persian or Lydian landlords or to more recent rural magnates; their rural activities at least were confined to the very narrow bounds of an individual *polis*. The aristocracy had been set apart in its way of life from the rest of the population for only a short time. Located in a system which was evolving rapidly in every respect, the aristocracy had had a superb opportunity to seize political and economic advantage, often in unjust fashion, and then to capitalize on its position; yet the inheritance of the past also prevented men from rejecting their sense of communal structure and responsibility. Landholders and peasants had earlier been bound together in a tight web of tribe, phratry, and other social, religious, and political units, the power of which was not broken all at once; Greece in the seventh century was still a simple land where the rich and the not so rich served side by side in the infantry phalanx.

In Sparta and elsewhere special conditions made it feasible for the upper classes to reduce the smaller farmers to formally dependent status, but across the Greek world as a whole that process either never began or was seriously curbed by the late seventh and early sixth centuries. The Greeks could not prevent—and did not try to halt—the consolidation of the aristocracy as their pace-setting social element, but the strengths of the *polis* could check economic domination by aristocrats. Middling farmers, in particular, took advantage of the opening up of opportunities in the seventh century; though Hesiod assails the "bribe-swallowing *basileis*," he nevertheless speaks in an independent tone and visualizes the possibility of gaining economic strength through hard work on the farm.

If we may take Attica as an example, by 500 the rural world consisted of many small and middling farmers who were subject mainly to the constraints of the marketplace. Here men no doubt came together "to cheat each other and foreswear themselves," but also engaged in more honest exchanges. The dominance even of the market, which has often operated in more recent times against its rural components, was restricted by problems of land transport, which ensured that more distant villages lived almost in self-sufficiency.

The tendency of Hasebroek and others to place agriculture and commerce-industry in polar opposition is based to some degree on the political theory of fourth-century thinkers, which set *autarkeia* over against *chrematistike*.[55] It is dangerous to project such views back into the age of expansion, just as it is impossible to sunder "economic" aspects of that era from social, religious, political and other alterations. We ourselves may seek to analyze the ways of gaining a livelihood as agricultural, commercial, and industrial, but progress in any one area was closely linked to expansion in another. The agricultural landscape and the nascent cities interacted upon each other, and in Greece proper the farmers never sank into helotry in any district which had real urban markets.[56]

In Chapter II I have given an estimated index for the relative rates of growth in the seventh and sixth centuries. Even if we make proper reserves for our incomplete information and keep clearly in mind the dangers of extrapolating from temples and statues, the conclusion that activity was in the range of three times as great after 600 seems to me of the right order. It also appears to be clear that this rate did not continue in the fifth and fourth centuries—not that there was an absolute decline in the classic era, but that the rapidity of expansion slowed.

If that be so, then several lines of explanation might be offered. By the fifth century the *polis* had become well consolidated and had absorbed a great deal of the surplus of its citizens in war and in public buildings (there were city walls then as well as political and religious edifices); Athens' citizens were supported by means of payment of salaries or even of recompense for attending the assembly.[57]

It could also be argued that economic concerns really did bulk larger in the minds of the upper classes until the fifth century, when the economic structure of the advanced Greek *poleis* had become well established; thereafter they devoted a larger part of their interest to political contention and the aristocratic way of life. In Solon's day "the calling of a merchant was actually held in honor," but Plato and Aristotle disdained money-getting;[58] the comedies of Menander, composed toward the end of the fourth century, exhibit a *rentier* spirit as a backdrop of their tales of mistaken identity and the travails of young lovers. Other students, of technological bent, would suggest that the Greek world had either too weak a metallurgical base or too limited a scientific/technological interest to continue the earlier advances in techniques and skills. And one must not omit the argument that slavery had begun to show its evil effects and that social exploitation had became ingrained in classical society; though I have not magnified the role of slavery in the archaic age, it did exist then and grew thereafter, especially at Athens.

The focus of these pages, however, has been on an earlier period, and proof of economic growth in that period most certainly can be found in the physical record. The one single factor of greatest weight in spurring it was an increasingly conscious economic interest, shared by aristocrats and non-aristocrats alike. A rigorous logician might point out that this statement is tautological, i.e., that growth implies interest, even if so subjective a concept cannot be quantified; but in truth those scholars who have considered early Greek economic development have often thrown it out entirely. We need not import modern entrepreneurial theory into ancient Hellas, but cardinal premises of the present discussion have been, first, that men of the era did desire to gain the fruits of economic progress and, secondly, that their very interest did help promote the development of a more complicated economic structure than the world had ever seen. Let us at the end listen again to three men whose voices we have often heard in earlier pages:

HESIOD: Potter is angry with potter, and craftsman with craftsman . . . as he hurries after wealth.

SOLON: Those who are richest have twice the eagerness that others have.

ALCAEUS: "Wealth makes the man"; and no poor man is noble or held in honor.

Notes

ABBREVIATIONS

AA   *Archäologischer Anzeiger*

AJA   *American Journal of Archaeology*

AM   *Mitteilungen des deutschen archäologischen Instituts, Athenische Abteilung*

BCH *Bulletin de correspondance hellénique*

BSA *Annual of the British School at Athens*

CAH *Cambridge Ancient History* (2d edition)

CP   *Classical Philology*

FGrH *Fragmente der griechischen Historiker,* ed. F. Jacoby (Leiden, 1923—)

FHG *Fragmenta historicorum graecorum,* ed. C. Muller, II (Paris, 1878)

JHS   *Journal of Hellenic Studies*

NC   *Numismatic Chronicle*

PW   *Real-Encyclopädie der classischen Altertumswissenschaft,* ed. Pauly, Wissowa, *et al.*

Ruschenbusch E. Ruschenbusch, *Solonos Nomoi* (*Historia,* Einzelschrift 9, 1966)

Trade and Politics in the Ancient World Proceedings of the 2d International Conference of Economic History (Aix-en-Provence), vol. I, *Trade and Politics in the Ancient World* (Paris, 1965)

Fragments of the Greek poets are cited according to the editions of T. Bergk, E. Diehl, F. Lasserre, and A. Bonnard (for Archilochus), and E. Lobel and D. Page (for Sappho and Alcaeus). References to Aristotle's *Politics* are to the running heads in the Teubner text (which will not correspond to those in several English translations).

The casual reader may feel that the following pages, devoted to notes, are overabundant. If the notes had been placed at the ends of chapters, as originally planned, their volume might not be so noticeable; but it is my responsibility to suggest the major sources and modern studies which bear on the many topics considered in this work. I have, indeed, pruned my references sharply; to make them more easily intelligible I have used only the abbreviations just listed. Short titles of modern works can be tracked down in the section on Bibliographical Information.

CHAPTER I

[1] Herodotus VII. 102. This famous statement must be construed in opposition to Persian royal ostentation; *penie* (*penia* in classical Greek) meant not destitution but the necessity to work for one's living. Greek farmland, if limited, was fertile; today, interestingly, Greece has a variety of potential sources of energy (oil, lignite, peat, and uranium) and important deposits of bauxite, asbestos, etc.; see briefly the *Economist* survey of Greece, Sept. 20, 1973.

[2] Here I need not point out factual or theoretical weaknesses in H. Michell, *The Economics of Ancient Greece* (2d ed.; Cambridge, 1957); F. M. Heichelheim, *An Ancient Economic History*, I–II (Leiden, 1958–64); or earlier works. Some specific aspects will appear in later comments. On the other hand, August Boeckh, *Die Staatshaushaltung der Athener* (3d ed.; Berlin, 1886), remains valuable though it was first published in 1817.

[3] Hesiod, *Works and Days* 202–12; cf. G. B. Ford, *Orpheus,* XII (1965), pp. 3–9.

[4] My views on Homer may be found more fully in Chester G. Starr, *The Origins of Greek Civilization, 1100–650 B.C.* (New York, 1961), pp. 46–47, 156–69, 264–68, with bibliography of some major works. See also Albin Lesky, *History of Greek Literature* (London, 1966); G. S. Kirk, in *CAH,* II. 2, chap. xxxix (b). Amintore Fanfani, *Poemi omerici ed economia antica* (2d ed.; Milan, 1962), assembled evidence from Homer and Hesiod.

[5] The term "Greek" will denote in this work only that coherent structure of thought and art which flourished in the great achievements of classical Hellenism and its direct roots, as visible in the pottery of the Dark Ages and in the epic. Many inhabitants—though not all—of the Aegean in the second millennium spoke Greek, but their culture was not "Greek" in the sense just stated. This is not an idle precision; there was a great gulf between "Mycenaean" and "Greek" times once they passed beyond the simplest level of rural life. From this point of view the period 800–500 B.C. may be called the time of "early Greece," but I shall also use the terms "age of expansion" and, less often, "archaic era" (an expression which comes from artistic time-divisions).

[6] Pro: A. W. H. Adkins, *Moral Values and Political Behaviour in Ancient Greece* (London, 1972), p. 10; M. I. Finley, "The World of Odysseus Revisited," *Proceedings of the Classical Association,* LXXI (1974), pp. 13–31. Con: A. M. Snodgrass, "An Historical Homeric Society?," *JHS,* XCIV (1974), pp. 114–25.

⁷ John Chadwick, *CAH,* II. 2, chap. xxxix (a); Paul Mazon, *Introduction à l'Iliade* (Paris, 1948), on repeated passages.

8 Lesky, *History of Greek Literature,* provides a good bibliography on the authors mentioned; Hesiod will be considered more fully in chap. VI.

⁹ L. H. Jeffery, *Local Scripts of Archaic Greece* (Oxford, 1961).

¹⁰ S. C. Humphreys, "Economy and Society in Classical Athens," *Annali,* Scuola normale superiore di Pisa, classe di lettere, storia, e filosophia, 2. ser. XXXIX (1970), pp. 1–26, places the changes within a conceptual framework of the primitivist/modernist debate (on which see below).

¹¹ M. I. Finley, "Aristotle and Economic Analysis," *Past and Present,* no. 47 (1970), pp. 3–25. Michell, *Economics,* p. 35, comments with justice that "we may reasonably doubt whether [the ancient Greeks] would have been helped a great deal if Aristotle had been the Adam Smith of his day."

¹² H. Bolkestein, *Economic Life in Greece's Golden Age* (Leiden, 1958), pp. 146–47.

¹³ Alfred Zimmern, *The Greek Commonwealth* (Oxford paperback, 1961), p. 229; cf. E. Will, *Le Monde grec et l'Orient: le Vᵉ siècle (510–403)* (Paris, 1972), pp. 630–32. M. I. Finley, *The Ancient Economy* (Berkeley, 1973), p. 21, observes that "economics" did not become a standard term until 1890, when Alfred Marshall published the first volume of his *Principles of Economics.* Finley's first chapter is an absorbing study of the "ancient economy" as a concept, which rested on a "common cultural-psychological framework" (p. 34).

¹⁴ See generally E. Will, "Archéologie et histoire économique; problèmes et méthodes," *Études d'archéologie classique,* I (*Annales de l'Est,* no. 19; 1958), pp. 147–66; and "Limites, possibilités et tâches de l'histoire économique et sociale du monde grec antique," *Études archéologiques,* ed. P. Courbin (Paris, 1963), pp. 153–66 (the essay in this volume by G. Le Rider on coinage as a source of economic history, pp. 175–92, is largely on later periods); S. C. Humphreys, "Archaeology and the Social and Economic History of Classical Greece," *Parola del Passato,* XXII (1967), pp. 374–400.

¹⁵ The point seems obvious but is sometimes overlooked; cf. Ettore Lepore, "Problemi dell'organizzazione della chora coloniale," *Problèmes de la terre en Grèce ancienne,* ed. M. I. Finley (Paris/Hague, 1973), pp. 15–47.

¹⁶ Starr, *Origins,* pp. 225–30; J. N. Coldstream, *Greek Geometric Pottery* (Oxford, 1968), p. 330. On the chronological problems in Sicilian colony dates see Starr, *Origins,* p. 228; R. M. Cook, *BSA,* LXIV

(1969), pp. 13–15; K. J. Dover, *Historical Commentary on Thucydides,* IV (Oxford, 1970), pp. 198–210.

[17] Phyllis Deane and W. A. Cole, *British Economic Growth 1688–1959: Trends and Structure* (2d ed.; Cambridge, 1967), p. xiv.

[18] Deane and Cole, *British Economic Growth,* p. xvii. Later (p. 62) they note that detailed agricultural statistics began in England only in 1866.

[19] J. D. Gould, *Economic Growth in History: Survey and Analysis* (London, 1972), p. 15, an excellent, cautious study to which I am much indebted. On macroeconomic studies he comments (p. 125) that they sometimes seem to be part of a parlor game "in which points are scored according to the degree of skill shown in marshalling evidence to support a pre-determined result."

[20] P. Goubert, "Historical Demography and the Reinterpretation of Early Modern French History: A Research Review," *Journal of Interdisciplinary History,* I (1970), pp. 37–48, suggests the results which can be attained, and also the great variations in areas even in parts of France.

[21] The era from about 1300 to 1450 is less illuminating for present purposes (cf. Harry A. Miskimin, *The Economy of Early Renaissance Europe, 1300–1460* [Englewood Cliffs, N.J., 1969]) even if one discounts the theses advanced by J. Z. Titow, *Winchester Yields* (Cambridge, 1972), and M. M. Postan, "Some Economic Evidence of Declining Population in the Later Middle Ages," *Economic History Review,* 2. ser., II (1950), pp. 221–46.

[22] Will, *Annales,* IX (1954), p. 7, suggests, but seems to oppose, the employment of "hypothèses inspirées par les réalités mieux étudiés de l'histoire économique médiévale ou moderne." Perhaps it should be emphasized that in the text I am not speaking of formulating hypotheses; my footnotes, to quote Henry Carr's remark on learning of James Joyce's research into the *Odyssey* and the Dublin Street Directory (Tom Stoppard's *Travesties*), will present "an unusual combination of sources, but not wholly without possibilities." I have drawn attention solely to the works which I have found useful, and can but ask indulgence if the citations are an incomplete reflection of modern economic and sociological scholarship.

Anyone who has lived for extended periods in Greece will inevitably draw parallels between modern and ancient beliefs and customs (as C. M. Woodhouse, *The Philhellenes* [London, 1969], p. 26, also notes for nineteenth-century travelers). These parallels may be privately illuminating, but I judge them too subjective to be advanced very often in formal argument.

[23] Summaries may be found in *Geras: Studies Presented to G. Thomson*

(Prague, 1963), pp. 183, 185; E. C. Welskopf, *Die Produktionsverhält-nisse im Alten Orient und in der griechisch-römischen Antike* (Berlin, 1957), gives at length the views of Marx, Engels, Lenin, and Stalin. G. Thomson, *Studies in Ancient Greek Society: The Prehistoric Aegean* (new ed.; London, 1954) and *The First Philosophers* (London, 1955), are both efforts "to reinterpret the legacy of Greece in the light of Marxism." Others who follow Marxist lines will be cited in later chapters.

[24] Simply to give illustrative examples: Coldstream, *Greek Geometric Pottery*, p. 351, describes eighth-century Athens as "a prosperous maritime city"; D. van Berchem, *Museum Helveticum*, XVII (1960), p. 24, asserts that Ephesus, Miletus, and Halicarnassus had a commercial objective in their foundation.

[25] Karl Bücher, *Die Entstehung der Volkwirtschaft* (Tübingen, 1893; 17th ed., 1926); Max Weber, *Gesammelte Aufsätze zur Sozial- und Wirtschaftsgeschichte* (Tübingen, 1924), pp. 7–8, related Bücher to Rodbertus; E. Will, "Trois quarts de siècle de recherches sur l'économie grecque antique," *Annales*, IX (1954), pp. 7–22, gives an excellent summary of the ensuing debate; see also F. Oertel's appendix to R. von Pöhlmann, *Geschichte der sozialien Frage und des Sozialismus in der antiken Welt* (3rd ed.; Munich, 1925).

[26] E.g., E. Meyer, "Die wirtschaftliche Entwicklung des Altertums," *Kleine Schriften,* I (Halle, 1910), pp. 79ff.

[27] In *Zeitschrift für die gesamte Staatswissenschaft,* XCII (1932), pp. 334–35, as quoted by Finley, *Trade and Politics in the Ancient World,* p. 12. Hasebroek published two polemical works, better in detail than in their overstated main thrust, *Staat und Handel im alten Griechenland* (Tübingen, 1928) = *Trade and Politics in Ancient Greece* (London, 1933); and *Griechische Wirtschafts- und Gesellschaftsgeschichte bis zur Perserzeit* (Tübingen, 1931).

[28] Finley, *Trade and Politics in the Ancient World,* p. 13.

[29] Iris Murdoch, *The Nice and the Good* (London, 1968), p. 165.

[30] Marshall Sahlins, *Stone Age Economics* (London, 1974), p. 76, is a study of modern simple societies which provides many useful examples to be cited later, but I shall not seek to enter into sociological contentions on the theoretical side.

[31] *Klassenkampf* in its modern sense, however, has become a standard ingredient in the explanation of Greek history and even appears in the pages of G. Busolt, *Griechische Staatskunde,* I (3d ed.; Munich, 1920), pp. 210ff.; see more directly J. P. Vernant, "Remarques sur la lutte de classe dans la Grèce ancienne," *Eirene,* IV (1965), pp. 5–19, and S. Lauffer, "Die Bedeutung des Standesunterschiedes im klassischen

Athen," *Historische Zeitschrift,* CLXXV (1958), pp. 497–514. Margaret O. Wason, *Class Struggles in Ancient Greece* (London, 1947), is firmly Marxist.

[32] So, for example, L. Whibley, *Greek Oligarchies* (London, 1896), p. 49, interpreted the shift from aristocracy to oligarchy as due to commercial and industrial development: "henceforth economic forces had free play, and to these forces the changes in the strength of classes must be chiefly attributed." As between Marxist and capitalist theories I hope to stand, like Solon, "with a strong shield thrown before the both sorts, and would have neither to prevail unrighteously over the other" (fr. 5), which will please neither modern Right nor modern Left; but then Solon himself was not totally successful.

CHAPTER II

[1] Thucydides I. 2. There is an interesting echo in Hobbes (*Leviathan,* Part I, chap. 13), ending with the famous remark that the life of man in a state of nature is "solitary, poore, nasty, brutish, and short."

[2] Herodotus I. 153.

[3] Radomir Pleiner, *Iron Working in Ancient Greece* (Prague, 1969); A. M. Snodgrass, *The Dark Age of Greece* (Edinburgh, 1971), chap. 5. The Marxist interpretation of the shift to iron as a basic cause for general change (Wason, *Class Struggles in Ancient Greece,* p. 29; R. F. Willetts in *Geras,* p. 257) is both simplistic and faulty on chronological grounds. Heichelheim, *Ancient Economic History,* I, pp. 193–97, is not much better.

[4] In a Palmyrene tariff of the Roman Empire a camel load was assessed as five times that of a donkey (*Orientis Graecae Inscriptiones Selectae,* no. 629 = *Corpus Inscriptionum Semiticarum,* II, no. 3913); in and near cities, however, the ox cart yielded only slowly (cf. R. W. Bulliet, *The Camel and the Wheel* [Cambridge, Mass., 1975]).

[5] Henri Frankfort, *The Art and Architecture of the Ancient Orient* (Penguin paperback, 1970), pp. 279ff., provides a good summary; a bibliography on ivory, metal, etc. is given in Starr, *The Origins of Greek Civilization, 1100–650 B.C.,* pp. 201–2.

[6] Starr, *Origins,* chap. 6. The opening chapter of S. Mazzarino, *Fra Oriente e Occidente: ricerche di storia greca arcaica* (Florence, 1947), gives a good conspectus of early opinions on the place of the Near East; see also T. J. Dunbabin, *The Greeks and Their Eastern Neighbours* (London, 1957). L. H. Jeffery, *Archaic Greece: The City-States c. 700–500 B.C.*

(London, 1976), pp. 26–27, suggests, reasonably, that even Greek shipbuilding profited from Eastern knowledge.

[7] Cook, *CAH,* II. 2, chap. xxxviii, places the inception of settlement *c.* 1000.

[8] Herodotus VIII. 144.

[9] The swiftness of change at that time is stressed in Starr, *Origins,* pp. 222–30.

[10] Here I draw on my essays "The Early Greek City State," *Parola del Passato,* XII (1957), pp. 97–108, and "The Decline of the Early Greek Kings," *Historia,* X (1961), pp. 129–38, as well as *Origins,* pp. 123–29. The *Historia* essay has received its Marxist commentary from P. Oliva, "Patrike Basileia," *Geras,* pp. 171–81, who argues that the *polis* emerged primarily to end the privileged position of the aristocracy and give voice to commercial and industrial classes. A. Fanta, *Der Staat in der Ilias und Odyssee* (Innsbruck, 1882), is still an excellent discussion of its subject; see also W. Hoffmann, "Die Polis bei Homer," *Festschrift Snell* (Munich, 1956), pp. 153–65. It should be noted that any one area, such as Athens or Ascra, might have had several *basileis* over tribal or other contingents.

[11] *Iliad* XVIII. 490ff; cf. E. Wolf, *Griechisches Rechtsdenken,* I (Frankfort, 1950), pp. 88ff.

[12] Mason Hammond, *The City in the Ancient World* (Cambridge, Mass., 1972), properly emphasizes this point.

[13] Phocylides fr. 4; Hesiod, *Theogony* 901–2, makes Eunomia, Dike, and Eirene sisters (cf. bibliography, Starr, *Origins,* p. 343).

[14] Aristotle, *Politics* IV. 9. 1295b.

[15] Thomson, *Studies,* II, pp. 205–6, gives this a Marxist stress; F. G. Bailey, *Stratagems and Spoils* (New York, 1969), p. 59, points out that leadership is scarcely necessary until "there is a need to take decisions *which are also innovations,*" a remark applicable to the emergence of the *polis.* The expression "Adelpolis" or "Adelstaat," used by Weber (*Gesammelte Aufsätze,* pp. 37ff.) and others is misleadingly compact.

[16] Corinth vs. Megara: N. G. L. Hammond, *BSA,* XLIX (1954), p. 97. The Lelantine war is commented on in chap. VIII below.

[17] On the phalanx and the hoplite, see H. L. Lorimer, "The Hoplite Phalanx," *BSA,* XLII (1947), pp. 76–138; more generally, see F. E. Adcock, *The Greek and Macedonian Art of War* (Berkeley, 1957); on the armor, Paul Courbin, "Une tombe géométrique d'Argos," *BCH,* LXXXI (1957), pp. 322–86, and A. M. Snodgrass, *Arms and Armour of the Greeks* (London, 1967); together with his thoughtful essay, "The Hoplite Reform and History," *JHS,* LXXXV (1965), pp. 110–22.

[18] *Hymn to Apollo* 147ff. K. Lehmann-Hartleben, *Die antiken Hafenanlagen des Mittelmeers, Klio,* Beih. XIV (1923), pp. 50–52; but H. Gallet de Santerre, *Délos primitive et archaïque* (Paris, 1958), p. 220, not certain that the quay should be placed so early.

[19] A. W. Lawrence, *Greek Architecture* (2d ed.; Harmondsworth, 1967), p. 96; W. B. Dinsmoor, *The Architecture of Ancient Greece* (3d ed.; London, 1950), p. 52. H. Drerup, *Griechische Baukunst in geometrischer Zeit* (*Archaeologia Homerica,* II, pt. O; Göttingen, 1969), has a good discussion of the earliest temples; for other bibliography see Starr, *Origins,* pp. 247–52.

[20] J. J. Coulton, "Lifting in Early Greek Architecture," *JHS,* XCIV (1974), pp. 1–19; on cranes see also Pleket, *Talanta,* V (1973), pp. 22–24.

[21] D. G. Hogarth, *The Archaic Artemisium* (London, 1908), p. 120; Jeffery, *Local Scripts,* p. 339, no. 33. D. van Berchem, *Museum Helveticum,* XVIII (1960), p. 26, takes the last item as an octroi or tax on locally manufactured wares, and is uncertain whether the receipts were for the new temple or for cult maintenance. His inference that Ephesus was a theocratic state, however, is doubtful; the religious activities of the *polis* were those which most required specific cash revenues.

[22] W. Kendrick Pritchett, *Ancient Greek Military Practices,* I (University of California Publications in Classical Studies, VII, 1971), p. 100. The Peisistratid temples of Athens, the sixth-century temple of Apollo at Delphi, and others had no visible connection with the fruits of any war. On contracts see Bolkestein, *Economic Life,* pp. 46–47, 136; A. Burford, *The Greek Temple Builders at Epidauros* (Liverpool, 1969).

[23] These counts rest on the standard architectural surveys by W. B. Dinsmoor, A. W. Lawrence, R. Martin, D. S. Robertson, and C. Wickert; on publications of specific sites such as Delos, Delphi, and Olympia; and on specialized studies by Lucy T. Shoe and E. D. Van Buren. I have made no use of purely literary references to early temples, which cannot usually be dated to a specific century, the so-called treasuries or *naiskoi,* and buildings for the celebration of the mysteries at Eleusis, etc. *The Princeton Encyclopedia of Classical Sites,* ed. R. Stillwell (Princeton, 1976), was available in time for me to check my lists against its valuable summations.

[24] G. M. A. Richter, *Korai: Archaic Greek Maidens* (London, 1968), and *Kouroi* (3d ed.; London, 1970). I have added in the addenda of the last; the Sunium group, which she dates 615–590, I have assigned to the seventh century. From the Ptoon group 20, placed at 520–485, I have assigned half to the sixth century.

[25] Gyges: Athenaeus VI. 231bff. Hecataeus: Herodotus V. 36 (so too Corinth suggested use of the riches of Olympia and Delphi at the beginning of the Peloponnesian war in Thycydides I. 121; cf. Will, *Annales de l'Est,* no. 44 [1975], p. 99). Temple treasuries: A. M. Andreades, *History of Greek Public Finance,* I (Cambridge, Mass., 1933), pp. 190–93; R. Bogaert, *Banques et banquiers dans les cités grecques* (Leiden, 1968), pp. 279–304. Only much later did temples make loans (as in Meiggs and Lewis, *Greek Historical Inscriptions,* nos. 53 and 62); cf. Humphreys, *Parola del Passato,* XXII (1967), p. 381, n. 24.

[26] Plutarch, *Solon* 2.

[27] Deane and Cole, *British Economic Growth,* p. 98; J. D. Chambers, *Population, Economy, and Society in Pre-Industrial England* (Oxford, 1971), pp. vi–vii, 7. As E. A. Wrigley, *Population and History* (New York, 1969), p. 49, bluntly puts it, "It is naïve to treat the demography of a society as a result of its economic constitution." Cf. also D. E. C. Eversley in *Population and History,* ed. D. V. Glass and D. E. C. Eversley (London, 1965), pp. 23ff.

[28] L. Gernet, *Anthropologie de la Grèce antique* (Paris, 1968), pp. 21–61 and 271–81, has republished interesting essays on this rural quality of life.

[29] Tyrtaeus fr. 5 suggests that Messenian helots had to yield half their crops; but this is still today one of the most fertile areas of Greece.

[30] D. W. Amundsen and C. J. Diers, "The Age of Menarche in Classical Greece and Rome," *Human Biology,* XLI (1969), pp. 125–32; Keith Hopkins, "The Age of Roman Girls at Marriage," *Population Studies,* XVIII (1965), pp. 309–27. This figure may be most applicable to the upper classes; girls were probably less well fed than boys were (cf. Xenophon, *On the Spartan Constitution* 1. 3–4). See generally J. M. Tanner, "Earlier Maturation in Man," *Scientific American,* Jan. 1968, pp. 21–27.

[31] Hesiod, *Works and Days* 695ff. (some scholars doubt the authenticity of this passage, but its factual content is of the right order). Solon fr. 19 suggests the same age for a man; Xenophon, *Oeconomicus* 7.5ff. later pictures an ideal marriage of a man 30 years and a wife of 14. Aristotle, *Politics* VII, 16. 1335a settles on 37 and 18. M. Hombert and C. Préaux, *Recherches sur le recensement dans l'Égypte romaine* (Leiden, 1952), find late male marriage there in the Roman era.

[32] J. Hajnal, in *Population and History,* pp. 101ff., discusses the modern European pattern; on pp. 124, 133–34, he points out that in the medieval centuries a man had to have his own farm before marriage. Even so, sons would not on the average have been over 24 at their fa-

ther's death. We do not, unfortunately, know the type of family common in early rural Greece. I am much indebted to Hopkins for discussions over the years, but he is not responsible for any demographic errors perpetrated in these pages.

Homosexuality, incidentally, was officially encouraged in Crete to reduce births according to Aristotle, *Politics* II. 7. 1272a.

[33] J. J. B. Mulder, *Quaestiones nonnullae ad Atheniensium matrimoniam vitamque coniugalem pertinentes* (Utrecht, 1920); G. Raepsaet, "A propos de l'utilisation de statistiques en démographie grecque: le nombre d'enfants par famille," *Antiquité classique,* XLII (1973), pp. 536–43; Wrigley, *Population and History,* p. 17; A. J. Coale, *Scientific American,* Sept. 1974, p. 44, who observes that if the average female life were 20 years, then 31.6 percent "survive to the mean age of childbearing, and those who live to the age of menopause have the average of 6.5 children." If the average life expectancy were 25, then a figure of five would be more likely (Eversley and Glass, *Population and History,* pp. 12–16, 46–52). Aristotle, *History of Animals* VII. 588a, noted that most infant deaths took place before the child was a week old.

[34] Keith Hopkins, "On the Probable Age Structure of the Roman Population," *Population Studies,* XX (1966), pp. 245–64, skeptically put the range between 20 and 30 but endorsed the parallel of Athenian and Roman mortality given by A. H. M. Jones, *Athenian Democracy* (Oxford, 1957), pp. 82–83. Hopkins also suggests caution with regard to the common view that women died much earlier than men. In a paper of 1973 J. L. Angel gave average longevity for males of 45.0 years and for females of 36.2 years (Sarah B. Pomeroy, *Goddesses, Whores, Wives, and Slaves* [New York, 1975], p. 68); these estimates seem to me insufficiently based.

Fundamental statistical studies are *The Determinants and Consequences of Population Trends* (UN Population Report 17, New York, 1953) and *Methods for Population Projections by Sex and Age* (Report 25, New York, 1956).

[35] Solon fr. 19; J. C. Russell, *British Medieval Population* (Albuquerque, 1948), pp. 162–64; Julius Beloch, *Die Bevölkerung der griechisch-römischen Welt* (Leipzig, 1881), pp. 14, 62. H. D. F. Kitto, *The Greeks* (Harmondsworth, 1951), p. 33, gave far too optimistic a picture of Greek longevity. Arthur Schlesinger, Sr., in his last work, *The Birth of the Nation* (New York, 1968), p. 200, also cited a series of long lives (Jefferson 83, John Adams 91, etc.), but pointed out that life expectancy in Massachusetts and New Hampshire in 1789 was only 35 years; of Cotton Mather's 16 children but one survived him.

[36] A. W. Gomme, *The Population of Athens in the Fifth and Fourth Centuries B.C.* (Oxford, 1933), pp. 9–10, 67–73. D. Herlihy, *Medieval and Renaissance Pistoia* (New Haven, 1967), pp. 283–86, shows that over one-third his population was 14 or under.

[37] G. Kaibel, *Epigrammata Graeca ex lapidibus conlecta* (Berlin, 1878), no. 11; Herodotus I. 94; Thucydides II. 54; Hesiod, *Works and Days* 243. The cemetery at Smyrna (*BSA,* LIII/IV [1958–59], pp. 44ff.) has been taken by D. C. Kurtz and John Boardman, *Greek Burial Customs* (Ithaca, N.Y., 1971), p. 190, to attest an epidemic; but the excavators explicitly denied such an interpretation.

[38] Miskimin, *The Economy of Early Renaissance Europe,* pp. 26–27; Alcman fr. 16.

[39] K. D. White, *Roman Farming* (Ithaca, N.Y., 1970), p. 111; Michell, *Economics,* p. 7; and many others. In chap. VII below some evidence will be given to suggest that Greek farming was not so inadequate.

[40] J. L. Angel, "Ecology and Population in the Eastern Mediterranean," *World Archaeology,* IV (1972), pp. 88–105, and "The Length of Life in Ancient Greece," *Journal of Gerontology,* II (1947), pp. 18–24 (with a more cautious view in *Khirokitia,* ed. P. Dikaios [London, 1953], p. 417). R. P. Charles, *BCH,* LXXXII (1958), pp. 267–313, and *Études péloponnésiennes,* III (Paris, 1963), pp. 74–76, suggested a decline *c.* 1000 from the Late Bronze Age; but evidence from Argive burials is quite restricted. Interesting comparative material from Anatolia, but for an earlier period, was published by M. Senyürek, *Anatolia,* II (1957), pp. 95–110.

[41] Coldstream, *Greek Geometric Pottery,* p. 360.

[42] D. Faucher, "Les Conditions naturelles de la vie agricole en Grèce continentale," *Mélanges de la société toulousaine d'études classiques,* I (1946), pp. 5–22, noted that Chateaubriand saw Albanian flocks on the ruins of Athens and Corinth in a later period of nomadism. In *Kypria* fr. 1 overpopulation is accounted a cause of the Trojan war as the gods sought to reduce the number of the heroes (echoed in Euripides, *Helen* 38ff. but not in Hesiod's *Catalogue*). Such divine displeasure was already a theme in the Atrahasis epic (*Ancient Near Eastern Texts Relating to the Old Testament,* ed. J. B. Pritchard [Princeton, 1950], pp. 104–6; cf. H. Frankfort, *The Birth of Civilization in the Near East* [New York reprint, 1968], pp. 51–52). The passages about a ravening belly in *Odyssey* XVII. 286–89 (cf. XVII. 473–74 and XV. 343–45) also cannot be accounted significant.

[43] Cf. the tremendous growth by natural causes in the population of

British North America in the eighteenth century, which exercised Malthus (J. F. Shepherd and G. M. Walton, *Shipping, Maritime Trade, and the Economic Development of Colonial North America* [Cambridge, 1972], p. 36, set it at 26–40 percent per decade). Cf. J. Potter, *Population and History,* p. 643.

[44] The phrase is that of C. A. Roebuck, *Trade and Politics in the Ancient World,* p. 98; the relation of the three aspects, by Aymard, *Annales de l'Est,* no. 22 (1959), p. 18.

[45] B. H. Slicher van Bath, *The Agrarian History of Western Europe, A.D. 500–1850* (London, 1963), p. 12. So too Sahlins, *Stone Age Economics,* p. 49, notes that " 'pressure on land' is not in the first instance a function of technology and resources, but rather of the producers' *access* to *sufficient* means of livelihood," and the cause is "a specification of the cultural system." Zimmern, *Greek Commonwealth,* p. 327, comments on the concept of a stationary population in Plato and Aristotle; cf. J. Moreau, "Les Théories démographiques dans l'antiquité grecque," *Population,* IV (1949), pp. 597–614 (J. Bérard, "Problèmes démographiques dans l'histoire de la Grèce antique," *Population,* II [1947], pp. 303–12, is a desultory essay).

[46] H. S. Bennett, *Life on the English Manor: A Study of Peasant Conditions, 1150–1400* (4th ed.; Cambridge paperback, 1960), pp. 239–40; Russell, *British Medieval Population,* p. 280, argued for a tripling, but cf. the critique in *English Historical Review,* LXIV (1949), p. 389. On the eighteenth-century expansion see T. McKeown and R. G. Brown in *Population in History,* pp. 285–307; Geoffrey Hawthorn, *The Sociology of Fertility* (London, 1970), suggests how many cultural factors go into birth rates. J. L. Myres, "The Causes of Rise and Fall in the Population of the Ancient World, *Geographical History in Greek Lands* (Oxford, 1953), pp. 172–208, is not very useful; M. I. Finley, *Journal of Roman Studies,* XLVIII (1958), pp. 157–58, is more direct.

[47] Beloch, *Bevölkerung,* pp. 54–214, summarized in the table on p. 506 (omitting Macedonia); Mitchell, *Economics,* pp. 21–22, gives a range about 2.5 million; C. A. Doxiadis, *Ekistics,* XXXV (1973), pp. 7–16, recently proposed the incredible figure of over 8 million. Fifth-century calculations were needed at Athens for the grain distribution of 445/4 (Philochorus, *FGrH* 328 F 119; Plutarch, *Pericles* 37) and are reflected in the reckonings of strength in Thucydides II. 13.

[48] T. J. Dunbabin, *The Western Greeks* (Oxford, 1948), pp. 77, 81; Busolt, *Staatskunde,* II, pp. 354–56; Aristotle, *Politics* II. 5. 1267b; Will, *Le Monde grec,* p. 642.

[49] Herodotus V. 97, VIII. 65; Gomme, *Population of Athens,* p. 26,

would give a higher estimate of 140,000. Beloch, *Bevölkerung,* p. 42, points out the ancient practice of assessing men of military age as one-quarter of the population but himself multiplies by a factor of three (cf. p. 53). He thus reaches a maximum of 90,000 citizens in the era of the Persian wars (p. 99) and an over-all total of scarcely more than 150,000, counting slaves and metics.

[50] Hesiod, *Works and Days* 380. On the modern side see Davis, *Rise of the Atlantic Economies,* pp. 15–16; Deane and Cole, *British Economic Growth,* pp. 98, 133–35; Chambers, *Population, Economy, and Society,* p. 17 (citing H. J. Habbakuk, "Population Growth and Economic Development," *Lectures on Economic Development* [Istanbul, 1958], 30–31).

[51] As does Finley, *Ancient Economy,* pp. 44ff. On "class" see below, chap. VI.

[52] Zimmern, *Greek Commonwealth,* p. 226, thus contrasts Greek aristocratic views with the modern "senseless greed for more"—the very charge Solon made against his contemporaries, as will be noted below.

[53] *Odyssey* VIII. 159–64; cf. the "piling up of *chremata*" in XIV. 285–86 (also IV. 90–91); and *Hymnn to Apollo* 397, 453–55.

[54] See chap. IV on the interest in gain by craftsmen.

[55] Hesiod, *Works and Days* 307; Solon fr. 1.

[56] Theognis 1157–60. The sayings of the Seven Sages vary: "wealth is insatiable" (Pittacus 11), but "do not become rich unjustly" (Thales 4), in B. Snell, *Leben und Meinungen der Sieben Weisen* (3d ed.; Munich, 1952), pp. 102–3. By the time of Bacchylides 29. 159ff. the eagerness for wealth has become a platitude.

[57] Alcaeus fr. 360 (quoted also by Pindar in *Isthmian* 2. 9ff.).

[58] Solon fr. 14 = Theognis 719ff.; *Iliad* V. 612–14. Finley, *Past and Present,* no. 47 (1970), p. 15; cf. Sahlins, *Stone Age Economics,* pp. 83–84, on the tendency to produce "useful" things in simple societies. Clay granaries in eighth-century Athenian graves: Kurtz and Boardman, *Greek Burial Customs,* p. 63; the suggestion of Smithson, *Hesperia,* XXXVII (1968), p. 96, that the one illustrated here attested membership in the uppermost class of *pentekosiomedimnoi* seems poorly founded.

[59] E.g., Alcaeus fr. 360; Solon frr. 1, 24; Tyrtaeus fr. 6; Mimnernus fr. 2; Theognis frequently; cf. J. Hemelrijk, *Penia en Ploutos* (Diss. Utrecht, 1925).

[60] Aristotle, *Politics* I. 3. 1256b lists freebooting as one of the five ways of independently securing a livelihood; H. A. Ormerod, *Piracy in the Ancient World* (Liverpool, 1924), remains a standard treatment.

[61] Jeffery, *Local Scripts,* p. 355; Meiggs and Lewis, *Greek Historical*

Inscriptions, no. 7. Gyges: Plutarch, *Greek Questions* 45; Mazzarino, *Fra Oriente e Occidente,* p. 139; Archilochus may not mean "mercenary" in his references to *epikouroi* (fr. 6, 27, etc.). In general see A. Aymard, "Mercenariat et histoire grecque," *Annales de l'Est,* no. 22 (1959), pp. 16–27; Pritchett, *Ancient Greek Military Practices,* I, pp. 53–84 (especially on booty); M. M. Austin, *Greece and Egypt in the Archaic Age* (Proceedings of the Cambridge Philological Society, suppl. 2; 1970), pp. 15–17, who cites the varied evidence but draws the strange conclusion that mercenary activity was very limited; R. Drews, "The First Tyrants in Greece," *Historia* XXI (1972), pp. 129–44.

[62] Alcaeus fr. 350; on other Greeks in the east cf. *Ancient Near Eastern Texts,* p. 308; Mazzarino, *Fra Oriente ed Occadente,* p. 288, and *Athenaeum,* n.s., XXI (1943), p. 76, on a scholion suggesting Alcaeus' brother served against the Jews.

[63] Bolkestein, *Economic Life,* pp. 140–41. Booty compacts: *Digest* XLVII. 22. 4 = Ruschenbusch F 76a; Aristotle, *Nicomachean Ethics* VIII.9.1160a. Heichelheim, *Ancient Economic History,* II, p. 93, comments for a later era that "accounting and book-keeping in writing were, in our period, used more carefully in registering income from campaigns by sea or land than in the case of peaceful economic activities."

[64] F. Redlich, "De Praeda Militari: Looting and Booty, 1500–1815," *Vierteljahrschrift für Sozial- und Wirtschaftsgeschichte,* Suppl. XXXIX (1956); Georges Duby, *Guerriers et paysans VII–XIIe siècle* (Paris, 1973), pp. 60–67, 89–90, "ravir, offrir: ces deux actes complémentaires gouvernment pour une très large part les échanges de biens."

[65] Meiggs and Lewis, *Greek Historical Inscriptions,* no. 16.

[66] P. Gauthier, *Symbola: les étrangers et la justice dans les cités grecques* (*Annales de l'Est,* no. 42; 1972), pp. 19–23; cf. M. I. Finley, *The World of Odysseus* (New York paperback, 1965), p. 107.

[67] Roebuck, *Trade and Politics in the Ancient World,* p. 103; Thomson, *Studies,* II, pp. 192–94. As parallels cf. the role of Portuguese nobility in the early expeditions down the African coast (J. H. Parry, *The Discovery of the Sea* [London, 1975]) and the place of younger sons of English nobles (as in L. A. Stone, *Explorations in Entrepreneurial History,* X [1957], p. 61, etc.; or F. Redlich, "European Aristocracy and Economic Development, *Explorations,* VI [1953], pp. 78–91).

[68] Plutarch, *Solon* 2, who goes on to observe "some say that he travelled to get experience and learning rather than to make money," but points out, with some historical sensitivity, that "the calling of a merchant was actually held in honor" in early Greece; this remark is to

be taken as a contrast with the aristocratic ethos prevalent after Plato and Aristotle. Heichelheim, *Ancient Economic History,* I, p. 247, however, thinks Solon took goods only to live off their proceeds and discounts the role of nobles in overseas trade. Alcaeus made his way to Egypt (fr. 432) and Sappho reportedly to Syracuse, but these excursions were not commercially oriented.

[69] Colaeus: Herodotus IV. 152; B. Freyer-Schauenberg, "Kolaios und die westphönizischen Elfenbeine," *Madrider Mitteilungen* (Deutsche Archäologische Institut), VII (1966), pp. 89–108, on an ivory comb of a type found on the Guadalquiver in Spain and also on Samos; Hasebroek, *Trade and Politics,* p. 69, takes Colaeus as a fifth-century invention and also minimizes the place of nobles in trade (pp. 13–14). The latest study of the Tartessus problem is by U. Täckholm, Skrifter utgivna av Svenska Institutet i Rom: *Opuscula romana* X. 3 (1974), pp. 41–57.

Sostratus: Herodotus IV. 52; M. Torelli, *Parola del Passato,* XXVI (1971), pp. 56ff.; A. M. Johnston, *Parola del Passato,* XXVII (1972), pp. 416–23. Another early religious dedication as a tithe of trade is noted in the Lindian temple chronicle (*FGrH* 532).

[70] Solon fr. 3. Later possibilities of profit from public position were given by Critias fr. 45 (Diels). In modern societies wealth in cash was achieved more by holding office than from the land; cf. A. Goodwin, ed., *The European Nobility in the Eighteenth Century* (2d ed.; London, 1967), pp. 6–7, 92–93, 104–5, 140–41.

[71] Solon fr. 4 = Theognis 315–18; Herodotus I. 30; Phocylides fr. 9; "nothing but gold is of account," said Pythermus of Teos (Ananius fr. 2 West; for Ananius' own view cf. fr. 3).

[72] R. Firth, *Economics of the New Zealand Maori* (2d ed.; Wellington, 1959), p. 133, quoted by Sahlins, *Stone Age Economics,* pp. 139–40. Note also *Iliad* VI. 14–15, and Aristotle, *Ethics* IV. 1. 1119b, on liberality.

CHAPTER III

[1] Immanuel Wallerstein, *The Modern World-System: Capitalist Agriculture and the Origins of the European World-Economy in the Sixteenth Century* (New York, 1974), pp. 15–16 (the figure of 40 to 60 days is from Braudel/Fried).

[2] K. Honea, *AJA,* LXXIX (1975), p. 279, sums up evidence on seafaring in the eighth and seventh millennia as far as the Adriatic. On parallel export of obsidian from Lake Van, in earlier times, cf. G. A. Wright and A. A. Gordus, *AJA,* LXXIII (1969), pp. 75–77.

[3] Starr, *Origins of Greek Civilization, 1100–650 B.C.* pp. 49–53; Emily Vermeule, *Greece in the Bronze Age* (Chicago, 1964).

[4] B. Schweitzer, *Greek Geometric Art* (London, 1971), and Coldstream, *Greek Geometric Pottery, passim;* Starr, *Origins,* pp. 94–98, 138–44.

[5] I am much indebted to R. A. Higgins for information on the jewelry from Lefkandi (as yet unpublished); these specific items might have been made in Cyprus. There is no gold in Protogeometric tombs at Lefkandi, but the granulation technique was later used on pins and earrings found there.

[6] Kerameikos bowl: K. Kübler, *Kerameikos,* IV (Berlin, 1943), pp. 17, 30–31; V.1 (Berlin, 1954), p. 159, n. 121, and his essay in *Studies D. M. Robinson,* ed. G. Mylonas, II (St. Louis, 1953), pp. 25–29; T. J. Dunbabin, *Perachora,* II (Oxford, 1962), p. 80, n. 8, suggested it was Cypriote under Syrian influence. Agora: E. L. Smithson, "The Tomb of a Rich Athenian Lady, *ca.* 850 B.C.," *Hesperia,* XXXVII (1968), pp. 77–116. Other tombs: E. Kunze, *AM,* LV (1930), pp. 148–55; A. N. Skias, *Archaiologike ephemeris* 1898, pp. 106–10; H. C. Catling, *Archaeological Reports for 1973–74,* p. 19, on an interesting female tomb in central Greece; and, generally, Kurtz and Boardman, *Greek Burial Customs.*

[7] E. Porada, in *The Aegean and the Near East; Studies Presented to Hetty Goldman* (New York, 1956), pp. 197–98, on the development of seals in Cyprus and from the later ninth century on Rhodes; cf. E. Bielefeld, *Schmuck (Archaeologia Homerica,* I, pt. C; Göttingen, 1968), pp. 59–60. Three seals from Phoenicia or North Syria, of faience and steatite, turned up at Lefkandi. Their significance as marking off "personal" possessions will recur in chap. VII, below.

[8] E. Kunze, *Kretische Bronzereliefs* (Stuttgart, 1931), and on Cretan ivories, *AM,* LX–LXI (1935–36), pp. 218–33. Mainland ivories: R. M. Dawkins, *The Sanctuary of Artemis Orthia at Sparta* (London, 1929), on which cf. R. D. Barnett, *JHS,* LXVIII (1948), pp. 14–15; *Perachora,* II (and on scarabs *Perachora,* I, pp. 76–77).

[9] These have at times been explained as survivals of sagas, as testimony to real naval wars, or as evidence of the growth of shipping interests (Coldstream, *Greek Geometric Pottery,* p. 351); G. S. Kirk, *BSA,* XLIV (1949), pp. 144–47, is judicious in discounting most of these suggestions except as testimony to overseas adventure. Animal rows: D. Ohly, *Griechische Goldbleche des 8. Jahrhunderts v. Chr.* (Berlin, 1953), pp. 133–35; Kunze, *Kretische Bronzereliefs,* pp. 153–65.

[10] Coldstream, *Greek Geometric Pottery,* pp. 386–87, who cites the view of W. Culican that the vases were local imitations of Greek ware.

[11] This is a prime defect in the analysis by John Hicks, *A Theory of Economic History* (Oxford, 1969), who asserts (p. 43) that "the trade is unlikely to get started unless, to begin with, it is a handsome profit." Recent debate on Homeric gift-societies was noted above, chap. I; see also Finley, *World of Odysseus,* pp. 68–73, 107–8, and Bolkestein, *Economic Life,* p. 104 (who was apparently not influenced by Mauss).

[12] *Hymn to Apollo* 453–55. Heichelheim, *Ancient Economic History,* I, p. 225, put it that "plunder, booty, political presents, trophies for athletes, and keepsakes acquired by sailors, merchants, mercenaries, and travellers were more common imports [until the seventh century] than proper trade goods."

[13] *Iliad* VI. 234–36.

[14] Sahlins, *Stone Age Economics,* pp. 298ff.

[15] *Odyssey* I. 179–84; note also the supplying of the Achaean host (*Iliad* VII. 472ff.) with wine, paid for in bronze, iron, hides, cattle, and slaves (though ancient Homeric critics rejected line 475 on slaves).

[16] Solon fr. 1, lines 43–46; Semonides fr. 1.

[17] Al Mina: J. Boardman, *JHS,* LXXXV (1965), pp. 12–15, with references, and *The Greeks Overseas* (Harmondsworth, 1964); Starr, *Origins,* p. 215, for earlier publications. Tell Sukas (explored more recently): *Sukas,* I, ed. P. J. Riis (Copenhagen, 1970); II, ed. Gunhild Ploug (1973); [III is on the Neolithic era]. J. N. Coldstream, *AJA,* LXXIX (1975), pp. 155–56, suggests a move from Al Mina and doubts that the early temple at Tell Sukas was Greek.

[18] Will, *Trade and Politics in the Ancient World,* p. 56, gives references; see, more recently, Austin, *Greece and Egypt.* The earliest Corinthian pottery is Transitional to Early Corinthian, usually put at 625–20 (John Boardman, *Athenian Black Figure Vases* [London, 1974], p. 194); but see Austin, p. 60.

[19] An example of the sophistication of Near Eastern thought as early as the second millennium is given in an Ugarit bilingual dictionary entry under "cost": "The price; high price; low price; poor price; fixed price; good price; stiff price; fair price; price in town" (C. F. A. Schaeffer, *Cuneiform Texts of Ras Shamra* [London, 1939], p. 40).

[20] *Iliad* XXIII. 741–45 (cf. VI. 289ff.); *Odyssey* XIII. 272ff., XIV. 288ff., XV. 415ff; Starr, *Origins,* pp. 212ff., to the references of which may be added W. A. Ward, ed., *The Role of the Phoenicians in the Interaction of Mediterranean Civilizations* (American University of Beirut, 1968).

[21] O. Masson and M. Sznycer, *Recherches sur les Phéniciens à Chypre* (Geneva, 1972); M. G. G. Amadasi, *Le iscrizioni fenicie e puniche delle coloni in occidente* (Rome, 1967); J. D. Muhly, *Copper and Tin: The Dis-*

tribution of Mineral Resources and the Nature of the Metals Trade in the Bronze Age (Transactions of the Connecticut Academy of Arts and Sciences, XLIII. 4 [New Haven, 1973]), pp. 182, 184, 268–69, for recent archeological discoveries. Phoenician activity inland is discussed by A. Leo Oppenheim, "Essay on Overland Trade in the First Millennium B.C.," *Journal of Cuneiform Studies,* XXI (1967), pp. 236–54.

[22] The bibliography is far too massive to list; see generally J. M. Cook, *The Greeks in Ionia and the East* (London, 1962), and A. G. Woodhead, *Greeks in the West* (London, 1962); for Russian work, E. Belin de Ballu, *L'Histoire des colonies grecques du litteral nord de la Mer Noire* (2d ed.; Leiden, 1965).

[23] A. Gwynn, "The Character of Greek Colonization," *JHS,* XXX-VIII (1918), pp. 88–123, emphasized its agricultural character; cf. E. Kirsten, *Die griechische Polis als historisch-geographisches Problem des Mittelmeerraumes* (Bonn, 1956), pp. 66–76; Hasebroek, *Trade and Politics,* pp. 105–10; Heichelheim, *Ancient Economic History,* I, pp. 494–97, for bibliography; and the judicious remarks of G. Vallet in *La Città e il suo territorio* (7th Congress of Studies on Magna Graecia, Naples, 1968), pp. 72-73. For disagreement at least to some degree see A. Blakeway (*BSA,* XXXIII [1932–33], pp. 170–208, and *Journal of Roman Studies,* XXV [1935], pp. 129–49); P. Demargne (*La Crète dédalique* [Paris, 1947], pp. 321–25); H. P. Drogemüller, "Untersuchungen zur Anlage und zur Entwicklung der Städte 'Grossgriechenlands,' " *Gymnasium,* LXXII (1965), pp. 27–62; Roebuck, *Trade and Politics in the Ancient World,* pp. 98ff., is balanced. Velia was a late colony (*c.* 535), but East Greek pottery appeared there before colonization (*Archaeological Reports for 1972–73,* p. 36).

[24] G. Buchner, *Expedition,* VIII. 4 (1966), p. 12; cf. *Archaeological Reports for 1966–67,* p. 30. Apparently iron was worked at Motya in the early eighth century (B. S. J. Isserlin *et al., Annual of Leeds University Oriental Society,* IV [1962–63], pp. 129ff); cf. Muhly, *Copper and Tin,* p. 187, who also (p. 227) comments on the role of other islands, such as Tilmun.

[25] *Archaeological Reports for 1972–73,* p. 36, on expansion inland from Siris and Metapontum; for Sicily see the interim reports of D. Adamesteanu, E. de Miro, V. Tusa, and A. di Vita, *Kokalos,* II (1956) and VIII (1962); and also *Metropoli e colonie di Magna Grecia* (3d Congress of Studies on Magna Graecia; Taranto, 1963).

[26] M. Guarducci, "Iscrizioni greche su vasi locali di Caere," *Archaologica classica,* IV (1952), pp. 241–44; the career of Demaratus (Blakeway, *Journal of Roman Studies,* XXV [1935], pp. 147–49); on Gravisca,

the reports of M. Torelli in *Parola del Passato,* XXVI (1971), pp. 44–67, and *Notizie delle Scavi* 1971, pp. 195–299.

[27] A. J. Graham, *Colony and Mother City in Ancient Greece* (Manchester, 1964).

[28] As C. R. Whittaker observes, *Proceedings of the Cambridge Philological Society,* no. 200 (1974), p. 77, "Trade empires, commercial monopolies and even regular trade routes implied by the term 'commerce' are fantasies in the archaic period."

[29] Thucydides III. 88; Diodorus V. 9; Pausanias X. 11. 3.; R. J. Buck, *CP,* LIV (1959), pp. 35–39.

[30] E.g., F. Villard, *La Céramique grecque de Marseille (VIe-IVe siècle): essai d'histoire économique* (Paris, 1960); G. Vallet, *Rhégion et Zanclè: histoire, commerce et civilisation des cités chalcidiennes du détroit de Messene* (Paris, 1958); bibliography on pottery will be found in R. M. Cook, *Greek Painted Pottery* (2d ed.; London, 1972).

[31] H. Knorringa, *Emporos* (Amsterdam, 1926), pp. 133–39, sums up the argument between Bücher, arguing for luxuries only, and Beloch, for mass items, and eventually agrees with Bücher and Hasebroek; Heichelheim, *Ancient Economic History,* II, pp. 41, 52, posits a change to mass exports *c.* 560. S. Dimitriou, *Revue archéologique* 1973, p. 28, comments on the great increase in numbers of Athenian vases found in the Black Sea in the third quarter of the sixth century, "un caractère de masse," but then goes on to assert that such vases were always a luxury item.

On "staple" theory see briefly Gould, *Economic Growth in History,* pp. 102ff. Wallerstein, *Modern World System,* pp. 41–45, incidentally, counters the usual argument that medieval trade was a search for luxury and emphasizes the place of staples.

[32] Bolkestein, *Economic Life,* p. 105; Cook, *JHS,* LXVI (1946), p. 86, suggests the same pattern of trade; C. Roebuck, "The Grain Trade between Greece and Egypt," *CP,* XLV (1950), pp. 236–47, comments on other than grain items—such as timber, oil, and wine—in exchange for faience and alabaster, linen, and papyrus; as also Austin, *Greece and Egypt,* pp. 35–37.

[33] Shepherd and Walton, *Shipping, Maritime Trade, and the Economic Development of Colonial North America,* p. 113 (woolens were 40 per cent of all goods of British manufacture). In 1847 iron and steel provided 1.1 per cent of French national production, textiles 17.9 per cent (T. Zeldin, *France 1848–1945* [Oxford, 1973], p. 72); even today about 12 per cent of the total industrial employment in Europe is in textiles (*Economist,* June 29, 1974, p. 68). Cf. Davis, *Rise of the Atlantic Economies,* pp. 202–4, 306.

[34] *CAH,* I. 2, pp. 723–25; A. H. M. Jones, *The Roman Economy* (Oxford, 1974), pp. 350–64 (on purchase even by the poor); J. P. Wild, *Textile Manufacture in the Northern Roman Provinces* (Cambridge, 1970). Some later examples were found at Kertch (Mitchell, *Economics,* pp. 181–82); an example known through [Aristotle], *de mirabilibus auscultationibus* 96.838a is discussed by P. J. Jacobsthal, "A Sybarite Himation," *JHS,* LVIII (1938), pp. 205–16 (with corrections by D. S. Robertson, *JHS,* LIX [1939], p. 136). Wool and sheep were important in the Mycenaean age as well; cf. J. T. Killen, "The Wool Industry of Crete in the Late Bronze Age," *BSA,* LIX (1964), pp. 1–15.

[35] R. A. Higgins, *Catalogue of the Terracottas in the Department of Greek and Roman Antiquities,* British Museum, I (London, 1954), p. 146, no. 537, analyzes the drapery of an Artemisium figurine. Cf. Sappho fr. 22, 39, 44, 92, 100, 156; Ibycus fr. 10B; Anacreon fr. 109. On dying see Athenaeus XII. 525; M. Reinhold, *History of Purple as a Status Symbol in Antiquity* (Brussels, 1970), pp. 22–23; R. J. Forbes, *Studies in Ancient Technology,* IV (Leiden, 1964). The object weighed before king Arcesilas of Cyrene and then, in the lower register, being stored on shipboard is more probably wool than silphium (cf. P. E. Arias and M. Hirmer, *History of Greek Vase Painting* [London, 1962], p. 309, and others). Bales of wool appear on other vase paintings, as Metropolitan Museum 47. 11. 5.

[36] Amorgos: Aristophanes, *Lysistrata* 150, 735; and others. Miletus: scholiast on Aristophanes, *Frogs* 542; Athenaeus XII. 519d; references in D. Magie, *Roman Rule in Asia Minor,* I (Princeton, 1950), p. 47 with notes. Ionians (?) appear with textiles on the Persepolis staircases (E. F. Schmidt, *Persepolis,* I [Chicago, 1953], p. 88); Crawford Greenewalt, Jr., has given a paper on Lydian textiles not yet published (cf. *Archaeology,* XXVIII [1975], p. 201). Of the female slaves freed at Athens 340–20 B.C. (*Inscriptiones Graecae* [2], II, nos. 1553–1578), 47 had been engaged in manufacture: 44 in textiles, 2 in shoes, 1 seamstress.

[37] Xenophon, *Memorabilia* II. 7. 6. Later comedians refer to textiles from Sicily and Corinth (Eubulus fr. 132, T. Koch, *Comicorum Atticorum Fragmenta,* II (Leipzig, 1884), p. 211; Antiphanes fr. 236, Koch, II, p. 115. Carpets and pillows came from Carthage (Knorringa, *Emporos,* pp. 74–76); cf. O. Brendel, *Die Schafzucht im alten Griechenland* (Würzburg, 1934).

[38] *Works and Days* 420ff. R. Martin, *Manuel d'architecture grecque,* I (Paris, 1965), pp. 2–46, discusses the construction needs for timber fully; see also A. T. Hodge, *The Woodwork of Greek Roofs* (Cambridge, 1960), and more generally A. Wasowicz, *Woodworking in Ancient Greece* (*Bibliotheca Antiqua* 6; Warsaw, 1966). R. P. Legon, "The Megarian Decree and the Balance of Greek Naval Power," *CP,* LXVIII (1973),

pp. 161–71, offers an interesting case of the significance of naval timber trade (cf. Thucydides IV. 108).

[39] Plato, *Critias* lllc; the Athenian Phaenippus used six donkeys to carry firewood from his estate and estimated sales at 12 drachmas a day (Demosthenes 42.7).

[40] P. R. S. Moorey, *Catalogue of the Ancient Persian Bronzes in the Ashmolean Museum* (Oxford, 1971), p. 281, thoughtfully comments on the light thrown on economic and social life by metal objects "in a way which may supplement, if it does not actually supersede, that to be gleaned from ceramic evidence," both in ways of life, contacts, industrial skills, and supplies. Cf. Muhly, *Copper and Tin,* p. 168, on the significance of the metals trade.

[41] R. F. Willetts, *Aristocratic Society in Ancient Crete* (London, 1955), pp. 221, 250, notes that the iron equipment of a free man could not be pledged in Crete. A friendly critic argues that Seriphos was an important source of Greek iron.

[42] Muhly, *Copper and Tin,* pp. 250ff., suggests its rise before 500, when Carthage shut the Straits of Gibraltar; on Cypriote copper in the first millennium he notes (p. 350) that we really know very little. Cf. Gould, *Economic Growth in History,* p. 231.

[43] Finley, *Journal of the Royal Society of Arts,* Sept. 1970, p. 8.

[44] Boardman, *Athenian Black Figure Vases,* pp. 167–70, points out, however, that something like 1000 vases were given as prizes each time and also that the inventories of the desecrators of the herms in 415 B.C. listed over 100 such vases (sold at an average price of half a drachma each!).

[45] Herodotus II. 135; III. 48 (Periander sent 300 noble Corcyraean boys to Alyattes of Lydia to be eunuchs; not by way of trade, to be sure, and the castration was to take place at Sardis—but the tale suggests that Eastern courts could present a "demand"). Slaves from the East could also be sold under Greek auspices (Joel 3:6, Ezekiel 27:13).

[46] Pliny, *h.n.* XIV. 150, appositely quoted by Bolkestein, *Economic Life,* p. 49. Vallet and Villard, *Études archéologiques,* pp. 213–15, provide useful comments on distinguishing "containers" or mass pottery from "luxury" pottery and, in contradiction to Heichelheim's views, would consider Corinthian pottery more a mass production and Athenian vases less so. Cf. also Vallet, *Rhégion et Zancle,* pp. 199ff.

[47] Cook, *JHS,* LXVI (1946), p. 80. See generally his essay, "Die Bedeutung der bemalten Keramik für den griechischen Handel," *Jahrbuch des Deutschen Archäologischen Instituts,* LXXIV (1959), pp. 114–23; G. Vallet and F. Villard, "Céramique et histoire grecque," *Revue historique,* CCXXV (1961), pp. 295–318, and "Céramique grecque et his-

toire economique," *Études archéologiques,* pp. 205–17. Will, *Le Monde grec,* p. 664, n. 2, and Michell, *Economics,* p. 295, provide examples of proper caution.

[48] On Chiote pottery see, for example, Cook, *BSA,* XLIV (1949), pp. 154–61. As he observes in *Greek Painted Pottery,* we must distinguish between casual single finds and real evidence for continuous entry of a type of Greek pottery (a weakness of B. L. Bailey, "The Export of Attic Black-figure Ware," *JHS,* LX [1940], pp. 60–70). Vallet and Villard, *Études archéologiques,* p. 210, point out that most such studies demonstrate geographical expansion of Athenian pottery but are not usable for the history of Athenian commerce if they do not give the precise volume discovered at any one point; on p. 215 they present a chart of Athenian pottery found at Marseilles, which reached a peak *c.* 525. Another very specific but useful count is given by S. Dimitriou and P. Alexandrescu, "L'importation de la céramique attique dans les colonies du pont-Euxin avant les guerres médiques," *Revue archéologique* 1973, pp. 23–38, especially on the discoveries at Histria. The Black Sea evidence provides the same pattern as that of the pottery found at Naucratis from the sixth century; Alexandrescu infers that Ionian cities engaged in the trade to both areas.

[49] J. L. Benson, *Die Geschichte der Korinthischen Vasen* (Basel, 1953), p. 101, shows the great upsurge from Early to Middle Corinthian ware; in a very rough count of vases listed in J. D. Beazley, *Attic Black-figure Vase-painters* (Oxford, 1956), chapters i–xxiv (thus omitting especially *oenochoe* and *lekythoi*) one can suggest something on the order of 50 vases assigned to the seventh century, 550 to the first quarter of the sixth, 625 to the second, 1600 to the third, and 1400 to the fourth (I have not sought to incorporate material from his *Paralipomena*). By the fourth quarter red-figure vases should also be figured into the over-all Athenian total. The return export of Etruscan bucchero, which appeared at Corinth from *c.* 625 on, should also be kept in mind (J. MacIntosh, "Etruscan Bucchero Pottery Imports in Corinth," *Hesperia,* XLIII (1974), pp. 34–45; and *Perachora,* II, p. 386).

[50] An ingenious theory argues that the Greeks could not have penetrated the Black Sea until they had the *triere,* with more rowers, inasmuch as the currents out through the Hellespont run six knots; but this fails to take into account the common use of sailing craft. See B. W. Labaree, "How the Greeks Sailed into the Black Sea," *AJA,* LXI (1957), pp. 29–33; A. J. Graham, "The Date of the Greek Penetration of the Black Sea," *Bulletin of the Institute of Classical Studies,* University of London, V (1958), pp. 25–42.

[51] L. Casson, *Ships and Seamanship in the Ancient World* (Princeton),

1971), pp. 170–73; I may refer to this up-to-date study for detailed descriptions of ancient sailing ships, their speeds, and the hazards of maritime activity. On warships see also J. S. Morrison and R. T. Williams, *Greek Oared Ships, 900–322 B.C.* (Cambridge, 1968); Shepherd and Walton, *Shipping, Maritime Trade, and the Economic Development of Colonial North America,* p. 196, give the average size of vessels trading in the Caribbean in the eighteenth century as less than 100 tons.

[52] This is the main thrust of the study by Shepherd and Walton; Hasebroek, *Trade and Politics,* p. 83, overemphasizes the uncertainties of return cargoes in Greek overseas trade.

[53] N. M. Verdelis, "Der Diolkos am Isthmus von Korinth," *AM,* LXXI (1956), pp. 51–59; Lehmann-Hartleben, *Antiken Hafenanlagen;* Motya, *Archaeological Reports for 1972–73,* p. 46. Cf. Alcaeus fr. 426 and Herodotus III. 60.

[54] V. G. Vinogradov, *Vestnik drevnej istorii* 1971, no. 1, pp. 64–76, and no. 4, pp. 74–100; S. C. Humphreys was kind enough to inform me of a study on this material in *Dialogues d'histoire ancienne,* I (1975), which I have not yet seen. A. Schulten, *AA* 1933, cols. 519–22, published anew a lead tablet of the late sixth century from Spain, written in Ionic script but an Iberian language, which seems to record monetary transactions (Schulten suggests pay for leadminers). Hasebroek, *Trade and Politics,* p. 11, may generalize too far in calling the business world "quite untrained and illiterate."

[55] Gauthier, *Symbola,* pp. 24–61, though I fail to follow how he could observe (p. 9), "dans les cités archaïques les questions relatives aux étrangers ne se posent pas en termes d'institutions judiciares." M. B. Wallace, "Early Greek Proxenoi," *Phoenix,* XXIV (1970), pp. 189–208, would date the earliest use of *proxenos,* in Meiggs and Lewis, *Greek Historical Inscriptions,* no. 4 (the cenotaph of a Locrian at Corcyra), in the sixth rather than the seventh century.

[56] Such problems would be most difficult in the case of sealed containers of wine and olive oil. Amphoras of Thasos, Cnidus, Rhodes, etc., were later stamped; H. Seyrig, *Syria,* XLVII (1970), pp. 287–90, suggests state control. Cf. Pleket, *Vestigia,* XVII (1973), p. 251.

[57] Plutarch, *Solon* 23 = Ruschenbusch F 81; Aristotle, *Constitution of Athens* 47. Boeckh, *Staathaushaltung,* I, p. 6, asserted a fivefold inflation between Solon and Demosthenes, but without testimony.

[58] B. B. Shefton, *Archaeological Reports for 1969–70,* p. 60; D. Amyx, *University of California Publications in Classical Archaeology,* I (Berkeley, 1941), pp. 179–98; and *Hesperia,* XXVII (1958), pp. 275–310; T. B. L. Webster, *Potter and Patron in Classical Athens*

(London, 1972), pp. 274ff. A. W. Johnston, "Trade Marks on Greek Vases," *Greece and Rome,* 2. ser. XXI (1974), pp. 138–52, is invaluable.

[59] Roebuck, *CP,* XLV (1950), p. 247, n. 71, citing *Naukratis,* II, no. 768; cf. also A. Furtwängler, *Aegina* (Munich, 1906), pp. 455–56.

[60] M. M. Eisman, "Attic Kyathos Production," *Archaeology,* XXVIII (1975), pp. 76–83, and *AJA,* LXXIV (1970), p. 193; Beazley, *Attic Black-figure Vase-painters,* pp. 216ff. Almost all the amphoras (except nos. 50 and 55), are, moreover, from Cervetri as far as Beazley knew. "Tyrrhenian" amphoras were also made for the Etruscan market in early black-figure workshops (Beazley, pp. 94ff); most of the series was found at Etruscan sites, though an example comes from Megara Hyblaea and related specimens from Athens and Rhodes. Cf. also the Chalcidizing cups of later black-figure which seem to imitate a south Italian type (Beazley, *Attic Black-figure Vase-painters,* pp. 204–5). Roebuck, *Hesperia,* XLI (1972), p. 118, suggests that from the late eighth century on Corinthian ware such as globular aryballoi were made for export inasmuch as they are very rare in Corinth itself.

[61] Eisman, *Archaeology,* XXVIII (1974), p. 83. On possible mythical scenes for export, cf. Aeneas-Anchises (Boardman, *Athenian Black Figure Vases,* p. 197).

[62] Webster, *Potter and Patron,* p. 291; J. D. Beazley, *Attic Red-figure Vase-Painters* (2d ed.; Oxford, 1963), pp. 329, 333, 383.

[63] Boardman (as reported in *Archaeological Reports for 1971–72,* p. 40) suggests that the last purchasers of vases had only a limited range of remainders from which to choose—a reasonable suggestion, if unproven.

[64] Hasebroek opposes the idea of special shippers; Heichelheim, *Ancient Economic History,* II, p. 57, disagrees, as does Knorringa, *Emporos,* pp. 97–98. M. I. Finkelstein (= Finley), "Emporos, Naukleros and Kapelos," *CP,* XXX (1935), pp. 320–36, illustrates the lack of clarity in these terms, though later at least they quite often meant, respectively, foreign shipper, sea captain, and local trader; as Will, *Annales,* IX (1954), p. 19, observes, there is no agreement on this among modern students, "et pour cause." On the *kapelos* see also C. A. Roebuck, *Ionian Trade and Colonization* (New York, 1959), p. 59. In Demosthenes 35. 32 a ship carried fish and wine from Panticapaeum to Theodosia for a farmer.

[65] Herodotus I. 23–24.

[66] Webster, *Potter and Patron,* pp. 270–73; Johnston, *Greece and Rome,* 2. ser. XXI (1974), p. 143; Alexandrescu, *Revue archéologique* 1973, pp. 35–36.

[67] Herodotus VII. 147; on the coinage of Aegina see chap. V,

below. In the sixth century Aegina was far stronger on the sea than was Athens (Herodotus V. 82ff., VI. 87ff.); but Hasebroek, *Griechische Wirtschafts- und Gesellschaftsgeschichte,* p. 278, almost inevitably discounted Aegenetan maritime interest (as did H. Winterscheidt, *Aigina,* Diss. Köln, 1938).

[68] Bolkestein, *Economic Life,* pp. 112ff.; G. M. Calhoun, *The Business Life of Ancient Athens* (Chicago, 1926); in Demosthenes 34. 51 a money-lender asserts that without the support of men of his type "no ship, skipper or sailor can put to sea."

[69] *Digest* XLVII. 22. 4 = Ruschenbusch F 76a; guilds of *naukleroi* did exist at the Piraeus in the fifth century (*Inscriptiones Graecae*[4], I, nos. 127, 128[4]). The problems a captain could face with his companion merchants are well illustrated by the trip of Roger Bodenham to Chios in 1550 as described in Hakluyt's *Voyages and Discoveries.*

[70] Gould, *Economic Growth in History,* pp. 222, 253, 285ff. This caution needs to be applied to Roebuck's remark (*Trade and Politics in the Ancient World,* p. 103) that a comparison of the wealth and power of Greek states in the sixth century as against the eighth "indicates the effect of trade on the economy of Greece." Note also the possibility that too great a dependence on foreign trade can actually occasion a decline (Wallerstein, *Modern World System,* p. 219, quoting C. Cipolla).

[71] Douglass North, *The Economic Growth of the United States, 1790–1860* (Englewood Cliffs, N.J., 1961), p. 2, on the invigoration produced by external sectors. E. W. Fox, *History in Geographical Perspective: The Other France* (New York, 1971), pp. 25–26, 35–37, comments on commercial linkages.

[72] The Old Oligarch of the later fifth century and Aristotle in the fourth (*Politics* VII. 5. 1327a) both recognized the current need in a *polis* for "commodities which it does not itself produce."

[73] See the discussion by Austin, *Greece and Egypt,* pp. 39–40, with references to Dressel and Regling and others.

[74] Jones, *Athenian Democracy,* pp. 93–95, discusses the Athenian balance of trade in the fourth century. Finley, *Ancient Economy,* pp. 131–39, also takes up Athens but is led astray by his effort to depreciate the role of manufactured products (on their actual appearance on coinage see Plate V) in a manner reminiscent of Hasebroek, *Trade and Politics,* pp. 48ff.

CHAPTER IV

[1] Davis, *Rise of the Atlantic Economies,* pp. xi, 15. G. A. Johnson, *Local Exchange and Early State Development in Southwestern Iran* (University of Michigan Anthropological Papers 51, 1973), p. 158, suggests that in very early times local exchange was more influential than foreign trade "by increasing vertical specialization of the administrative hierarchy and by increasing information storage capacity of administrative technology."

[2] Pittacus 10 (Snell, *Die sieben Weisen*); Alcaeus fr. 34; Semonides fr. 1; Hesiod, *Works and Days* 236–37; A. Lesky, *Thalatta: Der Weg der Griechen zum Meer* (Vienna, 1947), c. 1.

[3] Roebuck, *Ionian Trade and Colonization,* p. 18; Finley, *Ancient Economy,* pp. 127, 205; A. M. Burford, "Heavy Transport in Classical Antiquity," *Economic History Review,* 2. ser. XIII (1960), pp. 1–18. Interesting theoretical light is shed by S. Plattner, "Rural Market Networks," *Scientific American,* May 1975, pp. 66–79 (after the work by W. Christaller).

[4] Hicks, *Theory of Economic History,* pp. 29–30; Duby, *Guerriers et paysans,* pp. 262–69.

[5] Hesiod, *Works and Days* 25–26; cf. H. Munding, *Hesiods Erga in ihrem Verhältnis zur Ilias* (Frankfurt, 1959).

[6] Sardis: G. M. A. Hanfmann, *From Croesus to Constantine* (Ann Arbor, 1975), p. 6; with J. Waldbaum in *Near Eastern Archaeology in the Twentieth Century: Essays in Honor of Nelson Glueck,* ed. J. A. Sanders (New York, 1970), pp. 307–26. The term *demiourgi* occasionally appears, and at least later means artisans (as well as public officials in some states); cf. C. M. van den Oudenrijn, *Demiourgos* (Diss. Utrecht, 1951); K. Murakawa, "Demiurgos," *Historia,* VI (1957), pp. 385–415. To take its meaning far, however, would be dangerous.

[7] The limited need for capital in early modern times is noted by Gould, *Economic Growth in History,* chap. 3; Davis, *Rise of the Atlantic Economies,* pp. 232–40; Deane and Cole, *British Economic Development,* p. 260; Hicks, *Theory of Economic History,* p. 142. The lack of ancient productive loans is stressed by Finley, *Economic History Review,* 2. ser. XVIII (1965), p. 37, and *Ancient Economy,* p. 141; but as Will, *Le Monde grec,* p. 654, justly observes, if an artisan did not attract capital it was probably because he did not seek it, "et donc qu'il n'en avait pas besoin." Michell, *Economics,* p. 32, expresses the same view.

[8] M. I. Finley, "Technological Innovation and Economic Progress in the Ancient World," *Economic History Review,* 2. ser. XVIII (1965), pp.

25–45, and A. M. Burford, *Craftsmen in Greek and Roman Society* (Ithaca, N.Y., 1972), pp. 114–19, concentrate on the lack of *continued* technological improvement to such a degree that the innovations in the age of expansion almost disappear from sight. H. W. Pleket, "Technology in the Greco-Roman World," *Talanta,* V (1973), pp. 6–47, is a refreshing survey of the theoretical and practical limitations on technological advance, and also its occasional appearance.

[9] Homeric references to *chalkeus, kerameus, skytotomos,* and *tekton* are given by Bolkestein, *Economic Life,* p. 42; cf. Hasebroek, *Griechische Wirtschafts- und Gesellschaftsgeschichte,* p. 25.

[10] Courbin, *Études archéologiques,* pp. 71–72, 98–100; *Archaeological Reports for 1966–67,* p. 5; *Excavations at Lefkandi, Euboea 1964–66* (British School at Athens, 1968), pp. 28–29.

[11] H. V. Herrmann, *Olympische Forschungen,* VI (Berlin, 1966), asserts that of 49 siren cauldrons from *c.* 700 on, 37 were made in the Near East and 12 are Greek adaptations; cf. his reduction of Urartian influence in *Jahrbuch des Deutschen Archäologischen Instituts,* LXXXI (1966), pp. 79–141.

[12] Kunze, *Kretische Bronzereliefs,* pp. 263–64, and Frankfort, *Art and Architecture of the Ancient Orient,* p. 259, n. 123, are very skeptical about the presence of Levantine workmen in the Aegean (as suggested by Dunbabin, *Greeks and Their Eastern Neighbours,* pp. 41, 49, Boardman, and others).

[13] S. Adam, *The Technique of Greek Sculpture in the Archaic and Classical Period* (London, 1966); C. Nylander, *Ionians in Pasargadae* (Acta Universitatis Upsaliensis, Boreas 1, 1970); A. B. Tilia, *Studies and Restorations at Persepolis and Other Sites of Fars* (Instituto Italiano per il Medio ed Estreme Oriente, Reports and Memoirs, XVI, 1972), pp. 127–65; I have discussed several aspects of these developments in *Greeks and Persians in the Fourth Century B.C.: A Study of Cultural Contacts before Alexander,* Part II (forthcoming in *Iranica Antiqua*).

[14] Gould, *Economic Growth in History,* pp. 357–58 (cf. p. 303 on the limited role of technology in growth); F. Braudel, *Capitalism and Material Life: 1400–1800* (New York, 1973), p. 244; Sahlins, *Stone Age Economics,* pp. 81–82, emphasizes the significance of skill as against tools.

[15] [Plato], *Epinomis* 987c.

[16] Vatican 413; Webster, *Potter and Patron,* p. 61, takes the inscription on the other side, "Already, already, more than half is gone" as a reflection on the passing of life rather than a depletion of the merchant's stock (Boardman, *Athenian Black Figure Vases,* p. 111, construes it more literally as an argument over filling the vase).

[17] Bolkestein, *Economic Life,* p. 50: "In general the power of the merchant is the greater the more primitive commerce is. For the merchant alone is cognizant of the distant market and not the producer." This point had been made earlier by H. Francotte, *L'Industrie dans la Grèce ancienne,* I (Brussels, 1900), p. 308.

[18] Cook, *Jahrbuch des Deutschen Archäologischen Instituts,* LXXIV (1959), pp. 114–23.

[19] Webster, *Potter and Patron,* p. 52; J. Boardman, *Athenian Red Figure Vases* (London, 1975), p. 88, appears skeptical.

[20] Against the view of K. Polanyi, *Trade and Markets in the Early Empires* (Glencoe, Ill., 1957), and elsewhere, see G. E. M. de Ste Croix, *Economic History Review,* 2. ser. XII (1960), pp. 510–11, who goes so far as to suggest that economically slavery and the free market might be set "among the basic reasons why Greek civilization advanced so far beyond anything that had gone before it." One cannot, however, say much of utility as to *how* Greek markets operated before 500, and I have not encumbered my text with ungrounded speculation on that aspect.

[21] *Economist,* Apr. 14, 1973, p. 6 (figures for 1967); cf. Gould, *Economic Growth in History,* p. 234, on the limit to productivity in increased size of cotton mills in nineteenth-century England. Hasebroek, *Trade and Politics,* pp. 48ff., may serve as an example of the minimization of industry.

[22] Burford, *Craftsmen,* pp. 62, 79; vases showing potters at work (21 in all) are discussed by D. Metzler, *AA* 1969, pp. 138–52, and J. Ziomecki, *Les Représentations d'artisans sur les vases grecques* (Bibliotheca antiqua 15; Warsaw, 1975). A. Trevor Hodge, *AJA,* LXXIX (1975), p. 342, ingeniously supports the hypothesis that only two gangs usually laid the foundations of a temple. On Erechtheum workgroups see *Inscriptiones Graecae* [2], I, nos. 372–74 (Francotte, *L'Industrie,* I, pp. 204–7).

[23] Xenophon, *Cyropaedia* VIII. 2. 5. Bolkestein, *Economic Life,* pp. 59–60; Finley, *Economic History Review,* 2. ser. XVIII (1965), p. 38; but cf. Pleket, *Talanta,* V (1973), pp. 15–16.

[24] H. Hommel *s.v.* Metoikoi (PW); for Athens, Gauthier, *Symbola,* chap. 3.

[25] Boardman, *Athenian Red Figure Vases,* pp. 9–10; Ohly, *AM,* LXV (1940), p. 68, n. 2, showing correspondence between Samian and at least Rhodian and Cumaean figurines; Jenkins in *Perachora,* I, pp. 230–31, 242 (Corinth/Argos). Greek potters in Etruria are well known; cf. also B. A. Sparkes, *JHS,* LXXXVII (1967), p. 120 (Attic potter active in Boeotia *c.* 600, making Corinthian types), p. 122 (Boeotian vase

in Taranto signed "Teisias the Athenian made me"). Cf. also Boardman, *Athenian Black Figure Vases,* p. 183.

[26] Herodotus I. 23–24.

[27] Xenophon, *Symposium* 2.1ff.

[28] Burford, *Temple Builders at Epidauros,* p. 201 (cf. Gould, *Economic Growth in History,* pp. 412, 432, on modern shortages of skilled labor).

[29] Hasebroek, *Trade and Politics,* pp. 22–43, is vehement on this matter for the reason suggested in my text; Roebuck, *Ionian Trade and Colonization,* p. 132, and A. Andrewes, *The Greeks* (New York, 1967), p. 132, are more rational. Demosthenes 57. 30 asserts that there was an Athenian law forbidding the reproach of male or female citizen engaged in trade in the Agora—both a suggestion of their status and also of their existence.

[30] R. T. Ridley, "The Economic Activities of the Perioikoi," *Mnemosyne,* XXVII (1974), pp. 281–92, is a fascinating survey of modern views and their limited ancient support.

[31] A. Fuks, "Kolonos misthios: Labour Exchanges in Classical Athens," *Eranos,* XLIX (1951), pp. 171–73; cf. also Isocrates 14.48; *Inscriptiones Graecae* [2], II, no. 1561, etc. (*misthotos*).

[32] Raubitschek, *Dedications from the Athenian Acropolis,* no. 380 (Athens NM 6837 is a small shield dedicated by Phrygia, a bakerwoman; but its date I failed to note); R. Green, "The Caputi Hydria," *JHS,* LXXXI (1961), pp. 73–75, presents a convincing argument that the workshop of Plate VI.b is not a pottery.

[33] Herodotus VI. 60, who seems to take this inheritance as exceptional. London: M. Dorothy George, *London Life in the XVIIIth Century* (2d ed.; London, 1930), pp. 168–69.

[34] The literature on slavery, already abundant, grows by leaps and bounds; W. L. Westermann, *The Slave Systems of Greek and Roman Antiquity* (Philadelphia: American Philosophical Society, 1955), summed up the evidence in an ill-digested work. My fundamental disagreement with much of this literature led me to publish "An Overdose of Slavery," *Journal of Economic History,* XVIII (1958), pp. 17–32, which was attacked on the American side two years later in the same journal in an article "Starr on Slavery" and on the Marxist side by J. A. Lencman, *Die Sklaverei im Mykenischen und Homerischen Griechenland* (Wiesbaden, 1966), p. 93. Since Lencman found me one of "die verbissenen Gegner des Marxismus" I would emphasize—without expecting my remark to be accepted—that I am not thinking of Marxism at all in describing the actual character and spread of Greek slavery. Marxist analyses are surveyed again by Wilhelm Backhaus, *Marx, Engels und die Sklaverei* (Düsseldorf, 1975), though largely in terms of the American South.

[35] J. W. Jones, *Law and Legal Theory of the Greeks* (Oxford, 1956), pp. 141–42.

[36] Herodotus II. 134, VIII. 75, 110. On rural slavery see below, chap. VII; and Jones, *Athenian Democracy,* p. 13.

[37] Theopompus, *FGrH* 115 F 122 (Athenaeus VI. 265ff., who quotes this passage, suggests that slaves were rare in early Greece); Posidonius, *FGrH* 87 F 38; Thucydides VIII. 40. G. L. Huxley, *The Early Ionians* (London, 1966), p. 83, notes we do not know when Chiote purchases began but suggest without warrant they might be reflected in the attention to the rights of citizens in the famous "constitution of Chios" *c.* 550. Periander: E. Will, *Korinthiaka* (Paris, 1955), pp. 510–12, who takes it as an effort to reduce rural slavery (Ephorus, *FGrH* 70 F 179; Heracleides of Pontus, *FHG,* II, p. 213; Nicolaus of Damascus, *FGrH* 90 F 58).

[38] S. Lauffer, *Die Bergwerkssklaven Laureion* (2d ed.; Wiesbaden, 1975).

[39] Burford, *Craftsmen,* pp. 58–59; Mitchell, *Economics,* pp. 162–63, proffers very theoretical figures on the capital costs of slaves, but Finley, *Ancient Economy,* pp. 83–84, correctly points out we lack the data to calculate the profitability of ancient slavery. Bolkestein, *Economic Life,* pp. 47–48, argues no differentiation in wages, but his example of a physician is poorly chosen in view of the rewards of Democedes (and Solon fr. 1).

[40] M. I. Finley, "The Servile Statuses of Ancient Greece," *Revue internationale des droits de l'antiquité,* 3. ser., VII (1960), pp. 165–89; it should be kept in mind that Marxist thought on slave-holding structures in antiquity admits considerable variation therein (Y. M. Zhukov, *Journal of World History,* II [1954], p. 490).

[41] *Iliad* XII. 433–35, XXI. 441ff.; Hesiod, *Works and Days* 370 (generally taken as spurious; cf. L. B. Quaglia, *Gli "Erga" di Esiodo* [Turin, 1973], p. 209). Bolkestein, *Economic Life,* p. 66, comments on the meaning of *ergodotes* (employer) and *ergolabos* (one who accepts a job, as Phidias took on the construction of the statue of Athena) and concludes that there was no *class* of wage-earners in ancient Greece; Finley, *Ancient Economy,* pp. 65ff. suggests the difficulty in conceptualizing "labor."

[42] *Odyssey,* XV. 319–20.

[43] Herodotus II. 167; W. R. Connor, *The New Politicians of Fifth-Century Athens* (Princeton, 1971), pp. 153–54.

[44] *Politics* III. 2. 1277b; Xenophon, *Oeconomicus* 4. 2, 6. 5; other references are given by Bolkestein, *Economic Life,* pp. 72–73. Cf. A. Aymard, "L'Idée de travail dans la Grèce archaïque," *Journal de psychologie,*

XLI (1948), pp. 29–45, and "Hiérarchie du travail et autarcie individuelle dans la Grèce archaïque," *Revue d'histoire de la philosophie et d'histoire générale de la civilisation,* XI (1943), pp. 124–46.

[45] George, *London Life,* p. 338, notes that three truss societies existed in London by 1807 and on p. 203 reports an estimate of 1842 that one-tenth of London's laborers suffered from hernias.

[46] *Politics* III. 3. 1278a; so too for potters, Plato, *Republic* IV. 421.

[47] Webster, *Potter and Patron,* pp. 297–300, probably exaggerates the familiarity.

[48] Munich, Antikensammlungen 2307 (A. Furtwängler and K. Reichhold, *Griechische Vasenmalerei* [Munich, 1904], p. 14). Zimmern, *Greek Commonwealth,* pp. 257ff., is a good example of overemphasis on pure delight in craftsmanship; Will, *Le Monde grec,* pp. 655–56, and *Annales,* IX (1954), p. 20, presents somewhat the same view on artistic artisans. Pleket, *Vestigia,* XVII (1973), p. 9, cites other examples of pride in one's skill (even that of a slave working in the Laurium mines).

[49] Webster, *Potter and Patron,* pp. 5ff. (who somehow drops Mnesiades out of his calculations); Raubitschek, *Dedications from the Athenian Acropolis,* no. 178.

[50] Doctors: Herodotus III. 129–37; Solon fr. 1, lines 57–62. Architects: Burford, *Temple Builders at Epidauros,* pp. 138–40; R. Holloway, "Architect and Engineer in Archaic Greece," *Harvard Studies in Classical Philology,* LXXIII (1968), pp. 281–90.

[51] Andrewes, *The Greeks,* p. 146, comments at the close of a thoughtful chapter on traders, craftsmen, and slaves that "there is room for a good deal more hard thinking about the place which trade and manufacture really occupied in the life of Greek society."

CHAPTER V

[1] Hammond, *City in the Ancient World,* pp. 6–8, 346–47, surveys efforts to define the term "city"; see also A. Giuliano, *Urbanistica delle città greche* (Milan, 1961); Finley, *Ancient Economy,* pp. 123ff.

[2] D. W. Roller, *AJA,* LXXVIII (1974), p. 154, cites Tanagra, Thera, etc.; generally W. A. McDonald, *The Political Meeting Places of the Greeks* (Baltimore, 1943), and R. Martin, *Recherches sur l'agora grecque* (Paris, 1951).

[3] A. von Gerkan, *Griechische Städteanlagen* (Berlin, 1924), argues that the acropolis was a center for aristocrats; the agora, for the general public. A. Wokalek, *Griechische Stadtbefestigungen* (Bonn, 1973), pp.

13ff., disproves this antithesis adequately and concludes (p. 23) that the aristocratic element in itself was scarcely a directing influence in urban planning.

[4] Drerup, *Baukunst,* pp. 97–99, provides a good summary. See generally F. Castagnoli, *Orthogonal Town Planning in Antiquity* (Cambridge, Mass., 1971), pp. 9ff.; F. E. Winter, *Greek Fortifications* (London, 1971), p. 29, compactly sums the evidence; J. B. Ward-Perkins, *Cities of Ancient Greece and Italy: Planning in Classical Antiquity* (New York, 1974), pp. 10–13, is brief and general.

[5] R. V. Nicholls's drawing, as in *BSA,* LIII–IV (1958–59), pp. 1ff. I do not find that anyone has ever noted or countered the cautious suggestion of Kirsten, *Griechische Polis,* p. 52, after personal inspection, that the wall appeared to him to be only a terrace support—"nur am seinem Westfuss liegen sichere Stadtmauerreste." See generally R. L. Scranton, *Greek Walls* (Cambridge, Mass., 1941); R. E. Wycherley, *How the Greeks Built Cities* (London, 1967 reprint), pp. 50ff., is judicious.

[6] K. Schefold, *Antike Kunst,* IX (1966), pp. 116ff., and *Archaeology,* XXI (1968), pp. 280–81.

[7] E. Vanderpool, in *Phoros* (Locust Valley, N.Y., 1974), pp. 156–60; Herodotus IX. 13 and Thucydides I. 89. Andocides, *On the Peace* 37–38; and Lysias 34. 2, however, asserted that Athens got its wall and fleets approximately at the same time; does this refer only to the Long Walls? Winters, *Greek Fortifications,* pp. 61–64, accepts a pre-Persian wall; F. G. Maier, *Griechische Mauerbauinschriften,* I (Heidelberg, 1959), pp. 19–20, and Wokalek, *Griechische Stadtbefestigungen,* p. 59, are more doubtful.

[8] Wycherley, *How the Greeks Built Cities,* p. 10.

[9] F. Tritsch, "Die Stadtbildungen des Altertums und die griechische Polis," *Klio,* XXII (1928), pp. 1–83.

[10] R. Martin, *L'Urbanisme dans la Grèce antique* (2d ed.; Paris, 1974), pp. 30–31. L. Mumford, *The Culture of Cities* (New York, 1938), pp. 18ff., discounts the role of trade itself in promoting the initial rise of medieval cities; cf. Duby, *Guerriers et paysans,* p. 154. On Chinese cities see P. Wheatley, *The Pivot of the Four Quarters* (Edinburgh, 1971).

[11] Hammond, *City in the Ancient World,* pp. 153, 170–71, 350; Wycherley, *How the Greeks Built Cities,* pp. 3–4.

[12] The "city" of the Phaeacians (*Odyssey* VI. 259–69) might be taken as evidence in this respect; but as Finley, *World of Odysseus,* p. 107, notes, there is no reference to Phaeacian trade, and the taunt that Odysseus was a merchant (quoted above, chap. II) was delivered there.

[13] Generally, I. T. Hill, *The Ancient City of Athens* (Cambridge,

Mass., 1953); W. Judeich, *Topographie von Athen* (2d ed.; Munich, 1931); and on the Agora, H. A. Thompson and R. E. Wycherley, *The Athenian Agora XIV: The History, Shape and Uses of an Ancient City Center* (Princeton, 1972).

[14] *Odyssey* VII. 81; cf. *Iliad* II. 546ff. Herodotus V. 71 speaks only of a statue.

[15] E. Brann, *Hesperia,* XXX (1961), p. 306. Parenthetically, it is intriguing that in Rome (always considered backward) the regularization of the Forum took place about the same date.

[16] Herodotus I. 60, 62 (compare I. 114 on the distinction of *kome* and *polis* in the story of Cyrus).

[17] C. A. Roebuck, "Some Aspects of Urbanization in Corinth," *Hesperia,* XLI (1972), pp. 96–127; more generally Will, *Korinthiaka,* pp. 572ff.

[18] Thucydides I. 10.

[19] Aristotle, *Constitution of Athens* 50.

[20] Cook, *CAH* II. 2, p. 800; and *BSA,* LIII–IV (1958–59), pp. 16–17.

[21] Braudel, *Capitalism and Material Life,* pp. 20—21, 375–77. Two anonymous critics of the present study sharply disagreed on my estimate for the city of Athens: one endorsed it completely, the other felt that Cleisthenes' reorganization attests a much larger urban population (on this point see J. S. Traill, *The Political Organization of Attica* [*Hesperia,* Suppl. XIV, 1975], pp. 55 and 71). F. J. Frost, *American Journal of Ancient History,* I (1976), p. 67, however, considers sixth-century Athens "small and little more than a marketing center for the rural hinterland"; he appropriately cites J. S. Boersma, *Athenian Building Policy* (Groningen, 1970), pp. 11–64.

[22] Boardman, *Athenian Red Figure Vases,* p. 221 (a point often noted and obvious in the decline of agricultural scenes).

[23] Aristotle fr. 510 Rose (= Athenaeus VIII. 348).

[24] Mumford, *Culture of Cities,* p. 5.

[25] B. Dunkley, "Greek Fountain-Buildings before 300 B.C.," *BSA,* XXXVI (1935–36), pp. 142–204; Busolt, *Staatskunde,* I, p. 405; Martin, *L'Urbanisme,* pp. 84–89. M. White, *JHS,* LXXIV (1954), p. 41, quotes a modern expert opinion that the Samos tunnel required ten years' work; J. Goodfield and S. Toulmin, "How Was the Tunnel of Eupalinus Aligned?" *Isis,* LVI (1965), pp. 46–55, suggests the problem was relatively simply solved in a practical manner.

[26] Weber, *Gesammelte Aufsätze,* p. 13; Braudel, *Capitalism and Material Life,* p. 373, calls cities both electric transformers and "oppressive,

parasitical formations"; Finley, *Ancient Economy,* p. 125, presents a view of a city as ranging "from complete parasitism at the one end to full symbiosis at the other." Cf. the cool assessment of the city as a market for the agricultural sector by Pleket, *Vestigia,* XVII (1973), p. 36, who points out that E. Le Roy-Ladurie, *Les Paysans de Languedoc* (Paris, 1968), pays almost no attention to the cities.

[27] S. Smith, "A Pre-Greek Coinage in the Near East?" *NC,* 5. ser. II (1922), pp. 176–85.

[28] As in an inscription from Gortyn (M. Guarducci, *Rivista di filologia classica,* n.s. XXII–XXIII [1944–45], pp. 171–80); on dating see Jeffery, *Local Scripts,* p. 313; L. Breglia, "I Precedenti della moneta vera e propria nel bacino del Mediterraneo," *Congresso internazionale numismatica,* I (Rome, 1965), pp. 7ff.; M. Balmuth, "Remarks on the Earliest Coins," *Studies Presented to George Hanfmann,* ed. D. G. Mitten *et al.* (Mainz, 1971), pp. 1–7. The Greek words obol and drachma are directly connected to iron spits as individual items and as "handfuls." Spits are surveyed by M. C. Oeconomides, *Athens Annals of Archaeology,* II (1969), pp. 436–45.

[29] G. K. Jenkins, *Ancient Greek Coins* (London, 1972), p. 9; Herodotus I. 94.

[30] P. Naster surveys reverse punches in *Numismatique antique: problemes et méthodes* (*Annales de l'Est,* no. 44, 1975), pp. 17–22. I accept here the common view that "dumps" preceded coins with designs, but firm proof for such development remains to be found.

[31] L. Weidauer, "Probleme der frühen Elektronprägung," *Typos,* I (1975), pp. 71ff., argues the Artemisium deposit was closed by the mid-seventh century; E. S. G. Robinson, *JHS,* LXXI (1951), pp. 156–67, and P. Jacobsthal, ibid., pp. 85–95, would give this material a date just after 600; Martin Price was kind enough to tell me he would lower it even further. See also S. Kiyonaga, "The Date of the Beginning of Coinage in Asia Minor," *Revue suisse de numismatique,* LII (1973), pp. 5–16, and a large number of other essays in earlier literature.

[32] Herodotus VII. 28; Plutarch, *Moralia* 262d-e preserves the information that Pythius had a mine on his lands which he worked with his own peasants.

[33] M. Laloux, "La Circulation des monnaies d'électrum de Cyzique," *Revue belge de numismatique,* CXVII (1971), pp. 31–69.

[34] The coinage of Aegina is usually dated just after 600 (as by R. R. Holloway, *American Numismatic Society Museum Notes,* XVII [1971], pp. 1–21; W. L. Brown, *NC,* 6. ser. X [1950], pp. 177–204, gave *c.* 610); M. Price and N. Waggoner, *Archaic Greek Silver Coinage of the Asyut*

Hoard (London, 1975), seek to lower it, but as my student Bruce Holle observes, it is difficult thus to compress over 500 dies known for Aeginetan coinage, the largest number from any sixth-century mint. For this and other information I am much indebted to his dissertation on the origins and effects of coinage on the Greek *poleis* in the age of expansion.

[35] C. M. Kraay, "The Archaic Owls of Athens," *NC,* 6. ser. XVI (1956), pp. 43–68; E. Levy, *Parola del Passato,* XXVIII (1973), pp. 88–91, still pushes the *Wappenmünzen* back into the era of Solon, and H. A. Cahn has defended early dates in unpublished lectures at London and New York. In *NC* 7. ser. XVI (1976), pp. 219–22, I have published a clay sealing from Persepolis which strongly suggests that the Athena/owl series began at about the point Kraay puts it.

[36] Himeran coinage is discussed in *Annali Istituto Italiano di Numismatica,* XVI–XVII (1971) and its circulation by A. M. Longo, XVIII– IX (1971–72), pp. 25–57; on Spanish silver see Dunbabin, *Western Greeks,* p. 248. For general bibliography on Greek mints cf. C. M. Kraay and M. Hirmer, *Greek Coins* (London, 1966), and Jenkins, *Ancient Greek Coins.*

[37] E. Will, "Les sources des métaux monnayés dans le monde grec," *Annales de l'Est,* no. 44 (1975), pp. 97–102.

[38] *Sylloge Inscriptionum Graecarum* [3], 218 (Olbia); R. S. Stroud, "An Athenian Law on Silver Coinage," *Hesperia,* XLIII (1974), pp. 157–88.

[39] E.g., L. Breglia, "Le antiche rotte di Mediterraneo documentate da monete e pese," *Rendiconti dell'Accademia di archeologia, lettere e belle arti di Napoli,* XXX (1955), pp. 211–326 (summarized and criticized by draay, *NC,* 6 ser. XVII [1957], pp. 289–95).

[40] C. M. Kraay, "Hoards, Small Change, and the Origin of Coinage," *JHS,* LXXXIV (1964), pp. 76–91. L. Lacroix, "La monnaie grecque et les problèmes de la circulation monétaire," *Bulletin de la classe des lettres,* Academie royale belgique, 5. ser. LV (1969), pp. 169–80, comes back to commercial utility, as does K. Christ, "Die Griechen und das Geld," *Saeculum,* XV (1964), pp. 214–29; cf. the survey by P. Vidal-Naquet, "Fonction de la monnaie dans la Gréce archaïque," *Annales,* XXIII (1968), pp. 206–8. M. J. Price discusses early copper coinage in *Essays in Greek Coinage Presented to Stanley Robinson* (Oxford, 1968), pp. 94–104; "dolphins" from Olbia may be even earlier than Sicilian copper (V. V. Lapin, "A Group of Olbian Dolphins from Berezan," *Materialy po Arkheologii Severnago Prichernomor'ia,* VII [1971], pp. 42–51).

[41] For the observation about small pieces at the Artemisium I am indebted to Holle (and indeed these small fractions will be found very

commonly in major collections). L. Breglia, "Il materiale proveniente dalla base centrale dell'Artemision di Efeso e le monete di Lidia," *Annali Instituto Italiano di Numismatica,* XVIII–XIX (1970–72), pp. 9–24, even suggests that the *trite* was the largest denomination struck until the early sixth century and should be termed the "starter."

[42] As at Siphnos (Herodotus III. 57) or Athens (VII. 144); cf. Will, *Korinthiaka,* p. 499. J. J. Buchanan, *Theorika* (Locust Valley, N.Y., 1962), deals essentially with later periods.

[43] A point stressed by R. M. Cook, "Speculations on the Origins of Coinage," *Historia,* VII (1958), pp. 257–62.

[44] [Aristotle], *Oeconomica* II. 2. 4.

[45] *Inscriptiones Graecae,* XIII. 9. no. 1273; Meiggs and Lewis, *Greek Historical Inscriptions,* no. 8 (= Jeffery, *BSA,* LI [1956], pp. 157–67). Huxley, *Early Ionians,* pp. 82–83, also thinks that the fines of Chios were set in terms of bullion; the 2000 staters given by Lydia to Alcaeus and his friends (fr. 69) were even more certainly in bullion (*contra* L. Breglia, *Quaderni Ticinesi* [1974], pp. 7–12).

[46] Duby, *Guerriers et paysans,* p. 79; cf. his remarks on the later spread of coinage (pp. 158, 241, 285).

[47] G. Le Rider, "Contremarques et surfrappes dans l'antiquité grecque," *Annales de l'Est,* no. 44 (1975), pp. 27–56, discusses the explanations given in the text and finds none by itself completely adequate. The London example is BMC Lydia no. 5.

[48] Xenophon, *Ways and Means* 4. 7; for other references see Knorringa, *Emporos,* pp. 17–18.

[49] *An Inventory of Greek Coin Hoards,* ed. M. Thompson *et al.* (New York, 1973), nos. 1–5, 354, 689, 1152–1164, 1176, 1478, 1632–1633, 1872–1874. Of these Martin Price would lower nos. 1, 3, and 1874 to 500 or later; I have added nos. 1 and 3, both from Asia Minor, in *Coin Hoards,* I (London, 1975). Cf. the larger Egyptian hoards (nos. 1636ff.) and the contents of the Asyut hoard of *c.* 475, published by Price and Waggoner.

[50] Braudel, *Capitalism and Material Life,* p. 348, observes of his period, "The monetary system in Europe suffered from two incurable diseases. On the one hand there were external flights of precious metals; on the other, metals were immobilized by being saved and hoarded. As a result the engine incessantly and irreparably lost some of its fuel." The latter problem, though present in early Greece, was evidently minor.

[51] J. V. A. Fine, *Horoi* (*Hesperia,* Suppl. IX [1951], pp. 116ff.); M. I. Finley, *Studies in Land and Credit in Ancient Athens, 500–200 B.C.* (New Brunswick, N.J., 1952), pp. 44ff., on *apotimema proikos.* H. J.

Habbakuk, in *The European Nobility in the Eighteenth Century,* ed. Goodwin, pp. 8–9, observes that loans of English nobles were often for dowries, given in cash, not land; an overabundance of daughters could ruin an estate more than the gaming table.

[52] E.g., Zimmern, *Greek Commonwealth,* p. 115; Adkins, *Moral Values and Political Behaviour,* chap. 3. As Will, *Études archéologiques,* p. 155, dryly noted, Heichelheim originally placed the beginning of money in the eighth century; in the English edition (I, p. 481) he accepted a much later dating but did not change the argument of his text as to its effects (pp. 215ff.).

[53] W. L. Brown, "Pheidon's Alleged Aeginetan Coinage," *NC,* 6. ser. X (1950), pp. 177–204. Michell, *Economics,* p. 316 (publ. 1957), still accepted the Pheidonian picture, which D. Kagan tried to revive in *Transactions of the American Philological Association,* XCI (1960), pp. 121–36.

[54] Christ, *Saeculum,* XV (1964), p. 218; Welskopf, *Produktionsverhältnisse,* pp. 305ff., gives the Marxist views.

[55] The introductory remark of M. M. Postan, "The Rise of A Money Economy," *Economic History Review,* XIV (1944), pp. 123–34; as he goes on to observe, "The term 'money economy' can be taken to mean the relative frequency of money payments, while the word 'rise' can be used to denote not their birthday but their general expansion," a useful comment for sixth-century Greece as well.

[56] Aristotle, *Ethics* V. 5. 1133a (again IX. 1. 1164a); and *Politics* I. 3. 1257a; cf. M. Giacchero, "Ragionamenti socratici sulla ricchezza e sulla moneta nel dialogo pseudoplatonico Eryxias," *Rivista italiana di numismatica,* 5. ser. XXI (1973), pp. 7–38. E. Will is thoughtful and original in "De l'Aspect éthique des origines grecques de la monnaie," *Revue historique,* CCXII (1954), pp. 209–31; he returns to the matter in *Annales de l'Est,* no. 44 (1975), pp. 233–46, where he discusses especially gifts as promoting social unity. Braudel, *Capitalism and Material Life,* pp. 325–36, provides useful parallels.

CHAPTER VI

[1] Thersites: *Iliad* II. 212ff.; cf. XII. 211ff. Beauty: *Odyssey* IV. 62–64 (quoted below), XIII. 223, XVIII. 217–19. Role in war: my essay, "Homeric Cowards and Heroes," *The Classical Tradition: Literary and Historical Studies in Honor of Harry Caplan,* ed. L. Wallach (Ithaca, N.Y., 1966), pp. 58–63. Fanta, *Der Staat,* pp. 13ff., provides abundant references.

[2] A. W. H. Adkins, *Merit and Responsibility* (Oxford, 1960), p. 34. The distinction stressed in the text may be found also in G. M. Calhoun, "Classes and Masses in Homer," *CP,* XXIX (1934), pp. 192–208; and H. Strasburger, "Der soziologische Aspekt der homerischen Epen," *Gymnasium,* LX (1953), pp. 97–114.

[3] A point stressed by R. Mousnier, *Social Hierarchies* (London, 1973). "Class" is a fiercely debated term; Finley, *Ancient Economy,* pp. 48–50, cites S. Ossowski, *Class Structure in the Social Consciousness* (London, 1963). On the acceptance of aristocracy, and its limits, see the essay by J. G. A. Pocock, "The Classical Theory of Deference," *American Historical Review,* LXXXI (1976), pp. 516–23, and his forthcoming study on Harrington.

[4] M. K. Langdon, *AJA,* LXXIX (1975), pp. 139–40; Jeffery, *Local Scripts,* pp. 15–16, thinks it the product of a literary person of non-Attic origin.

[5] As Julius Gerlack, *Aner Agathos* (Diss., Munich, 1932), showed, that term did not yet have a class significance in the seventh century; in Homer and even in Archilochus bravery and beauty do not necessarily go hand in hand (*Iliad* V. 801, 787). On later views of moral superiority cf. Whibley, *Greek Oligarchies,* pp. 25–29.

[6] Plutarch, *Nob.* 2 (ed. Bernadakis, VII); *Odyssey* IV. 62–64; Archilochus fr. 195 (cf. fr. 65).

[7] Sappho fr. 155. Raubitschek, *Dedications from the Athenian Acropolis,* pp. 464–67, is thoughtful on the difficulty in distinguishing aristocrats in our epigraphic evidence due to the lack of titles.

[8] Stobaeus, *Anthologium* IV. 29 (86. 25) = Aristotle fr. 92 Rose (cf. *Politics* V. 1. 1301b). The sentiment was repeated by Lord Burleigh, "Gentilie is naught but ancient riches" (Roy Perrott, *The Aristocrats* [London, 1968], p. 256). Busolt, *Staatskunde,* I, pp. 210–12, gives a list of terms applied to upper and lower classes. Athenian archons; Aristotle, *Constitution of Athens* 3; cf. *Politics* II. 8. 1273a and IV. 5. 1293b.

[9] G. E. M. de Ste Croix, *Ancient Society and Institutions* (Oxford, 1966), pp. 109–14, explodes the exaggerated views of the estate of Phaenippus and cites Lysias 19. 29, "more than 300 [square] plethra of land." In Mycenaean Pylos (M. Ventris and J. Chadwick, *Documents in Mycenaean Greek* [Oxford, 1956], p. 237) the king's *temenos* may have run 120 hectares; a medium holding, about 5 hectares. *The European Nobility in the Eighteenth Century,* ed. Goodwin, has estimates that one-third the cultivable land of Spain at that time was held by four great houses (p. 48); the Radziwill estate in the Ukraine was half the size of Ireland (p. 167).

[10] J. K. Davies, *Athenian Propertied Families 600–300 B.C.* (Oxford,

1971), pp. xxff. (though these later trierarchs were not necessarily landed aristocrats); Polybius XII. 5. 6. At Corinth the Bacchiad state had a governing class of essentially 200 members (Will, *Korinthiaka,* pp. 295ff.; Diodorus VII fr. 9); D. W. S. Hunt, *JHS,* LXVII (1947), pp. 68–76, suggests the countryside of Teos was held in the main by some 40 families.

[11] Phocylides fr. 3, cf. fr. 9, "Seek a living, and when thou hast a living, virtue." Sappho fr. 148 sharply observes that "wealth (*ploutos*) without worth (*aretas*) is no harmless housemate"; but their conjunction puts one on a peak.

[12] Whibley, *Greek Oligarchies,* pp. 41, 111; Michell, *Economics,* p. 42. Postan, *Economic History Review,* XIV (1944), p. 123, dryly comments on "how frequently the middle-class formula has been used to bridge gaps in historical knowledge."

[13] Davis, *Rise of the Atlantic Economies,* pp. 60, 279; H. J. Habbakuk, "English Landownership, 1680–1740," *Economic History Review,* X (1940), pp. 2–17.

[14] At some point toward 500 B.C. the Solonian classes were capitalized in terms of money; the *hippeis* thus had to have 3000 drachmas and the *zeugitai* 1000, the range in which Mnesiades and Andocides would have fallen. Busolt, *Staatskunde,* II, pp. 820–21, felt that definition of Solonian classes in terms of revenues had not been a part of Solon's own laws; R. Thomsen, *Eisphora* (Copenhagen, 1964), pp. 149ff., and others disagree.

[15] Plato, *Republic* VIII. 565a.

[16] Theognis 54–55; country-folk wear goatskins in Aristophanes, *Ecclesiazusae* 724, *Lysistrata* 1151 (cf. Pollux VII. 68). After reaching this view I was happy to find Will, *Annales de l'Est,* no. 44 (1975), p. 242, n. 36, also emphasizing the rural bearing of Theognis' passage; his discussion (pp. 241–45) bears chiefly on *kakoi* in the Old Oligarch and Aristophanes. Against this view one might wish to advance the emphasis in archaic poets on the mutability of wealth (e.g., Solon fr. 1, 15); but this could occur in a rural as well as a commercial setting.

[17] In the counties Habbakuk studied (*Economic History Review,* X [1940], pp. 2–17), interestingly enough, the income of a peer was, on the average, three times that of a squire.

[18] Hesiod may be considered the least studied and most poorly understood poet of our period (apart from philosophical investigation of his *Theogony*). J. Kerschensteiner, "Zu Aufbau und Gedankenführung von Hesiods Erga," *Hermes,* LXXIX (1944), pp. 149–91, gives full references to earlier work; see more recently F. Solmsen, *Hesiod and Aeschylus*

(Ithaca, N.Y., 1949); P. Walcot, *Greek Peasants, Ancient and Modern* (Manchester, 1971), and *Hesiod and the Near East* (Cardiff, 1966); Quaglia, *Gli "Erga" di Esiodo,* a study primarily in intellectual and ethical terms, is useful in the present connection for its careful examination of the authenticity of lines 381–694, some of which are quoted in these pages. Adkins, *Values and Political Behaviour,* pp. 24ff., thinks Hesiod was advising aristocrats of declining fortune; Roebuck, *Trade and Politics in the Ancient World,* p. 100, calls him a "substantial free-holding farmer," which is closer to the mark.

[19] *Works and Days* 589; in his later discussion of the days of the month slaves also appear.

[20] Phocylides fr. 12; cf. Theognis 219–20; 331–32, 335–36; Aristotle, *Ethics* X. 8. 1179a, who cites Solon and Anaxagoras to this end. So too Archilochus' carpenter (fr. 15) does not desire the power of a tyrant. The view carried on to Euripides, *Suppliants* 238ff., which distinguishes the rich, "a useless set that ever crave for more," the poor, and the midmost class which preserves a *polis.*

[21] M. Detienne, "En Grèce archaïque: géométrie, politique et société," *Annales,* XX (1965), pp. 425–41.

[22] On the inclusion of the aristocrats in the phalanx see the firm statement by Snodgrass, *JHS,* LXXXV (1965), p. 114, which has since been supported by the analysis of P. A. L. Greenhalgh, *Early Greek Warfare: Horsemen and Chariots in the Homeric and Archaic Ages* (Cambridge, 1973).

[23] Phocylides fr. 6.

[24] This desire of non-aristocratic elements to ape their betters can be abundantly documented from Theognis; a purported Solonian law (Ruschenbusch F 74) even forbade slaves to exercise in the gymnasium or to have boy-lovers.

[25] Three fairly recent essays may be cited though they bear more on the classic period (and all are unfavorable toward elites): R. R. Bolgar in R. Wilkinson, ed., *Governing Elites: Studies in Training and Selection* (New York, 1966), pp. 23–49; R. Seager in F. C. Jaher, ed., *The Rich, The Well Born and the Powerful* (Urbana, Ill., 1975), pp. 7–26; E. C. Welskopf, "Elitevorstellungen und Elitebildung in der hellenischen Polis," *Klio,* XLIII–V (1965), pp. 49–64. See more generally H. I. Marrou, *History of Education in Antiquity* (New York, 1956), pp. 5–13, 43–44. The dates of specialized studies on Greek aristocracy suggest the unwarranted neglect of the topic; Whibley's *Greek Oligarchies* appeared in 1896; G. Méautis, *L'Aristocratie athénienne* (Paris, 1927), is brief. Hasebroek, *Griechische Wirtschafts- und Gesellschaftsgeschichte,* pp.

73–135, is reasonably rounded. Even for modern times studies of aristocracies are not easy to come by; some of those which I cite for specific information are not major works, though useful.

[26] J. P. Vernant, "Le Mariage en Gréce archaïque," *Parola del Passato,* XXVIII (1973), pp. 51–74; Gernet, *Anthropologie,* pp. 344–59; Heuss, *Antike und Abendland,* II (1946), pp. 49–50. Herodotus VI. 126ff. on the courting of Agariste is a remarkable example; the ban by Andros on marriage with Parians in the mid-seventh century suggests an earlier general acceptance of interstate marriage rights (Plutarch, *Greek Questions* 30). Alcaeus attacked Pittacus, whose father may have been a Thracian (but was called *basileus*); Mazzarino, *Fra Oriente e Occidente,* p. 192; D. L. Page, *Sappho and Alcaeus* (Oxford, 1955), pp. 170–71.

[27] Solon fr. 13 (repeated in Theognis 1253–54).

[28] H. Troyat, *Pushkin* (New York 1950), p. 13; quoted by R. Redfield, *The Primitive World and Its Transformations* (Ithaca, 1953), p. 40. See also Redfield's *Peasant Society and Culture* (Chicago, 1956), pp. 64–68, 131–37; and for another modern parallel G. Bazin, *The Baroque* (Greenwich, Conn., 1968), p. 322.

[29] *Ethics* I. 5. 1095b, IX. 2. 1165a, X. 8. 1179a.

[30] Mazzarino, *Fra Oriente e Occidente,* pp. 8–9, gives a good summation; for Marxist examples in western literature see Thomson, *Prehistoric Aegean,* pp. 149ff., or Willetts, *Aristocratic Society in Ancient Crete,* pp. 87–88 (cf. review by J. Bleicken, *Gnomon,* XXIX [1957], pp. 271–72), though Willetts has a very good treatment of the masculine character of historic Cretan society. Cf. H. J. Rose, "Prehistoric Greece and Mother-Right," *Folk-Lore,* XXXVII (1926), pp. 213–44.

[31] *Odyssey* VII. 66ff; XI. 427.; Hesiod, *Works and Days* 373–75, 702–4; *Theogony* 591ff.; Semonides fr. 7 (recently translated and published by H. Lloyd-Jones); cf. Phocylides fr. 2.

[32] W. A. Müller, *Nacktheit und Entblössung in der altorientalischen und älteren griechischen Kunst* (Leipzig, 1906).

[33] A. Andrewes, "Phratries in Homer," *Hermes,* LXXXIX (1961), pp. 129–40; Busolt, *Staatskunde,* II, pp. 959–60; M. P. Nilsson, *Cults, Myths, Oracles and Politics in Ancient Greece* (Lund, 1951), pp. 150–70, sought to find a blood-relationship in the origins of phratries. An early grave at Argoes has fire irons and spits; Drerup, *Baukunst,* p. 127, makes the not impossible suggestion that the dead man had been leader of a phratry which had communal meals.

[34] B. E. Richardson, *Old Age among the Ancient Greeks* (Baltimore, 1933), collects the evidence. E. Bethe, "Die dorische Knabenliebe, Ihre

Ethik und Ihre Idee," *Rheinisches Museum,* LXII (1907), pp. 438–75, remains useful even if an error is suggested in the adjective in his title.

[35] Archilochus fr. 96 (cf. fr. 11, 241–42). *Payment* of some sort took place; the prostitutes of Sardis who erected the tomb of Alyattes with the market people and craftsmen (Herodotus I. 93) presumably contributed more than labor. Courtesans such as Rhodopis were sufficiently famous to gain attention from Herodotus II. 134–35.

[36] So on Lesbos (Alcaeus fr. 130). See generally Pomeroy, *Goddesses, Whores, Wives, and Slaves,* c. 3.

[37] *Politics* VII. 8. 1329a.

[38] Herodotus I. 30; cf. Callinus, Tyrtaeus fr. 4, 7, Mimnermus fr. 13, Solon fr. 2; B. Snell, *The Discovery of the Mind* (Harper paperback, 1960), pp. 170–77, is excellent on the elaboration of the idea of *arete.*

[39] F. Matz, *Geschichte der griechischen Kunst,* I (Frankfort, 1950), pl. 286a; British Museum B 421 (Boardman, *Athenian Black Figure Vases,* fig. 110). Cf. Bolkestein, *Economic Life,* pp. 35–36; H. G. Buchholz, G. Jährens, I. Maull, *Jagd und Fischfang (Archaeologia Homerica,* II, pt. J; Göttingen, 1973).

[40] H. W. Pleket, "Zur Soziologie des antiken Sports," *Mededelingen van het Nederlands Instituut te Rome,* XXXVI (1974), pp. 57–87. Contests occur from Archilochus fr. 217 onward; on the agonistic spirit see V. Ehrenberg, *Ost und West* (Brünn, 1935), pp. 63–96.

[41] Xenophanes fr. 2 (H. Fränkel, *Dichtung und Philosophie des frühen Griechentums* [Munich, 1962], pp. 384–86, compares Tyrtaeus fr. 9). G. Pugliese Carratelli, *Atti e Memorie della Società Magna Graecia,* n. s. VI (1965), pp. 13–17, as cited by Pleket, p. 67. Plutarch, *Solon* 23 (= Ruschenbusch F 143a), asserts that under Solon's laws an Athenian victor in the Olympic games received 500 drachmas (or *medimnoi*).

[42] Isocrates 16. 33. S. D. Markman, *The Horse in Greek Art* (Baltimore, 1943), is chronologically insecure; Greenhalgh, *Early Greek Warfare,* is generally excellent; J. K. Anderson, *Ancient Greek Horsemanship* (Berkeley, 1961). As Perrott, *The Aristocrats,* p. 246, puts it, English rural aristocracy was "centered very largely on the totem of the Horse" (though fox-hunting was largely a nineteenth-century development; cf. E. Wingfield-Stratton, *The Squire and His Relations* [London, 1956], p. 259).

[43] Heracleides, *FHG,* II, p. 217; cf. Aristotle, *Politics* VI. 3. 1289b.

[44] The description is by Franklin Blake in Wilkie Collins, *The Moonstone* (Second Period, Third Narrative), I omit the italics of the original. Cf. Trollope's picture of Sir Harry Hotspur, which may seem far afield from ancient Greece; but the nineteenth century was perhaps the last era

in which the role of a "gentleman" was accepted both by himself and by his "inferiors."

⁴⁵ As Adkins does in *Merit and Responsibility* and *Moral Values;* cf. Snell, *Discovery of the Mind,* pp. 69–70, and Starr, *Origins,* pp. 272–75, 295–98, 343–45. It is also possible that later Greeks selected from the work of Archilochus passages which best expressed his relative modernity. In a very different world R. Brentano, *Rome before Avignon* (New York, 1974), p. 208, observes that "clustering and role-playing seem naturally to complement each other. The individual Roman stepping forth from his group to act alone did so not only perhaps with compensatory brio, but also with the aid of a great type role to support him in his unwonted loneliness." H. Strasburger, "Der Einzelne und die Gemeinschaft im Denken der Griechen," *Historische Zeitschrift,* CLXXVII (1954), pp. 227–48, overstresses spiritual freedom from the *Gemeinschaft.*

⁴⁶ K. Kübler, *Altattische Malerei* (Tübingen, 1950), pp. 29–30, suggests this interesting parallel as connected "mit der äussersten Verfestigung der attischen Adelsmacht" and then its decline.

⁴⁷ Archilochus fr. 115–16, 118; Alcman fr. 23; H. Fränkel, "Man's 'Ephemeros' Nature according to Pindar and Others," *Transactions of the American Philological Association,* LXXVII (1946), pp. 131–45, and other works cited in Starr, *Origins,* p. 280.

⁴⁸ D. Asheri, *Distribuzioni di terre nell'antica Grecia,* Memorie dell'Accademia delle scienze di Torino, classe di scienze morali, storiche e filologiche, 4 ser. X (1966), p. 9. W. K. Lacey, *The Family in Classical Greece* (London, 1968), does not decide relations to the *genos* as against the phratry.

⁴⁹ E. R. Dodds, *The Greeks and the Irrational* (Beacon paperback, 1957), pp. 45–48, thus suggests the rise of difficulty between fathers and sons; but cf. Zeldin, *France,* pp. 316ff., who points out that in France of the Old Regime fathers and sons were often very distant on the aristocratic level (Chateaubriand froze on seeing his father). Also, "while their fathers were alive children could not get at their mothers."

⁵⁰ For the conventional view see Thomson, *Prehistoric Aegean,* pp. 325ff., and many others; C. Hignett, *A History of the Athenian Constitution to the End of the Fifth Century B.C.* (Oxford, 1952), pp. 61–67, notes that *gene* had no place in archaic Attic law. In a Sorbonne thesis, "Recherches sur la nature du *genos:* étude d'histoire sociale Athénienne, periodes archaïque et classique" (defended in the spring of 1975), F. Bourriot almost eliminates *gene* except at Sparta and in some priestly families. One must await publication of this radical work, but I am

much indebted to Mme. de Romilly in giving me a long résumé, and also to Sally Humphreys of the University of London for discussion of the *genos* (on which she is writing a dissertation).

[51] *Iliad* ix. 593–94, XII. 243, XV. 496–98; cf. P. A. L. Greenhalgh, "Patriotism in the Homeric World," *Historia,* XXI (1972), pp. 528–37. Some examples of deserters and traitors in later times are given in my *Political Intelligence in Classical Greece,* Mnemosyne, Supplement 31 (1974), pp. 12–15.

[52] Xenophanes fr. 10. Theognis 607–10 opposes lying, but elsewhere he talks much more of speaking fair and concealing one's thought. As Adkins, *Merit and Responsibility,* p. 181, notes, we cannot be sure it was *aischron,* or shameful, to lie in order to gain prosperity.

[53] Theognis 363–64.

[54] Braudel, *Capitalism and Material Life,* p. 124; parallel attitudes will be found in Finley, *Ancient Economy,* p. 144, or *Economic History Review,* 2 ser. XVIII (1965), p. 39; and others. Pleket, *Vestigia,* XVII (1973), p. 38, observes on the other hand that he is not preaching a sermon and so will not "censure this mentality."

[55] *Illustrated English Social History* (Penguin paperback), I, pp. 67, 179; II, pp. 153–56 (the latter giving a picture of hoarding in the Earl of Bedford's trunk). Davis, *Rise of the Atlantic Economies,* pp. 189, 238, notes that the transfer of capital from trade to land in his period was "not undertaken wholly because of the prestige of landowning; a place had to be found for surplus funds that could not be employed even by a very large-scale trader."

[56] Braudel, *Capitalism and Material Life,* p. 122.

[57] *Odyssey* viii. 236ff.; Xenophanes fr. 3; Athenaeus XII. 525f. (on the problems of attributing this fragment to Asius see G. L. Huxley, *Greek Epic Poetry* [Cambridge, Mass., 1969], pp. 96–97)l Thucydides I. 6 notes that in olden days Athenians also worn golden cicadas in their hair.

[58] On hair styles see S. Marinatos, *Haar- und Barttracht* (*Archaeologia Homerica,* I, pt. B; Göttingen, 1967); Matz, *Geschichte der griechischen Kunst,* I, pp. 472–73, thoughtfully observes that jewelry was not meant to impress the onlooker merely through its value but to give dignity and a sense of beauty befitting a lady, "einem höheren Lebenszusammenhang eingefügt und so über sich selbst erhöht." As J. Maxmin, *JHS,* XCV (1975), p. 178, points out again, female statues at times even had metal jewelry. Perfumes: Archilochus fr. 38; Alcaeus fr. 362; Semonides fr. 14; Athenaeus XV. 686ff.; the references in Sappho are discussed by Page, *Sappho and Alcaeus,* pp. 36, 71, 78–79 (with paral-

lels in Homer); a purported Solonian law against male activity in selling perfumes is Ruschenbusch F 73.

⁵⁹ Alcman fr. 33; Hipponax fr. 39; G. Bruns, *Küchenwesen und Mahlzeiten* (*Archaeologia Homerica,* II, pt. Q; Göttingen, 1970), does not go far down into our period. Drinking bouts occur from Archilochus and Alcaeus onward; in Sappho fr. 94 female symposia appear.

⁶⁰ S. Laser, *Hausrat* (*Archaeologia Homerica,* II, pt. P; Göttingen, 1968); G. M. A. Richter, *The Furniture of the Greeks, Etruscans and Romans* (London, 1966); on lamps, J. D. Beazley, "A Marble Lamp," *JHS,* LX (1940), pp. 22–49. On Athenian houses see J. Travlos, *Pictorial Dictionary of Ancient Athens* (London, 1971), *s. v. oikia.*

⁶¹ Herodotus VI. 86; cf. R. Bogaert, *Les Origines antique de la banque de dépôt* (Leiden, 1966), pp. 35–37.

⁶² Horos 14 in Finley, *Studies in Land and Credit,* lists a house and plot (rural) and a "house in the city" from the late fourth century. S. C. Humphreys, *Daedalus,* Spring 1975, p. 97, stresses the public quality of aristocratic life in the archaic era (though Homeric nobles generally lived in the central meeting place of their *ethnos;* Fanta, *Der Staat,* p. 42; Busolt, *Staatskunde,* II, p. 778).

⁶3 I. Bekker, *Anecdota,* I (Berlin, 1814), p. 257. Gomme, *Population of Athens,* pp. 37–39, points out that most Athenian noble families belonged to urban demes; and Raubitschek, *Dedications from the Athenian Acropolis,* p. 476, that almost all *kalos* names are of Athenians whose demes were urban.

⁶⁴ Sappho fr. 57. In medieval England *rusticus* was also opprobrious (G. G. Coulton, *The Medieval Village* [Cambridge, 1926], p. 91), partly because it inferred serfdom; C. Laye, *The Dark Child* (New York, 1954), p. 62, muses interestingly on the dignity and civil formality of "rustics."

⁶⁵ See generally Fränkel, *Dichtung und Philosophie;* Snell, *Discovery of the Mind;* M. Treu, *Von Homer zur Lyrik* (Munich, 1955).

⁶⁶ Thales: Diogenes Laertius I. 22. Hecataeus: Herodotus II. 143.

⁶⁷ A commonly stated point, though the inference is not entirely certain. Psammetichus, for example, was the name of a scion of the Cypselid family (Aristotle, *Politics* V. 9 1315b) and perhaps of the owner of a seventh-century Athenian vase (Austin, *Greece and Egypt,* p. 52); a man called Croesus died in war in Attica in the sixth century, but he may have been an East Greek (Richter, *Kouroi,* p. 115).

CHAPTER VII

[1] C. A. Doxiadis has produced interesting surveys of the numbers of such settlements; but the critique by J. M. Wagstaff, *JHS,* XCV (1975), pp. 163–68, is quite justified. J. Pečírka, "Homestead Farms in Classical and Hellenistic Greece," *Problèmes de la terre,* pp. 113–47, sums up evidence which he has treated in other more detailed analyses of Attica, Miletus, and the Crimea. See also D. Lazarides, *Athens Annals of Archaeology,* I (1968), p. 31. Pečírka (p. 114, n. 1) comments on the debate about *Streusiedlung* in early Greece and the lack of useful evidence.

[2] G. Vallet, *La Città e il suo territorio,* pp. 81–94, is a useful consideration of these aspects.

[3] Zeldin, *France,* p. 180; cf. Coulton, *Medieval Village,* pp. 174, 461; Bennett, *Life on the English Manor,* pp. 232–34. Rural use of iron: *Iliad* XXIII. 826ff.; but Hesiod, *Works and Days* 430, does not specifically mention iron. No iron plow-shares are listed from Greece by A. G. Drachmann *s.v.* Pflug in PW.

[4] Ovid, *Metamorphoses* VIII. 640ff.

[5] Aristotle, *Politics* VII. 9. 1330a, as a theoretical argument; Asheri, *Distribuzioni,* p. 10; D. M. Lewis in *Problèmes de la terre,* pp. 210–12.

[6] Finley, *Studies in Land and Credit,* p. 54.

[7] D. Asheri, "Laws of Inheritance, Distribution of Land, and Political Constitutions in Ancient Greece," *Historia,* XII (1963), pp. 1–21; F. Cassola, "Sull'alienabilità del suolo nel mondo greco," *Labeo,* XI (1965), pp. 206–19; M. I. Finley, "The Alienability of Land in Ancient Greece," *Eirene,* VII (1968), pp. 25–32; J. Pečírka, "Land Tenure and the Development of the Athenian Polis," *Geras,* pp. 183–201; Thomson, *Prehistoric Aegean,* pp. 297ff; Will, *Trade and Politics in the Ancient World,* pp. 64–68 (with the dissent of Andrewes, p. 114); and a variety of studies on Solonian Attica in particular which will be cited in chap. VII. On the asserted role of the *genos,* H. J. Rose, *Primitive Culture in Greece* (London, 1925), pp. 174–81, may serve as example; the Sorbonne thesis by F. Bourriot casts considerable doubt on the concept.

[8] Archilochus fr. 216 (Asheri, *Distribuzioni, passim*); Hesiod, *Works and Days* 341. The Greek is clear and terse, yet P. Guiraud, *La Propriété foncière en Grèce* (Paris, 1893), p. 101, called it "unique et douteux" and others have denied its implications especially for Attic conditions; cf. Will, *Revue des Études Anciennes,* LIX (1957), pp. 12–24. Herodotus II. 59, IX. 94; Vallet, *La Città e il suo territorio,* pp. 72–73, and *Problèmes de la terre,* pp. 83–94, raises the question as to how cemeteries, second

urban centers (Megara Hyblaea), and rural sanctuaries gained their plots.

[9] W. J. Woodhouse, *Solon the Liberator* (Oxford, 1938), p. 81; so too Fine, *Horoi;* Aristotle, *Politics* II. 6. 1270a, terms the sale of land at Sparta *ou kalon,* "not proper."

[10] Aristotle, *Politics* II. 3. 1265b. At Thebes Philolaus, of Corinthian origin, also sought to regulate the number of *kleroi* (II. 9. 1274a); on the colonies cf. Asheri, *Distribuzioni,* p. 9.

[11] A. R. W. Harrison, *The Law of Athens* (Oxford, 1968), pp. 132ff.; J. A. Newth in Molly Miller, *The Sicilian Colony Dates* (Albany, 1970), pp. 133ff.

[12] Vallet, *La Città e il suo territorio,* p. 104. Such communal storage had existed from very early times in Greece; Sp. Marinatos, "Greniers de l'Hélladique ancien," *BCH,* LXX (1946), pp. 337–51.

[13] Heichelheim sought to show an introduction of the three-field system in classic times, but M. I. Rostovtzeff, *Social and Economic History of the Hellenistic World,* II (Oxford, 1941), pp. 1186–87 (with notes) adequately disproved the theory; even in medieval times a two-year sequence was more suited to Mediterranean lands (Miskimin, *Economy of Early Renaissance Europe,* p. 18). In later times leases sometimes required a two-year sequence (Guiraud, *Propriété foncière,* p. 436).

See generally E. C. Semple, *The Geography of the Mediterranean Region* (London, 1932); White, *Roman Farming,* who compares (pp. 371ff.), not unfavorably, ancient and early modern agricultural efficiency; Rostovtzeff, *Social and Economic History,* who suggests that "primitive as the methods were, they were the best possible, and the Greeks applied them with patience and tenacity." One example of technological improvement, outside farming itself, was given by L. A. Moritz, *Grain Mills and Flour in Classical Antiquity* (Oxford, 1958).

[14] For Bangladesh the estimate by Roger Revelle, *Scientific American,* Sept. 1974, p. 162 (based on FAO tables) is 1800 calories per day. Climate, proper utilization of food, and other factors have their influence; see FAO, *Calorie Requirements,* Nutritional Studies, no. 15 (Rome, 1957); A. Keys, "Minimum Subsistence," *The Population Ahead,* ed. R. G. Francis (Minneapolis, 1958), pp. 27–39, estimates wastage of 20–25 per cent. (I may note that references to an area of study far removed from classical times are intended only to suggest my own sources for statistics and information.)

[15] Ruschenbusch F 89. Payne, *Perachora,* I, pp. 67–69, discussed the types of bread shown in dedications. There are interesting Boeotian sixth-century figurines of grinding grain, making bread, and baking in

the National Museum, Athens (e.g., 4431, 5773, 12980), see also *Catalogue raisonné des figurines et reliefs en terre-cuite grecs étrusques et romains,* I, ed. Simone Mollard-Besques (Paris, 1954), B. 101ff., and G. H. Chase in *Festschrift für James Loeb* (Munich, 1930), pp. 45–51. Braudel, *Capitalism and Material Life,* p. 68, quotes a remarkable statement that in Greece "the eaters of barley gruel have no desire to make war."

[16] Minor variations in estimates will be found in Gomme, *Population of Athens,* p. 32; Boeckh, *Staathaushaltung,* I, p. 114; Beloch, *Bevölkerung,* p. 33; A. Jarde, *Les Céréales dans l'antiquité grecque* (Paris, 1925), pp. 123–24, 128–35; Roebuck, *CP,* XL (1945), pp. 159–61, who comments that the measures found in the Agora essentially support Hultsch's estimate that an Attic *medimnos* equaled 52.5 liters (cf. M. Lang and M. Crosby, *Athenian Agora, X: Weights Measures and Tokens* [Princeton, 1964]). The modern quotation is from I. T. Sanders, *Rainbow in the Rock* (Cambridge, Mass., 1962), p. 88—the best recent English study of Greek rural population.

[17] See the recent work by J. M. Frayn, "Wild and Cultivated Plants," *Journal of Roman Studies,* LXV (1975), pp. 32–39.

[18] Jardé, *Céréales,* p. 60; A. French, *The Growth of the Athenian Economy* (London, 1964), p. 176; Slicher van Bath, *Agrarian History,* p. 173; cf. Bennett, *Life on the English Manor,* pp. 86–87. In medieval and early modern Europe seed requirements for barley could even run one-third to one-fourth the crop (Slicher van Bath, pp. 66–67, 172–73), though theoretical statements gave seed/yield ratios of 1 : 8.

[19] In the modern world there is one hectare of farmland for every 2.7 persons (Revelle, *Scientific American,* Sept. 1974, p. 167).

[20] At Metapontum a *kleros* was six hectares (Will, *Le Monde grec,* pp. 641–42). In one part of the Crimea plots of the fourth to second centuries B.C. were 4.5 hectares; in another, 26.4 where homesteads and large vineyards were included (Pečirka, *Problèmes de la terre,* pp. 140ff.; and also in "Country Estates of the Polis of Chersonesos in the Crimea," *Ricerche storiche ed economiche in memoria di Corrado Barbagallo,* I [Naples, 1970], pp. 459–77).

In the eastern part of England at the end of the thirteenth century 38 per cent of the farms were three hectares or less, 36 per cent were six hectares, 26 per cent 12 or more (Slicher van Bath, *Agrarian History,* pp. 134–36); but P. Goubert, "The French Peasant of the Seventeenth Century," *Past and Present,* no. 10 (1956), pp. 55–77, estimated that at that time only a peasant holding 12 hectares or more could be economically independent—the equivalent of a Solonian *zeugite.* In 1961, the average Greek farm ran 3.18 hectares (UN, *Monthly Bulletin of Statistics,*

XXVI 4 [Apr. 1972], XXVII. 11 [Nov., 1973]). In the Italian census of 1948 53 per cent of the farms were less than one hectare, and 93.4 per cent ran less than five (*Economist,* Jan. 21, 1961, p. 251).

²¹ See Olck *s.v.* Ackerbau in PW; White, *Roman Farming,* pp. 371, 413; Slicher van Bath, *Agrarian History,* p. 184, gives medieval English figures which suggest 5.5. to 6.25 days in harvesting per hectare (plowing then required 0.35 to 0.40 days per hectare).

²² Aristotle, *Constitution of Athens* 7; the doubts of Busolt as to the presence of precise figures in Solon's own law are noted in chap. VI, above.

²³ G. Glotz, *Ancient Greece at Work* (London, 1926), p. 247, gives essentially the same figures (cf. Finley, *Studies in Land and Credit,* pp. 58–59); French, *Growth of the Athenian Economy,* p. 19, gives 15 to 30.

²⁴ By the fifth and fourth centuries something less than half the Athenian population held enough land to serve in the phalanx (Beloch, *Bevölkerung,* pp. 24–25); Antipater eliminated 12,000 out of 21,000 citizens from active participation in government.

²⁵ Beloch, *Bevölkerung,* p. 56, estimated the total area of Attica at 2527 sq.km.; the figure in the text is hesitantly set forth by Jardé, *Céréales,* pp. 48–50 (French, *Growth of the Athenian Economy,* p. 6, gives only 34,000 hectares for the plains, without suggesting a source for that very deviant figure).

²⁶ *Odyssey* XI. 489–91. Asheri, *Distribuzioni,* pp. 13–16, argues that in original divisions of colonies equality was sought, but colonial experience cannot be transferred to conditions in the homeland; later (pp. 60ff.) he documents inequality of landholding abundantly.

²⁷ Bolkestein, *Economic Life,* p. 114; A. Biscardi, *Studi U. Paoli* (Florence, 1955), pp. 105–43.

²⁸ The arithmetic is as follows: 3450 hectares (10 per cent of the grainland) in wheat at 4 hl. (half the wheat yield) per hectare = 13,800 hl., divided by 3 hl. per person to feed a total of 4600 persons. 31,050 hectares in barley at 8 hl. per hectare = 248,400 hl., divided by 3.5 hl. per person to feed a total of 71,000 persons.

²⁹ *Inscriptiones Graecae* ² II, no. 1672. The figures are those of P. Foucart, *BCH,* VIII (1884), p. 211, taken over by Beloch, *Bevölkerung,* p. 32, and Jardé, *Céréales,* pp. 36–48. Gomme, *Population of Athens,* p. 28, gives only 28,500 *medimnoi* of wheat and 340,350 of barley. Beloch, *Bevölkerung,* p. 96, deducted one-sixth for seed and allotted seven *medimnoi* to each person to reach a total of 40,000–45,000 persons who could be fed from that year's crop.

³⁰ Here one need only note the intriguing argument by E. Fiumi that

Tuscan towns grew in the thirteenth century because the countryside was expanding (summarized by Herlihy, *Economic History Review,* 2 ser. XVIII [1965], p. 226) or the assignment of English agricultural change to the seventeenth century by E. Kerridge, *The Agricultural Revolution* (London, 1967) and *The Farmers of Old England* (Totowa, N.J., 1973).

[31] Michell, *Economics,* pp. 74–76, gives references from Theognis 864 onward; the chicken appears on sixth-century coins of Himera (Plate V.d) and elsewhere.

[32] The best, though inadequate, evidence is in W. A. MacDonald and G. R. Rapp, Jr., eds. *The Minnesota Messenia Expedition* (Minneapolis, 1972), pp. 49–50; the SOS amphoras which turn up as far west as Spain (J. de Hos Bravo, *Madrider Mitteilungen,* XI [1970], pp. 102–9), also suggest a growth in Athenian oil exports. For archeological evidence of concentration on grapes and olives in classic Athens see D. Lazarides; *Athens Annals of Archaeology,* I [1968], p. 31. For Solonian Athens cf. M. R. Cataudella, *Atene fra il VII e il VI secolo: aspetti economici e sociali dell'Attica arcaica* (Catania, 1966), pp. 109–24, and the caution of Will, *Trade and Politics in the Ancient World,* pp. 70–71; M. Detienne, *Problèmes de la terre,* pp. 293–306, is more concerned with religious aspects of the olive.

[33] Humphreys, *Parola del Passato,* XXII (1967), p. 378, cites the limited information.

[34] Finley, *Past and Present,* no. 47 (1970), p. 23.

[35] G. Mickwitz, "Economic Rationalism in Graeco-Roman Agriculture," *English Historical Review,* CCVIII (1937), pp. 577–89; R. Forster, *American Historical Review,* LXXV (1970), p. 1611, observes of French landowners in the eighteenth century an inability to determine "much about the relative efficiency or profitability of capital inputs." Yet with M. W. Frederiksen, *Journal of Roman Studies,* LXV (1975), pp. 168–69, I am not so certain we may totally dismiss economic interest; Plutarch, *Pericles* 16. 3–5, at least, provides one specific example of exactitude in accounting for sales and expenditures. Cf. also Pleket, *Vestigia,* XVII (1973), pp. 33–35.

[36] Xenophon, *Oeconomicus* 20. 22–26; but "all in all, there are not a dozen references in Greek literature to increasing the value of a farm or urban holding" (Finley, *Studies in Land and Credit,* p. 82). Import of sheep: Athenaeus XII. 540d.

[37] Sahlins, *Stone Age Economics,* pp. 41ff., 56–57, 68–69. Slicher van Bath, *Agrarian History,* p. 183, observes that the working day on English medieval manors was only from sunrise to noon (after Bennett, *Life on the English Manor,* pp. 104–6); in Russia man-days per worker in-

creased about 50 per cent from the 1920's to the 1950's (Gould, *Economic Growth in History,* p. 77).

[38] Among recent explorations see A. B. Appleby, "Agrarian Capitalism or Seigneurial Reaction? The Northwest of England, 1500–1700," *American Historical Review,* LXXX (1975), pp. 574–94; R. H. Hilton, "Rent and Capital Formation in Feudal Society," *2d International Economic History Congress* (1962), pp. 33–68, who shows that in fourteenth- and fifteenth-century England the rich tried to hoard and prevent cheating rather than to increase production; R. G. Witt, "The Landlord and the Economic Revival of the Middle Ages in Northern Europe, 1000–1250," *American Historical Review,* LXXVI (1971), pp. 965–88, suggests "a development in which the haves, in pursuit of even more, played the primary role."

[39] Davis, *Rise of the Atlantic Economies,* p. 115.

[40] Decrease in farm size: Slicher van Bath, *Agrarian History,* p. 314; Wrigley, *Population and History,* p. 136, is rather skeptical. Productivity: FAO, *Production Yearbook,* 1971, pp. 10–11, 21–23; R. McNamara, *One Hundred Countries, Two Billion People* (New York, 1973), p. 67; R. Forster, *American Historical Review,* LXXV (1970), p. 1601, who concludes that "what the development economists rather coldly call 'motivational structure' can play a large part in increasing productivity."

[41] Aristotle, *Constitution of Athens* 16.6; but conditions of security and availability may at times lead to the cultivation of poorer rather than better land (as an example, for Pistoia see Herlihy, *Economic History Review,* 2. ser. XVIII [1965], p. 237).

[42] *Works and Days* 640; T. P. Howe, "Linear B and Hesiod's Breadwinners," *Transactions of the American Philological Association,* LXXXIX (1958), pp. 44–65, argues that grain-raising only slowly replaced livestock.

[43] Andrewes in *Phoros,* p. 26, commenting on Pollux VII. 151; as he observes, money rents may not have become standard till the end of the sixth century.

[44] Demosthenes 53. 19–21 and 57. 45; see also Jones, *Athenian Democracy,* p. 13.

[45] Bennett, *Life on the English Manor,* pp. 65ff., 302; Frank Aydelotte, *Elizabethan Rogues and Vagabonds* (London, 1913); Hasebroek, *Griechische Wirtschafts- und Gesellschaftsgeschichte,* pp. 138–39, hypothesizes a "vagabundierenden Proletariat"; did it really exist?

[46] Aristotle, *Politics* VI. 5. 1323a. Ste Croix, *Economic History Review,* 2. ser. XII (1960), pp. 510–11, and others would naturally stress rural slavery much more.

[47] E. R. Wolf as quoted in Redfield, *Peasant Society and Culture,* p. 27, who is later cautious about finding a uniform peasant type.

[48] E. R. Wolf, *Peasants* (Englewood Cliffs, N.J., 1966), pp. 2–4; cf. T. Shanin, ed., *Peasants and Peasant Societies* (Harmondsworth, 1971), p. 105.

[49] Wolf, p. 11.

[50] Herodotus I. 17ff.; S. Vryonis, *The Decline of Medieval Hellenism in Asia Minor and the Process of Islamization from the Eleventh through the Fifteenth Century* (Berkeley, 1971), p. 173, reports the plan of sultan Ala al-Din to devastate the lands of Amid in the first year, to prevent entry of food-stuffs in the second, and so in the third to force its surrender.

[51] Andreades, *Greek Public Finance,* p. 230, discusses the heavy expenses of sacrifices; the sale of hides therefrom produced nearly two talents in 334/3 at Athens.

[52] Pollux III. 83; D. Lotze, *Metaxy eleutheron kai doulon* (Berlin, 1959), and for Crete esp. Willetts, *Aristocratic Society in Crete,* pp. 46ff. On the *penestai* little can be said; the helots have never been properly treated. One might add in colonial areas parts of Sicily and the Black Sea (D. M. Pippidi in *Problèmes de la terre,* chap. 3). Serfdom does not appear in Homer; cf. Hasebroek, *Griechische Wirtschafts- und Gesellschaftsgeschichte,* p. 22; Guiraud, *Propriété foncière,* pp. 407–18.

[53] Wingfield-Stratton, *Squire and His Relations,* pp. 65–66, discusses the yeoman as a "cormorant"; cf. Ronald Blythe's delightful *Akenfield* (New York, 1969), pp. 50–51, 143.

[54] Habbakuk, *Economic History Review,* X (1940), p. 12; in the nineteenth century about 30–40 per cent of the land about Paris was bought by the city dwellers (Zeldin, *France,* p. 152; cf. Fox, *History in Geographical Perspective,* p. 114). Finley, *Ancient Economy,* p. 107, suggests it was the wealthier landowners who acquired lands near cities and shrines.

[55] Heichelheim, *Ancient Economic History,* II, pp. 113–16.

[56] Herodotus VII. 147, 158.

[57] Austin, *Greece and Egypt,* p. 35, properly notes the lack of early testimony, but like most scholars still explains the rise of Naucratis as reflecting the export of grain.

[58] Meiggs and Lewis, *Greek Historical Inscriptions,* no. 30.

[59] Braudel, *Capitalism and Material Life,* pp. 84–86, comments that large traders regularly specializing in grain did not exist even in sixteenth-century Venice, Genoa, and Florence (except perhaps the Bardi Corsi), though these cities were dependent on imported grain. The first significant shipment of grain from the North American colonies to England occurred only a few years before the American Revolution (Davis, *Rise of the Atlantic Economies,* p. 285). E. F. Hecksher, *The Continental*

System (Oxford, 1922), pp. 336ff., guesses that in the period after 1805 England imported perhaps 6.5 per cent of its grain; the Continent was self-sufficient except for coffee, tobacco, sugar, and other colonial items (pp. 289ff.)

[60] T. S. Noonan, "The Grain Trade of the Northern Black Sea in Antiquity," *American Journal of Philology,* XCIV (1973), pp. 231–42, and his essay on Panticapaeum in *AJA,* LXXVII (1973), pp. 77–81, countering the arguments of Roebuck, *CP,* XLVIII (1953), pp. 9–16, who places the origins of the Black Sea grain trade at the end of the seventh century (cf. also *CP,* XLV [1950], pp. 236–47). Heichelheim *s.v.* Sitos (PW, Supplementband VI) accepted imports on a large scale only in the fifth century.

[61] FAO, *Production Yearbook,* 1971, pp. 10–11, 21–23.

CHAPTER VIII

[1] Will, *Études archéologiques,* p. 154, describes the work of Rostovtzeff and Heichelheim as "une somme d'études, d'esquisses si l'on préfère, et il n'en pourra jamais être autrement."

[2] Dodds, *Greeks and the Irrational,* is a valiant effort on which some of my comments below rest; see also Starr, *The Origins of Greek Civilization, 1100–650 B.C.,* pp. 278–92, 318–23.

[3] Copenhagen NM 727; a sherd from Tenos is even more macabre: it shows a warrior with four gaping wounds whose private parts are being devoured by a bird of prey (Kunze, *Kretische Bronzereliefs,* pp. 250–51).

[4] Hesiod, *Theogony* 954–55, 530–31; F. Brommer, *Herakles: Die zwölf Taten des Helden in antiker Kunst und Literatur* (Münster/Köln, 1953); Boardman, *JHS,* XCV (1975), pp. 1–2, presents a count of mythical scenes suggesting that over one-quarter of sixth-century decorated wares (metal and ceramic) depicted Heracles, and at Athens almost one-half did.

[5] Thucydides II. 15; Boardman, however, counts in the first quarter of the fifth century still 19.4 per cent of mythical scenes referring to Heracles, only 13.2 per cent to Theseus.

[6] Bailey, *Strategems and Spoils,* p. 59, as cited in chap. II, above.

[7] Will, *Annales,* IX (1954), pp. 7–22; Bolkestein, *Economics,* pp. 135ff. Marxists, true, seek to uncover commercial and industrial exploitation as early as possible; P. Oliva, *Raná Řecká Tyrannis* (Prague, 1959), thus found commercial and industrial elements more important than agricultural aristocrats by the time of Pisistratus at Athens; cf. Welskopf, *Produktionsverhältnisse,* pp. 352ff.

[8] A. R. Burn, "The So-called 'Trade Leagues' in Early Greek History and the Lelantine War," *JHS,* XLIX (1929), pp. 14–37; cf. Forrest, *Historia,* VI (1957), pp. 161–64, Will, *Korinthiaka,* pp. 391ff.

[9] Michell, *Economics,* pp. 224–30, is a reasonably balanced counter.

[10] A point stressed in Karl Polanyi's work; cf. S. C. Humphreys, "History, Economics and Anthropology; The Work of Karl Polanyi," *History and Theory,* II (1969), pp. 165–212.

[11] Xenophon, *Hipparchicus* 4. 7; cf. Aristotle's discussion of the advantages and disadvantages of trade in *Politics* VII. 5. 1327a.

[12] In the sixth century Cyzicus granted a man exemption from all save fees on slave-dealing, horse-dealing, public scales, and perhaps ferry tax (H. Solmsen, *Inscriptiones Graecae ad inlustrandas dialectos selectae* [4th ed.; Leipzig, 1930], no. 51); on trade taxes see also Knorringa, *Emporos,* pp. 132–33; Andreades, *Greek Public Finance,* pp. 137–54; Hasebroek, *Trade and Politics,* pp. 151ff., views the matter as "economic tyranny."

[13] Finley, *Ancient Economy,* pp. 95–96, argues that in principle land was free from taxation; (as did Boeckh); but Busolt, *Staatskunde,* I, p. 610, gives examples; Pleket, *Vestigia,* XVII (1973), pp. 251–52, is balanced.

[14] Gould, *Growth in Economic History,* pp. 218–19; Herodotus I. 165.

[15] Diogenes Laertius I. 98; Nicolaus, *FGrH* 90 F 58; Heracleides, *FHG,* II, p. 213.

[16] K. Köster, *Die Lebensmittelversorgung der altgriechischen Polis* (Berlin, 1939), seriously antedates public care and is otherwise inadequate.

[17] Thucydides I. 13; Herodotus VI. 21.

[18] Herodotus V. 94–95; Zimmern, *Greek Commonwealth,* pp. 27–28, on the currents; Page, *Sappho and Alcaeus,* pp. 152–58; French, *Growth of the Athenian Economy,* pp. 44–50.

[19] Herodotus VI. 33ff.

[20] The later seventh-century activity of Athens at Sigeum, however, is less easily explained; Huxley, *Early Ionians,* p. 87, admits the problem and suggests Phrynon and his followers may have been exiles following the Cylonian conspiracy (though this seems remote from 607/6).

[21] V. Martin, *La Vie internationale dans la Grèce des cités (VIe-IVe s. av. J. C.)* (Paris, 1940); we know nothing of any treaty with explicit trade provisions such as that between Rome and Carthage at the beginning of the Republic (H. Bengtson, *Die Staatsverträge des Altertums,* II [Munich, 1962], no. 121).

[22] J. A. Schumpeter, *Capitalism, Socialism and Democracy* (3d ed.; London, 1950), p. 145.

[23] H. Berve, *Die Tyrannis bei den Griechen* (Munich, 1967), 2 vols., is a full account; for Corinth, see Will, *Korinthiaka*.

[24] P. N. Ure, *The Origin of Tyranny* (Cambridge, 1922).

[25] Aristotle, *Politics,* II. 3. 1265b; III. 5. 1279b; III. 11. 1288a; IV. 10. 1297b; VII. 4. 1321a; A. Andrewes, *The Greek Tyrants* (London, 1956), p. 34; Snodgrass, *JHS,* LXXV (1965), pp. 110–22, gives an extremely valuable analysis which ends with the words "Hoplites, in short, were an instrument before they became a force." He also makes a telling point (p. 115) that middling farmers forced to serve in the ranks of the new phalanx may not have done so with enthusiasm. Weber, *Gesammelte Aufsätze,* pp. 40ff., gives considerable weight to the "Hopliten polis."

[26] Andrewes, pp. 35–36; A. Forti-Messina, "Demos in alcuni lirici," *Antidoron Paoli* (Genoa, 1956), pp. 227ff. (which I have not seen). Snodgrass, parenthetically, draws attention to the statement by Aristotle, *Politics* IV. 10. 1297b that those who were not aristocrats were weak in "organization" (syntaxis).

[27] So Andrewes, p. 8, states that the causes lay "in the oppressiveness or inadequacy of the aristocracies" and comments on the preceding page that "personal ambition and public necessity cannot be neatly disentangled." Cf. Hasebroek, *Griechische Wirtschafts- und Gesellschaftsgeschichte,* p. 172; Heuss, *Antike und Abendland,* II (1946), pp. 45–48; Drews, *Historia,* XXI (1972), pp. 129–44.

[28] Herodotus V. 68; Ephorus, *FGrH* 70 F 179; other references in Starr, *Origins,* p. 344; Busolt, *Staatskunde* I, pp. 384–86, even called these policies anti-capitalistic!

[29] B. D. Meritt, *Hesperia,* VIII (1939), pp. 59ff.; Thucydides VI. 54 asserts, however, that these had to be supporters of Pisistratus.

[30] Thucydides I. 17; Andreades, *Greek Public Finance,* pp. 112–24; Busolt, *Staatskunde,* I, p. 601, puts it that "grössere Finanzwirtschaften sind wohl zuerst von Tyrannen geführt worden."

[31] The last of these three elements must definitely be assumed; E. R. Wolf, *Peasant Wars of the Twentieth Century* (London, 1971), p. 291, finds the locus of peasant unrest—i.e., its necessary leadership—in "either landowning 'middle peasantry' or a peasantry located in a peripheral area outside the domains of landlord control." Sixth-century Athens had both.

[32] Herodotus V. 28–29; Plutarch, *Greek Questions* 32; Cook, *CAH,* II, 2, p. 800; Athenaeus XII. 524a; Roebuck, reviewing Huxley in *Gnomon,* XL (1968), p. 53, suggests that the Cheiromacha were "hand-

fighters" of landless [or light-armed] military units. Difficulties at Megara over debts (Plutarch, *Greek Questions* 18, 59) are obscure and undatable.

[33] Solon fr. 10.3. Plutarch, *Solon* 12, emphasizes the factional division of Attica in the time of Cylon and asserts that Solon played a major part in securing a fair trial of the family of Megacles; but then in cc. 13–14 he gives the common ancient interpretation of a strife between rich and poor as the primary cause of difficulties.

[34] Cataudella, *Atene,* pp. 93–124, surveys exhaustively the reasons advanced in modern literature and argues (pp. 47–48) the problem was not a specifically agricultural or economic crisis but the general situation of the small landowners.

[35] E.g., Woodhouse, *Solon the Liberator;* with earlier references; Fine, *Horoi,* who moves from the fact that *horoi* did not actually exist before the late fifth-fourth centuries; F. Cassola, "La proprietà del suolo in Attica fino a Pisistrato," *Parola del Passato,* XXVIII (1973), pp. 75–87, who argues Solon distributed commons land in the 570's; N. G. L. Hammond, "Land Tenure in Attica and Solon's Seisachtheia," *JHS,* LXXXI (1961), pp. 76–98; (criticized by French in *Historia,* XII [1963], pp. 242–47); J. H. Thiel, "On Solon's System of Property Classes," *Mnemosyne,* 4. ser. III (1950), pp. 1–11, does accept alienability.

[36] *Constitution of Athens* 2.2, 9. 1; cf. Plutarch, *Solon* 15. Although some scholars have argued the share paid to creditors was 5/6, that is outside the bounds of agricultural reality (on the metic "sixth part" in the fourth century of Demosthenes 22. 61 cf. Thomsen, *Eisphora,* p. 99). Cataudella, *Atene,* pp. 7–23, argues the *hektemoroi* were debtors who paid in six equal yearly installments.

[37] Fine, *Horoi,* pp. 178ff.; N. Lewis, "Solon's Agrarian Legislation," *American Journal of Philology,* LXII (1941), pp. 144–56.

[38] French, *Growth of the Athenian Economy,* pp. 12–14, cheerily asserts that "it is not difficult to imagine how the peasants had come to fall into debt" and creates a picture of overpopulation as a result of which peasants were driven off the land. Such overpopulation is less than likely, and there was no major increase in productivity to render farming labor surplus. If there had been such a surplus would Solon have encouraged immigration?

[39] *Works and Days* 477–78, 349–51; as Sahlins, *Stone Age Economics,* pp. 217–18, observes, food in simple societies is given or shared; "food has too much social value . . . to have exchange value."

[40] So Fine, *Horoi,* pp. 182, and others. Note the appearance of rural debt in fourth-century Rome as it entered a market system (T. Frank, *Economic Survey of Ancient Rome,* I [Baltimore, 1937], pp. 28–32).

[41] Cataudella, *Atene,* pp. 112ff.

[42] E.g., R. Seager, "Lysias and the Corn-dealers," *Historia,* XV (1966), pp. 172–84.

[43] Ruschenbusch F 65–70.

[44] Fr. 1 lines 63ff. A "law of Solon" which purportedly limited the size of farms (Ruschenbusch F 66) is generally rejected (cf. Asheri, *Distribuzioni,* pp. 69–70).

[45] Ruschenbusch F 56.

[46] Aristotle, *Constitution of Athens* 2.

[47] Ruschenbusch F 72; Kurtz and Boardman, *Greek Burial Customs,* pp. 90, 200–201 (Iulis and Gortyn); Will, *Korinthiaka,* pp. 512–14, on sumptuary measures by the Cypselids at Corinth.

[48] Andrewes, *Phoros* (Locust Valley, N.Y., 1974), pp. 21–28. Examples of Solonian laws which are rejected have been given immediately above and elsewhere; one notorious problem is Ruschenbusch F 38 ordering every citizen to take up sides in civil strife, which seems contrary to Lysias 31. 27–28 (as Hignett, *History of the Athenian Constitution,* p. 27, pointed out). Ruschenbusch suggests Aristotle misunderstood a provision requiring service in *external* war; J. A. Goldstein, "Solon's Law for an Activist Citizenry," *Historia,* XXI (1972), pp. 538–45, seeks to get around the surface meaning of Lysias' statements.

[49] *Constitution of Athens* 10; Plutarch, *Solon* 15. (Ruschenbusch omits this ordinance altogether.) In an extensive bibliography cf. T. Fischer, "Zu Solons Mass-, Gewichts- und Münzreform," *Chiron,* III (1973), pp. 1–14, with full bibliography; K. Kraft, "Zur solonischen Gewichts- und Münzreform," *Jahrbuch für Numismatik,* XIX (1969), pp. 7–24, reenforcing his earlier essay in X (1959–60), pp. 21–46; E. Will, "Soloniana," *Revue des Études Grecques,* LXXXII (1969), pp. 104–16, a review of Cataudella, *Atene;* C. M. Kraay, "An Interpretation of *Ath. Pol.,* ch. 10," *Essays in Greek Coinage Presented to Stanley Robinson* (Oxford, 1968), pp. 1–9. M. Crawford, *Eirene,* X (1972), pp. 5–8, rejected any change at all; P. J. Rhodes, *NC,* 7. ser. XV (1975), pp. 1–11, presents a conclusion very similar to mine.

[50] Herodotus VI. 127; T. Kelly, *History of Argos* (Minneapolis, 1977).

[51] French, *Growth of the Athenian Economy,* p. 182, rightly observed that "we are always in danger of attributing to Solon motives more sophisticated than he himself felt," but he too worries about the prob-

lem of coinage and concludes it *must* have existed even though Kraay showed it began twenty years later. Boardman, *Athenian Black Figure Vases,* p. 212, observed, almost casually, that in the sixth century "like is weighed against like, not against weights" on vases (as on Plate VII.b); note too that weights were far from uniform (*Athenian Agora* X, pp. 15–16, shows the remarkable variations even for "staters" or double minas). It may be significant that the weight found on Pithecusa (*Archaeological Reports for 1970–71,* p. 66) was connected with a metal-working shop, not in an agricultural context.

[52] Thucydides II. 14, 16; [Aristotle], *Oeconomica* I. 6. 1344bff.

[53] Alcaeus fr. 426.

[54] Jones, *Athenian Democracy,* p. 90.

[55] So especially O. Erb, *Wirtschaft und Gesellschaft im Denken des hellenischen Antike* (Basel, 1938), who found therein an antagonism which eventually destroyed the unity of the *polis.*

[56] Redfield, *Peasant Society and Culture,* pp. 131–37, reflects that the interpretations of the relations of peasantry and gentry as oppressed/oppressor are very incomplete; Andrewes, *Trade and Politics in the Ancient World,* p. 108, felt "there is some danger of making the contrast between mercantile and agrarian too sharp."

[57] French, *Growth of the Athenian Economy,* pp. 172–75, suggests the ordinary Athenian citizen was no better off after the creation of an empire; cf. the balanced assessment by R. Meiggs, *The Athenian Empire* (Oxford, 1972), pp. 255ff.

[58] Plutarch, *Solon* 2.

Bibliographical Information

This section is not a general bibliography, which would require another volume, nor is it even a list of all studies cited in preceding pages. Its aim is rather to help the reader find bibliographical information on works cited in footnotes of several chapters under short titles. In a monograph such as the present one, which draws on both classical and non-classical research, it might otherwise be a frustrating matter to search back for the page on which data of publication were first presented. Fuller information on works concerning coinage, slavery, agriculture, and other topics may be found via the Index.

COLLECTIONS OF ESSAYS

Archaeologia Homerica: Die Denkmäler und das frühgriechische Epos, ed. Friedrich Matz and H. G. Buchholz (Göttingen, 1967–).

La Città e il suo territorio (7th Congress of Studies on Magna Graecia; Naples, 1968).

Geras: Studies Presented to G. Thomson (Prague, 1963).

Metropoli e colonie di magna Grecia (3d Congress of Studies on Magna Graecia; Taranto, 1963).

Problèmes de la terre en Grèce ancienne, ed. M. I. Finley (Paris/Hague, 1973).

Trade and Politics in the Ancient World, ed. M. I. Finley (2d International Conference of Economic History, Aix-en-Provence; Paris/Hague, 1965).

GENERAL WORKS (AND INSCRIPTIONS)

Boeckh, August, *Die Staatshaushaltung der Athener,* 2 vols. (3d ed.; Munich, 1886).

Bolkestein, H., *Economic Life in Greece's Golden Age* (Leiden, 1958).

Busolt, George, *Griechische Staatskunde,* 2 vols. (3d ed.; Munich, 1920–26).

Dunbabin, T. J., *The Greeks and Their Eastern Neighbours* (London, 1957).

———, *The Western Greeks* (Oxford, 1948).

Finley, M. I., *The Ancient Economy* (Berkeley, 1973).

French, A., *The Growth of the Athenian Economy* (London, 1964).

Hammond, Mason, *The City in the Ancient World* (Cambridge, Mass., 1972).

Heichelheim, F. M., *An Ancient Economic History,* vols. I–II (Leiden, 1958–64).

Mazzarino, Santo, *Fra Oriente e Occidente: ricerche di storia greca arcaica* (Florence, 1947).

Meiggs, R., and D. M. Lewis, *A Selection of Greek Historical Inscriptions to the End of the Fifth Century B.C.* (Oxford, 1969).

Michell, H., *The Economics of Ancient Greece* (2d ed.; Cambridge, 1957).

Raubitschek, A. E., *Dedications from the Athenian Acropolis* (Cambridge, Mass., 1949).

Starr, Chester G., *The Origins of Greek Civilization, 1100–650 B.C.* (New York, 1961).

Thomson, George, *Studies in Ancient Greek Society: The Prehistoric Aegean* (new ed.; London, 1954), and *The First Philosophers* (1955).

Will, Edouard, *Le Monde grec et l'Orient: le Ve siècle (510–403)* (Paris, 1972).

Zimmern, Alfred, *The Greek Commonwealth* (Oxford paperback, 1961).

SPECIALIZED ECONOMIC STUDIES

Andreades, A. M., *A History of Greek Public Finance,* I (Cambridge, Mass., 1933).

Asheri, D., *Distribuzioni di terre nell'antica Grecia,* Memorie dell'Accademia delle scienze di Torino, classe di scienze morali, storiche e filologiche, 4. ser. X (1966).

Austin, M. M., *Greece and Egypt in the Archaic Age* (Proceedings of the Cambridge Philological Society, suppl. 2; 1970).

Aymard, A., "Mercenariat et histoire grecque," *Annales de l'Est,* no. 22 (1959), pp. 16–27.

Burford, A. M., *Craftsmen in Greek and Roman Society* (Ithaca, N.Y., 1972).

————, *The Greek Temple Builders at Epidauros* (Liverpool, 1969).

Cataudella, M. R., *Atene fra il VII e il VI secolo: aspetti economici e sociali dell'Attica arcaica* (Catania, 1966).

Fine, J. V. A., *Horoi (Hesperia,* Supplement IX, 1951).

Finley, M. I., "Aristotle and Economic Analysis," *Past and Present,* no. 47 (1970), pp. 3–25.

————, "Emporos, Naukleros and Kapelos," *Classical Philology,* XXX (1935), pp. 320–36.

————, "Technological Innovation and Economic Progress in the Ancient World," *Economic History Review,* 2. ser. XVIII (1965), pp. 25–45.

————, *Studies in Land and Credit in Ancient Athens, 500–200 B.C.* (New Brusnwick, N.J., 1952).

Francotte, H., *L'Industrie dans la Grèce ancienne,* 2 vols. (Brussels, 1900–01).

Gauthier, P., *Symbola: les étrangers et la justice dans les cités grecques (Annales de l'Est,* no. 42, 1972).

Guiraud, P., *La Propriété foncière en Grèce* (Paris, 1893).

Hasebroek, Johannes, *Staat und Handel im alten Griechenland* (Tübingen, 1928) = *Trade and Politics in Ancient Greece* (London, 1933).

————, *Griechische Wirtschafts- und Gesellschaftsgeschichte bis zur Perserzeit* (Tübingen, 1931).

Humphreys, S. C., "Economy and Society in Classical Athens," *Annali, Scuola normale superiore di Pisa, classe di lettere, storia, e filosophia,* 2. ser. XXXIX (1970), pp. 1–26.

Jardé, A., *Les Céréales dans l'antiquité grecque* (Paris, 1925).

Knorringa, H., *Emporos* (Amsterdam, 1926).

Muhly, J., *Copper and Tin: The Distribution of Mineral Resources and the*

Nature of the Metals Trade in the Bronze Age (Transactions of the Connecticut Academy of Arts and Sciences, XLIII. 4, 1973).

Pleket, H. W., "Economic History of the Ancient World and Epigraphy," *Vestigia,* XVII (1973), pp. 243–57.

————, "Technology in the Greco-Roman World," *Talanta,* V (1973), pp. 6–47.

Ridley, R. T., "The Economic Activities of the Perioikoi," *Mnemosyne,* XXVII (1974), pp. 281–92.

Roebuck, C. A., "The Economic Development of Ionia," *Classical Philology,* XLVIII (1953), pp. 9–16.

————, "The Grain Trade between Greece and Egypt," *Classical Philology,* XLV (1950), pp. 236–47.

————, *Ionian Trade and Colonization* (New York, 1959).

Thomsen, Rudi, *Eisphora* (Copenhagen, 1964).

Weber, Max, "Agrarverhältnisse im Altertum," *Gesammelte Aufsätze zur Sozial- und Wirtschaftsgeschichte* (Tübingen, 1924), pp. 1–288.

Welskopf, E. C., *Die Productionsverhältnisse im Alten Orient und in der griechisch-römischen Antike* (Berlin, 1957).

White, K. D., *Roman Farming* (Ithaca, N.Y., 1970).

Will, Edouard, "Archéologie et histoire économique: Problèmes et méthodes," *Études d'archéologie classique,* I (*Annales de l'Est,* no. 19; 1958), pp. 147–166.

————, "De l'aspect éthique des origines grecques de la monnaie," *Revue historique,* CCXII (1954), pp. 209–31.

————, "Limites, possibilités et tâches de l'histoire économique et sociale du monde grec antique," *Études archéologiques,* ed. P. Courbin (Paris, 1963), pp. 153–66.

————, "Trois quarts de siècle de recherches sur l'économie grecque antique," *Annales,* IX (1954), pp. 7–22.

Woodhouse, W. J., *Solon the Liberator* (Oxford, 1938).

SOCIAL AND DEMOGRAPHIC STUDIES

Adkins, A. W. H., *Merit and Responsibility* (Oxford, 1960).

————, *Moral Values and Political Behaviour in Ancient Greece* (London, 1972).

Beloch, Julius, *Die Bevölkerung der griechisch-römischen Welt* (Leipzig, 1881).

Davies, J. K., *Athenian Propertied Families 600–300 B.C.* (Oxford, 1971).

Finley, M. I., *The World of Odysseus* (New York paperback, 1965).

Gernet, Louis, *Anthropologie de la Grèce antique* (Paris, 1968).

Gomme, A. W., *The Population of Athens in the Fifth and Fourth Centuries B.C.* (Oxford, 1933).

Hopkins, Keith, "The Age of Roman Girls at Marriage," *Population Studies,* XVIII (1965), pp. 309–27.

————, "On the Probable Age Structure of the Roman Population," *Population Studies,* XX (1966), pp. 245–64.

Humphreys, S. C., "Archaeology and the Social and Economic History of Classical Greece," *Parola del Passato,* XXII (1967), pp. 374–400.

Kurtz, Donna C., and John Boardman, *Greek Burial Customs* (Ithaca, N.Y., 1971).

Pleket, H. W., "Zur Soziologie des antiken Sports," *Mededelingen van het Nederlands Instituut te Rome,* XXXVI (1974), pp. 57–87.

Strasburger, H., "Der Einzelne und die Gemeinschaft im Denken der Griechen," *Historische Zeitschrift,* CLXXVII (1954), pp. 227–48.

————, "Der soziologische Aspekt der homerischen Epen," *Gymnasium,* LX (1953), pp. 97–114.

Walcot, P., *Greek Peasants, Ancient and Modern* (Manchester, 1971).

Wason, Margaret O., *Class Struggles in Ancient Greece* (London, 1947).

Willetts, R. F., *Aristocratic Society in Ancient Crete* (London, 1955).

POLITICAL AND MILITARY CHANGES

Cook, R. M., "Ionia and Greece in the Eighth and Seventh Centuries B.C.," *Journal of Hellenic Studies,* XLVI (1946), pp. 67–98.

Drews, Robert, "The First Tyrants in Greece," *Historia,* XXI (1972), pp. 129–44.

Fanta, A., *Der Staat in der Ilias und Odyssee* (Innsbruck, 1882).

Greenhalgh, P. A. L., *Early Greek Warfare: Horsemen and Chariots in the Homeric and Archaic Ages* (Cambridge, 1973).

Heuss, Alfred, "Die archaische Zeit Griechenlands als geschichtliche Epoche," *Antike und Abendland,* II (1946), pp. 26–62.

Hignett, C., *A History of the Athenian Constitution to the End of the Fifth Century B.C.* (Oxford, 1952).

Huxley, G. L., *The Early Ionians* (London, 1966).

Jones, A. H. M., *Athenian Democracy* (Oxford, 1957).

Kirsten, E., *Die griechische Polis als historisch-geographisches Problem des Mittelmeerraumes* (Bonn, 1956).

Pritchett, W. Kendrick, *Ancient Greek Military Practices,* I (University of California Publications in Classical Studies, VII, 1971).

Snodgrass, A. M., "The Hoplite Reform and History," *Journal of Hellenic Studies,* LXXXV (1965), pp. 110–22.

Whibley, Leonard, *Greek Oligarchies* (London, 1896).

Will, Edouard, *Korinthiaka* (Paris, 1955).

STUDIES OF INTELLECTUAL DEVELOPMENT

Dodds, E. R., *The Greeks and the Irrational* (Beacon paperback, 1957).

Fränkel, Hermann, *Dichtung und Philosophie des frühen Griechentums* (Munich, 1962).

Jeffery, L. H., *Local Scripts of Archaic Greece* (Oxford, 1961).

Lesky, Albin, *History of Greek Literature* (London, 1966).

Page, D. L., *Sappho and Alcaeus* (Oxford, 1955).

Quaglia, L. B., *Gli "Erga" di Esiodo* (Turin, 1973).

ART, ARCHITECTURE, ARCHEOLOGY, POTTERY

Bailey, B. L., "The Export of Attic Black-figure Ware," *Journal of Hellenic Studies,* LX (1940), pp. 60–70.

Beazley, J. D., *Attic Black-figure Vase-painters* (Oxford, 1956).

Boardman, John, *Athenian Black Figure Vases* (London, 1974).

———, *Athenian Red Figure Vases* (London, 1975).

Coldstream, J. N., *Greek Geometric Pottery* (Oxford, 1968).

Cook, R. M., "Die Bedeutung der bemalten Keramik für den griechischen Handel," *Jahrbuch des Deutschen Archäologischen Instituts,* LXXIV (1959), pp. 114–23.

———, *Greek Painted Pottery* (2d ed.; London, 1972).

Dimitriou, S., and P. Alexandrescu, "L'Importation de la céramique attique dans les colonies du Pont-Euxin avant les guerres médiques," *Revue archéologique* 1973, pp. 23–38.

Drerup, H., *Griechische Baukunst in geometrischer Zeit (Archaeologia Homerica,* II, pt. 0; Göttingen, 1969).

Frankfort, Henri, *The Art and Architecture of the Ancient Orient* (Penguin paperback, 1970).

Johnston, A. W., "Trade Marks on Greek Vases," *Greece and Rome,* 2. ser. XXI (1974), pp. 138–52.

Kunze, Emil, *Kretische Bronzereliefs* (Stuttgart, 1931).

Lehman-Hartleben, K., *Die antiken Hafenanlagen des Mittelmeeres, Klio,* Beiheft XIV (1923).

Martin, Roland, *Manuel d'architecture grecque,* I (Paris, 1965).

————, *L'Urbanisme dans la Grèce antique* (2d ed.; Paris, 1974).

Matz, Friedrich, *Geschichte der griechischen Kunst,* I (Frankfort, 1950).

Ohly, D., *Griechische Goldbleche des 8. Jahrhunderts v. Chr.* (Berlin, 1953).

Richter, G. M. A., *Kouroi* (3d ed.; London, 1970).

Roebuck, D. A., "Some Aspects of Urbanization in Corinth," *Hesperia,* XLI (1972), pp. 96–127.

Snodgrass, A. M., *The Dark Age of Greece* (Edinburgh, 1971).

Webster, T. B. L., *Potter and Patron in Classical Athens* (London, 1972).

Vallet, G., *Rhégion et Zanclè: histoire, commerce et civilisation des cités chalcidiennes du détroit de Messene* (Paris, 1958).

Villard, F., *La Céramique grecque de Marseille (VIᵉ–IVᵉ siècle): essai d'histoire économique* (Paris, 1960).

Wokalek, A., *Griechische Stadtbefestigungen* (Bonn, 1973).

Wycherley, R. E., *How the Greeks Built Cities* (London, 1967 reprint).

MEDIEVAL AND MODERN STUDIES

Bailey, F. G., *Stratagems and Spoils* (New York, 1969).

Bennett, H. S., *Life on the English Manor: A Study of Peasant Conditions, 1150–1400* (4th ed.; Cambridge paperback, 1960).

Braudel, F., *Capitalism and Material Life: 1400–1800* (New York, 1973).

Chambers, J. D., *Population, Economy, and Society in Pre-Industrial England* (Oxford, 1971).

Coulton, G. G., *The Medieval Village* (Cambridge, 1926).

Davis, Ralph, *The Rise of the Atlantic Economies* (Ithaca, 1973).

Deane, Phyllis and W. A. Cole, *British Economic Growth 1688–1959: Trends and Structure* (2d ed.; Cambridge, 1967).

Duby, Georges, *Guerriers et paysans VII–XIIᵉ siècle* (Paris, 1973) = *The Early Growth of the European Economy: Warriors and Peasants from the Seventh to the Twelfth Century* (Ithaca, N.Y., 1974).

Fox, E. W., *History in Geographical Perspective: The Other France* (New York, 1971).

George, M. Dorothy, *London Life in the XVIIIth Century* (2d ed.; London, 1930).

Glass, D. V., and D. E. C. Eversley, *Population in History* (London, 1965).

Goodwin, A., ed., *The European Nobility in the Eighteenth Century* (2d ed.; London, 1967).

Gould, J. D., *Economic Growth in History: Survey and Analysis* (London, 1972).

Habbakuk, H. J., "English Landownership, 1680–1740," *Economic History Review,* X (1940), pp. 2–17.

Herlihy, David, "Population, Plague and Social Change in Rural Pistoia, 1201–1430," *Economic History Review,* 2. ser. XVIII (1965), pp. 225–44.

Hicks, John, *A Theory of Economic History* (Oxford, 1969).

Miskimin, H. A., *The Economy of Early Renaissance Europe, 1300–1460* (Englewood Cliffs, N.J., 1969).

Perrott, Roy, *The Aristocrats* (London, 1968).

Postan, M. M., "The Rise of a Money Economy," *Economic History Review,* XIV (1944), pp. 123–34.

Redfield, R., *The Primitive World and Its Transformations* (Ithaca, N.Y., 1953).

———, *Peasant Society and Culture* (Chicago, 1956).

Russell, J. C., *British Medieval Population* (Albuquerque, 1948).

Sahlins, Marshall, *Stone Age Economics* (London, 1974).

Shepherd, J. F. and G. M. Walton, *Shipping, Maritime Trade, and the Economic Development of Colonial North America* (Cambridge, 1972).

Slicher van Bath, B. H., *The Agrarian History of Western Europe, A.D. 500–1850* (London, 1963).

Wallerstein, Immanuel, *The Modern World-System: Capitalist Agriculture and the Origins of the European World-Economy in the Sixteenth Century* (New York, 1974).

Wingfield-Stratton, Esmè, *The Squire and His Relations* (London, 1956).

Wrigley, E. A., *Population and History* (New York, 1969).

Zeldin, T., *France 1848–1945* (Oxford, 1973).

Index